CYNCOED LEARNING CENTRE
U
C
CARDIFF
CF23 6XD

MANCHESTER
1824
Manchester University Press

The marketing of political parties

Political marketing at the 2005 British general election

edited by
Darren G. Lilleker,
Nigel A. Jackson and
Richard Scullion

Manchester University Press
Manchester and New York
distributed exclusively in the USA by Palgrave

Published by Manchester University Press
Oxford Road, Manchester M13 9NR, UK
and Room 400, 175 Fifth Avenue, New York, NY 10010, USA
www.manchesteruniversitypress.co.uk

Distributed exclusively in the USA by
Palgrave, 175 Fifth Avenue, New York,
NY 10010, USA

Distributed exclusively in Canada by
UBC Press, University of British Columbia, 2029 West Mall,
Vancouver, BC, Canada V6T 1Z2

British Library Cataloguing-in-Publication Data
A catalogue record for this book is available from the British Library

Library of Congress Cataloging-in-Publication Data applied for

ISBN   0 7190 7300 6 *hardback*
EAN   978 0 7190 7300 7

ISBN   0 7190 7301 4 *paperback*
EAN   978 0 7190 7301 4

First published 2006

15 14 13 12 11 10 09 08 07 06   10 9 8 7 6 5 4 3 2 1

Typeset in Charter ITC BT 10.5/12.5pt
by Servis Filmsetting Ltd, Manchester
Printed in Great Britain
by CPI, Bath

Contents

List of illustrations

List of tables

List of contributors

Dianne Dean is Lecturer in Marketing at the Hull University Business School. She has written several papers on political marketing, as well as working on other specialist areas such as consumer studies of electronic in-home retailing and marketing on the Internet. Prior to coming into academic life she worked for a number of years in a marketing consultancy, having started her marketing career in the pharmaceutical industry. She graduated from the University of Hull with a degree in politics and is completing a doctorate at the University of Stirling.

Janine Dermody is a Senior Lecturer in Marketing, Gloucestershire Business School, University of Gloucestershire. Her background is in consumer behaviour and the potential persuasive impacts of communication. She is chair of the Academy of Marketing special interest group Political Marketing and has been actively involved in researching on British elections from a marketing communications perspective since 2000. Her research interests include sustainable marketing and public attitudes to politics. Her most recent area of research activity is in electoral engagement and trust.

Ivor Gaber is Professor Emeritus of Broadcast Journalism at Goldsmiths' College, University of London, and is a journalist and broadcaster. He gained wide experience in political journalism as a reporter and producer for the BBC, ITN and Sky News. He has also acted as a consultant and trainer on political campaigning in the UK and overseas. He has published widely on the topic, including *Westminster Tales: The Twenty-first-century Crisis in Political Journalism* (with S. Barnett) and *Culture Wars: The Media and the British Left* (with J. Curran and J. Petley).

Stuart Hanmer-Lloyd is a Reader in Marketing at the University of Gloucestershire Business School and founder and Director of the Centre for Research in Service (CeReS). His research interests include youth attitudes to politics (non)voting behaviour, negative political advertising, (political) trust and distrust, channel management and marketing and the NHS. He has authored papers on financial and public-sector services, environmental responsibility and voter disengagement. He conducted independent research into the advertising employed in the 2005 General Election (with Janine Dermody).

Stephan C. Henneberg is a Lecturer and Co-director of the International Marketing and Purchasing Research Centre at the School of Management, University of Bath. His research interests are in the areas of strategic marketing, relational marketing, consumer behaviour, strategic competences, and social and political marketing. He has organised several international conferences on political marketing at the University of Cambridge. Stephan has published extensively on issues of political marketing in the *Journal of Marketing Management, Journal of Public Affairs* and *Journal of Political Marketing*, and co-edited *The Idea of Political Marketing* with N. O'Shaughnessy.

Nigel A. Jackson is Senior Lecturer in Public Relations at Bournemouth Media School. His practical experience covers the political marketing sphere, having worked for a political party, MP and pressure group in the political world, and then in commercial public relations and marketing. His research interests focus on how politicians interact with voters via unmediated communication, especially the use of information technology. Recent research projects have considered the use by political actors of Web sites, e-mail and e-newsletters. He has reviewed papers on e-government and political marketing and produces the newsletter of the PSA political marketing group.

Darren G. Lilleker is Senior Lecturer in the Bournemouth Media School and worked previously in the Centre for Mass Communication Research at the University of Leicester. His research interests relate to the ways in which politicians interact with society and citizens. Recent publications include a study of the effects of class dealignment (*International Review of Social History* 47: 65–85) and a number of articles covering the professionalisation of political communication, the use of political marketing and the impact of such trends. He was co-editor of *Political Marketing in Comparative Perspective*. In addition Dr Lilleker has researched the ideological debates surrounding British and European defence policy (*Against the Cold War*). He has reviewed papers in political marketing and, at November 2005, is chair of the PSA political marketing group.

Jenny Lloyd is employed as a Research and Teaching Associate at the University of the West of England and is in the final year of her Ph.D. She returned to academia following ten years' practitioner experience in the fields of brand management, advertising and direct marketing, She has published in the *Journal of Nonprofit and Public Sector Marketing* and has presented a number of papers pertaining to the nature of the political 'product' and 'brand' at national and international conferences.

Robert P. Ormrod holds a B.A. (Hons) in Economics and Danish from the University of East Anglia and an M.Sc. in Business Administration from the Aarhus School of Business in Denmark. He is a freelance researcher in Aarhus. His research interests include the market orientation of political parties at the national and local levels, and lobbying activities carried out by non-profit organisations. He advises the Deputy Chairman of the Danish Social Liberal Party on communication and marketing activities and is a member of the Aarhus county election strategy committee. Robert has published work in the *Journal of Nonprofit and Public Sector Marketing,* the Institute for Democratic Communication's Political Communication Report series and has contributed to an edited book of readings, *Current Issues in Political Marketing*.

Heather Savigny is Lecturer in Politics at the University of East Anglia. She undertook her B.A. at Staffordshire University, her M.A. at Keele and has since completed a Ph.D. at the University of Birmingham. Her research interests centre on the use of political marketing and the democratic implications of its use. Recent publications include 'Political marketing: a rational choice?' (*Journal of Political Marketing* 31, 1; 'The media and the personal lives of politicians in the United States' (*Parliamentary Affairs* 57, 1; 'Political science as a broad church: the search for a pluralist discipline' (*Politics* 24, 3) with Dave Marsh and 'Public opinion, political communication and the Internet' (*Politics* 22, 1).

Richard Scullion is Senior Lecturer in the Bournemouth Media School, specialising in marketing communications. He worked in commercial marketing for ten years before moving into academia. His research has to date focused on political marketing with particular emphasis on political advertising. He has published several journal articles in this area. Along with a colleague he carried out extensive empirical research during the General Election of 2001 surrounding the strategies and perceptions of the advertising used by the three main parties. He is Secretary of the Political Marketing Special Interest Group of the Academy of Marketing and has reviewed a number of papers and chaired a number of sessions in that capacity. He is conducting doctoral research in the area of 'consumer choice and its transfer to the political arena'.

Preface

The complexities of modern politics are never clearer than during elections. At these moments all the shifts in politics and society become apparent and shape the campaign. Given the plethora of studies that offer observations as to the professionalisation and indeed the marketisation of politics, we would expect these to come to the fore particularly at this time. It is the extent of the marketisation that interests us in this volume. While there are many volumes that conceptualise political marketing, the aim here is to assemble a series of chapters that empirically test the assumption that politics is undergoing a process of marketisation and, if so, to what effect. The chapters, all of which are discrete pieces of research on an aspect of the campaign from a marketing perspective, may not provide a definitive view of modern politics or political marketing; that was not our explicit intention. Instead this study aims to assess UK politics at the turn of the twenty-first century and determine the extent to which marketing principles have been introduced by political leaders and their strategists, and to detect the resultant changes for parties' behaviour and citizen engagement. Our contributors all adopt differing perspectives and foci on which to base their analysis – these are diverse but in sum present a picture of the parties, the political system and the electorate through a marketing lens. We hope these will provide the reader with an insight into politics in the UK that will stimulate thought and discussion.

We would like to thank all the contributors for keeping to deadlines, producing very thought-provoking studies and supporting us throughout the process. Anthony Mason at Manchester University Press has shown constant enthusiasm for the project, mirroring his support to the field of political marketing over the last five years or so; we thank him for that. On a personal note we would like to thank our respective families for their patience: their help as always is intangible and immeasurable but we could not have survived without it.

Darren, Nigel and Richard

1

Introduction

Darren G. Lilleker, Nigel A. Jackson and Richard Scullion

Political marketing is a highly contested concept. To some it is anathema; politics and marketing are simply alien to one another (Moloney 2004) with marketing's apparent manipulative approach and focus on style over substance. Politicians critique marketing on the basis that it is their job to persuade electors of what society should look like, rather than relying on marketing research to tell them what citizens believe policy should be. Others are happy to argue that marketing could re-engage citizens with the body politic (Lees-Marshment 2001). Indeed, Miller (1997) goes further, arguing that consumption is a very political act and so marketing is rightly influential. The contention is demonstrated in the following quotes. Steve Mattey (2005), an experienced consultant on consumer behaviour, suggests that politicians could learn a lot from marketing:

> Surely it would be commercial suicide for any business to ignore its own customers and prospects for four years at a time. What sort of business or brand would first have the stupidity to do this, and secondly have the barefaced cheek to go on to ask you to buy from them? Unfortunately these are the very brands currently shopping for your vote to run the country.

Underpinning Mattey's argument is recognition that there are profound shifts in the attitudes of the voter towards politics. Grant Mercer (2005), CEO of marketing consultancy Tequila, notes that 'customers find political parties, like banks, to be out of touch and untrustworthy'.

An underlying suggestion here is that more marketing is required to effect a re-engagement between the body politic and citizenry in the UK. However, there are those, even in the world of marketing, who are quick to hail *vive la différence*. In this vein Hugh Burkitt (2005), CEO Marketing Society, raises the important point that 'Marketing has an important role to play in democracy and in winning elections, but the parallels between marketing in business and marketing in politics should not be pushed too far'. These differences of opinion and

emphasis lie at the heart of debates within the field of political marketing. This raises the question, can it be both a cause of, and potential
solution to, the same problem: an electorate disengaged from mainstream politics?

Inevitably there are problems in deciding whether political marketing's contribution is good or bad and to what extent political marketing
is actually a feature of the modern political terrain. This has led to
varying levels of attention awarded in studies of political party behaviour. Literature on recent election campaigns appears to approach the
use of marketing principles and practices in two contrasting ways. It
either sees them as centre-stage: the ultimate cause of party/candidate
gains and losses (Newman, 1999; Lees-Marshment 2001); or it treats
marketing as synonymous with the traditional study of political campaign communication. The latter suggests that little of real substance
has changed with the encroachment of marketing actors into the political sphere. (For example, see the Nuffield studies.) While during elections it is true that the marketing communication output is the most
visible element of the party marketing strategies, it would be wrong to
reduce marketing simply to communication. It is increasingly the case
that, as with corporate communication, the underlying marketing strategy, and orientation of the organisation, drive the communication – in
terms of style, tone, media used and content.

This study of the 2005 UK General Election places political marketing
at the heart of our analysis, with the aim of assessing the extent to which
politics, as a process, has become marketised. We do not, however,
impose a single definition of this concept; instead all our authors take
as a starting point the notion that marketing principles and practices are
consciously applied within political campaigns by both the individual
and the organisations involved. It sets out to discover the extent to
which marketing informs party behaviour at all levels and whether it is
appropriate to use marketing theory to explain party behaviour, communication, the successes and failures and, importantly, the response
from the electorate.

The stance of the authors in this text is not that marketing is either a
curse or a panacea. Evidence shows that marketing is being used, to
greater or lesser extents, by all competitors in all elections, either strategically or simply through experiences of using marketing in previous
non-political roles, from segmenting voters (target audiences) through
to the use of marketing language. This means that both the overt and
the more subtle use of a marketing orientation and the associated tools
and techniques will be studied in order to understand the nature of election campaigning in 2005. We are not saying that marketing determines

the victor, this is clearly due to a range of factors, and only some of these may be linked to long-term strategies that themselves rely on the use of marketing concepts. However, it is our intention to contextualise the role of marketing within an election campaign as well as relate the various aspects of a campaign to marketing theory and practice.

Our contention is that marketing has permeated society (Gabriel and Lang 1995; Wernick 1991). It influences the way that society operates in quite profound ways (Holt 2002). We find a whole range of groups that would normally be considered in other ways, citizens, audiences, students and employees, increasingly acting with consumerist views and therefore being treated increasingly as consumers (Lewis *et al.* 2005). Voters appear to be following a similar paradigm shift. As there is less partisan attachment, and an increase in the phenomenon popularised as 'pocket book voting' in the US, voters are thinking about political choice in a more individualised manner. Thus they ask would-be representatives, 'If I vote for you, what's in it for me?' Political candidates have responded. They do not necessarily target individuals, but groups of like-minded individuals. Thus we find core messages and related communication tailored for consumption; this shifts politics away from convictions and ideologies to being responsive, to some extent, to market forces. This change is manifest in such things as short-term public relations battles. Though it is debatable how long-term parties look when setting out their promises, and so whether they are following short-term demands or long-term social needs (see Ormrod and Henneberg in the next chapter for a broader debate), it is the normative view that the locus of power over various elements of political party and governmental behaviour has shifted away from parties to the voters.

Given the changes in society referred to above, we would expect marketing to have an increasing role within parties and campaigns, and for voters to respond to this in part because they are familiar (as consumers) with it. It is indications and evidence that we and our other chapter authors are seeking in order to determine whether the 2005 UK General Election can indeed be accurately referred to as the political marketing election. In other words is this the election where political marketing comes of age and is identifiable at all levels, going beyond assumptions that policies are market-led simply because they match voter priorities (Lilleker and Negrine 2006). Prior to discussing how this volume examines the extent to which marketing informed the offerings and election strategies of UK political parties, we introduce political marketing for the reader. We then discuss the context of elections in the UK in terms of how they operate and issues specific to this particular contest prior to outlining the structure of the volume.

Political marketing: an introduction

Political marketing refers to the use of marketing tools, concepts and importantly principles within the fields of policy development, campaigning and internal relations within political parties and organisations. It is seen as a reaction to the rise of political consumerism, where members of the electorate increasingly engage in political choice as they do when confronted with commercial brand offerings. In addition it is a feature of the collapse of partisanship, in Western democratic societies. A textbook definition of marketing speaks of 'understanding, creating, communicating, and delivering customer value and satisfaction . . . at a profit' (Kotler and Armstrong 2001: 5). Such notions may initially appear alien to politics, be it campaigning or policy development. Politics, normatively, is associated with ideas and ideologies, and political parties are seen as united around a body of core ideas that bind together its members, and that are subscribed to by a significant proportion of the electorate. The real battle is then waged for the votes of the undecided and those without ideological predilections. Within such an understanding of politics and the political process, political campaigning is intended to persuade and mobilise voters. The only tools of marketing that are traditionally considered to be used within this conception of politics are the promotional tools: advertising, messages, events, etc. (O'Shaughnessy 1990; Wring 2002).

The increasingly non-partisan electorate, however, has changed much of this. With a mass non-partisan electorate, parties are forced to become professional campaigners (Blumler and Kavanagh 1995; Negrine and Lilleker 2003; Norris *et al.* 1999) and their point of cohesion moves from promoting a set of ideals to the desire to win power. This may seem implausible, that parties at some point did not seek power. However, it was not previously seen as the overriding purpose of forming a political party. In the UK the Conservatives were formed to gain electoral power in order to deliver a codified set of political objectives; Labour in slight contrast was formed to promote the rights of the working man (and woman). With the collapse of partisanship, however, all major parties appear to have adopted the underlying Conservative philosophy that winning is the primary objective. Thus we hear of parties responding to economic models of voting behaviour (Downs 1957), and viewing voters through the lens of economic behaviourist models. As voters calculate their choice on a mental profit and loss account with the intention of increasing their personal 'profit' (Heath *et al.* 2001) parties attempt to demonstrate how they will provide that which a sufficient number of voters want. This leads to the concept of the electoral professional party, where all activities and resources are directed into campaigning, both during short intense periods and between these in the so-called permanent campaign, with a view to maintaining a lead over rivals (Panebianco 1987). We can therefore trace the birth of political marketing to changes in society during the 1960s and 1970s, since which the nature of electioneering has steadily evolved with marketing principles having a greater role in determining strategy (Wring 2005). By the 2000s we find a situation where neo-liberal concepts relating to the dominance of markets have so infiltrated both public and private life that is seems to have become a normative ontological perspective (Savigny 2005). Voters are now consumers of a political product and so parties must behave and communicate using the methods of for-profit organisations.

However, the notion that electors simply seek out the best party or candidate for their pocket is criticised by many studies of elections from rational choice or emotional perspectives. Voters, according to Popkin (1994), will seek out the party or candidate that most closely matches their personal ideas and values, that is, they will seek to elect not simply the most effective 'management team' but the team that most closely reflects their own vision of society. This means that marketing cannot simply be about identifying the basic needs and wants, but must also discover what motivates voters when they are considering politics. Parties seeking electoral success must somehow 'connect' with voters (Clarke *et al.* 2004), and, depending on how and where voters seek the information on which to base their decisions, they will regard one party or candidate as more acceptable than another. Thus there are various potential connection points parties may have to establish between their organisations and the electorate. These can be value-based, instrumental or simply points that promote managerial competence, yet all these are at once parts of a single package which broadly appeals to sufficient numbers of voters independent of their individual priorities. Given the above, it then becomes crucially important for political parties to ensure that the information they transmit – in effect, the messages about policies and positions which they wish to pursue – are considered likely to satisfy the needs and wants of the voter/consumer, or at the very least to satisfy them more than any other available alternative. As a result they want and need voters to digest their communication material and to elaborate on it in such a way that the information received connects with their own experiential knowledge and thus is considered salient. It becomes essential that political messages are self-evidently relevant to the lives of intended recipients.

Somewhat paradoxically, as marketing has increased in its 'colonisa-tion' of political campaigning and communication, the electorate appear less interested in mainstream Westminster politics (Coleman 2003; Coleman and Rowe 2005). The timing of these phenomena may instinc-tively suggest a causal relationship but this is thrown into doubt when this same electorate demands a right to be included in the policy-making process. (Bowler and Farrell 1992; Butler and Collins 2001; Lees-Marshment 2001).

According to Newman (1999), a political party or candidate must seek to persuade voters; they cannot simply hope that voters will connect with them or their party. They must discover what factors will facilitate that connection. The party must therefore use marketing research to discover what the voter/citizen wants, then develop a product that is linked, or can be made to link, directly with voter concerns, and promote it in such a way as to appeal to the voter. Additionally they must also make efforts to ensure the policies and positions they adopt are promoted in such a way as to be appealing to sections of the electorate and the media alike. In some respects this is fundamentally no different from any manu-facturer developing a product based on consumer research and then using a range of promotional techniques to raise awareness and then desire for that offering. (For a detailed discussion of political advertising used in recent election campaigns see Dermody and Scullion 2005 and for a similar discussion on the main parties' use of the Internet as a pro-motional tool see Jackson 2004.) Newman describes this process as follows:

> In politics, the application of marketing centers on the . . . analysis of needs . . . centers on voters and citizens; the product becomes a multifac-eted combination of the politician himself or herself, the politician's image, and the platform the politician advocates, which is then promoted and delivered to the appropriate audience. (Newman 1999: 3)

What has been termed a market orientation (Lees-Marshment 2001) suggests a fundamental shift in all aspects of behaviour; however, what some also argue is that a shift in thinking is also required. This necessi-tates the adoption of a marketing philosophy, which is a change in how we look at the way the world is and ought to be. To be responsive to a market an entire organisation must be committed to 'determining the needs and wants of target markets and delivering the desired satisfac-tions more effectively and efficiently than competitors' (Kotler 1991: 17). The notion of target markets may appear difficult to translate into political discourse. However, historically parties have always focused on target groups. Large groups characterised by economic status, C2s (a

grouping of low-level managerial workers) or 'Mondeo man' (characterised by driving a particular type of company car – which itself represents a certain lifestyle) being the sorts of groups that the British Labour
Party felt it had lost but which could be fertile for conversion (Gould
1998; Wring 2005; Lilleker 2005a, b). Of course these voters possessed
a combination of reasons for rejecting the Conservatives, only some of
which were based on the categories they were assigned by such segmentation. A market orientation may well have aided Labour in appealing at a number of different levels each responding to the things that
their target markets demanded.

It is useful to note that there are other potential orientations, and that
doubt can be cast on whether we can delineate parties easily as fitting
one particular type of behaviour or another as Lees-Marshment (2001)
does (Lees-Marshment and Lilleker 2005; Marland 2005; Ormrod 2005;
Rudd 2005). We can usually say that behaviour does or does not fit with
our understanding of a market orientation. We can argue thus that the
party's communication follows from this orientation and may show a
different pattern and set of motives from parties that follow other orientations. Previous to considerations of market orientation, academics
viewed behaviour as product-oriented or sales-oriented, where the
market played a submissive role in simply choosing from a range of
products on sale rather than having input into their production. These
models have been elaborated elsewhere (Shama 1976) and placed in a
political context (Lees-Marshment 2001). Indications are that within
the world of for-profit and not-for-profit the market-oriented organisation has an advantage over those that communicate using propaganda
and mass media models (Lees-Marshment 2001; Knuckey and Lees-
Marshment 2005).

With reducing turnout in the UK elections (Whiteley *et al.*. 2001;
Clarke *et al.* 2004) debates rage regarding who are the most important
groups that parties should communicate with. Equally, given the
concept of a market orientation, does this mean that UK party policy
becomes increasingly under the control of a small segment of voters:
the undecided voters in key marginal constituencies (Ormrod 2005),
those party strategists have identified as crucial voters whose support
will swing the result of the contest? If this is the case, as some evidence
suggests (Lilleker 2005a), it has the potential to alienate the remaining
partisan voters and members and contribute to the growing number of
disaffected electors. While segmentation is not always the best strategy
for every commercial organisation (Houston 1986; 85), never mind
political parties, a party seeking to win significant electoral support
appears to have the false choice of either developing an agenda so

broad and all-encompassing as to be meaningless to most or so specific that it would alienate significant parts of the potential electorate. The party needs, therefore, to provide a political agenda that will satisfy existing members and at the same time attract potential supporters. It means being aware of what competitors have to offer, creating a brand that is positioned strategically with reference to those offered by competitors and one that can credibly offer deliverable 'services' at the right cost that will appeal to a majority of voters (Kohli *et al*. 1993; McGee and Spiro 1988; Narver and Slater 1990). Hence parties are drawn into complex discussions of the balance between taxation (cost) and public spending (benefits) in an attempt to match the demands of the electorate.

If contemporary society necessitates political parties to adopt a market orientation, to develop a series of policies that match their needs and demands, as well as create an image of an organisation that appears able to achieve these demands in a way that voters desire, then we would expect the three main parties in the UK to evidence a market orientation in their thinking and behaviour (Lees-Marshment 2001; 2004; Lilleker and Lees-Marshment 2005).

A relationship marketing approach

Since the 1970s and early 1980s the traditional 'four Ps' approach of focusing primarily on the sale has been criticised by those who suggest that relationship marketing is a more appropriate tool (Gronroos 1994; Berry 1983; Christopher *et al*.. 1991). Relationship marketing is predicated on the belief that long-term profitability and success are based on developing the loyalty of customers and potential customers. Although all marketers need to attract new customers, the emphasis is on satisfying the needs of existing customers. Providing customers with added value, be it more information, special offers or a feel-good factor, encourages a sense of trust, which in turn leads to loyalty. Key to developing relationships are networks through which organisations communicate with customers (Gummesson 2002).

Relationship marketing does not necessarily apply to all industries, but there are certain sectors, such as the service industries – banking, leisure, property – where this 'paradigm shift' (Gronroos 1994) is viewed particularly appropriate. It is no coincidence that as politics is becoming increasingly viewed as similar to a service industry a number of commentators have suggested that political parties should adopt a relationship marketing approach (Scammell 1999; Dean and Croft 2001; Bannon 2003; Bowers-Brown 2003). Relationship marketing is not a quick fix: it takes time, energy and resources to build effective and meaningful relationships. It is therefore not a strategy which parties suddenly decide to use during an election campaign, it needs probably at least a year's lead time. Relationship marking is not necessarily an alien concept to parties who seek progression, first persuading citizens to vote for them, then encouraging them to join their party and then to become activists. The 'loyalty ladder' (Christopher *et al.* 1991) is a mechanism through which parties can conceptualise how they can potentially both attract floating voters and mobilise supporters. Relationship marketing is not a panacea for parties, but it is an alternative and legitimate means by which parties can contest general elections.

The emerging research agenda

The above briefly outlines some of the key conceptual developments in this field, and this certainly leaves scope for further enhancing the theoretical underpinning of the cross-disciplinary body of work that constitutes political marketing literature. One way to help bring this about is to carry out empirical work that loosely 'tests' the relevance of this body of knowledge by investigating the actual practices. A prime location for such a study is during a General Election when activity and commentary offer a brief period rich in potential data collection. This book's prime purpose is to offer perspectives on the notions within political marketing by applying it to and considering it alongside political marketing action. Each chapter is a research project in its own right and so a variety of methodological approaches have been undertaken, from content analysis, discourse analysis and quantitative surveys through to diary keeping. This perhaps tells us something about the approach to developing our understanding in this arena: we tend to use a wider range of methods, some borrowed from other more established disciplines, than is traditional within the confines of political science. These pieces of empirical work are integrated in the sense that we asked the individual authors to keep in mind what their findings might be telling us about the following questions. What do the practices of the main political actors tell us about the meaning of political marketing? What are the opinions of the various groups to such approaches?

As a result a key contribution of this book is to build up the research base in this discipline and to do so in a way that allows comparison, because each research project is based on the same event: a recent General Election. The end result, we hope, is an innovative investigation that exposes the reader to various perspectives about three core aspects of all elections: product, communication and consumer. It does not claim to be exhaustive, and there was no intention to produce guidance here on *how to* research political marketing. However, such a significant amount of empirical work is likely to generate issues related to potentially fruitful future research agendas; these will be briefly visited in the conclusion.

The preceding sections have presented the theoretical background to this study. Prior to introducing the chapters that attempt to assess the extent to which marketing influenced the political campaign of the 2005 General Election, we need to place this contest in context. Such a discussion allows an assessment of which models of marketing are the most appropriate and effective at this point in the history of UK politics.

The electoral context

As noted elsewhere (Lilleker and Lees-Marshment 2005), the electoral system and rules have an impact on the behaviour of the parties and on their ability to use political marketing. For example, within systems where power is allocated to groups proportionally, based on actual votes cast, there is more likely to be a larger number of parties and a greater potential for coalitions. This means that segmentation is fairly rigid and parties must primarily match their policies to their loyal voters, spending less time and effort selling these policies to the floating voters in the society.

In the UK, however, there are present the conditions that arguably necessitate the introduction of marketing philosophies and concepts. The reason for political marketing to be most prevalent in the UK and US are the 'winner takes all'-style electoral systems. In both nations the election is based on the number of seats won, which in turn is determined by who receives the most votes. This disadvantages minor parties, as they seldom gain sufficient support to win one local contest but may well accrue enough votes across the nation to warrant representation if the seats were apportioned proportionally, or at least more relative to the number of votes cast for a particular party. These systems mean that two parties are usually fighting over each seat, though there can be anything up to fifteen parties vying for the votes of the electorate locally. Each of the main parties, and some independents, may have a core of support contained within that geographical area, but crucially they will need to convince the floating voters to support them. A symptom of this is that parties may need to focus more on the non-partisan, disloyal voter segments, as these are key to their winning the contest nationally. As a result it is often the least involved, least committed electors who really count, a group that require a more intense marketing campaign to become engaged. With evidence of growing disengagement, the breakdown of the hegemony of class-based political allegiance and growing fragmentation within society, this all points to a context that increasingly demands a marketing approach.

A number of electoral factors helped shape the context within which party political marketers had to fight the 2005 General Election campaign. First, as in 1997 and 2001, the existing boundaries of seats were widely believed to benefit the Labour Party by some twenty to thirty seats. This provided Labour strategists with a slight 'cushion', and at the same time made the task of Conservative Party strategists that bit more difficult. Second, the boundaries of Scottish seats were changed. In some seats this meant a candidate 'lost' an area they had cultivated for years and 'gained' one they knew little about. As a result, at the individual seat level campaigners had to build some of their credibility, brand image and relationships from scratch. At the same time the number of seats in Scotland was reduced from seventy-one seats to fifty-nine. This limited the number of seats available to, especially, Labour, the Liberal Democrats and the Scottish National Party. Competition to win this reduced number of seats would naturally be harder. Third, there has been a general perception that a decline in voter turnout, especially in 2001, has set parties a challenge. By maximising the vote for their own party, collectively political marketers could potentially reverse this 'democratic deficit', though not of course if there were also moves to depress the opposition's vote. The electoral context was very fluid and, some strategists within the two major parties argued, offered strong potential for the skilful use of marketing to have an impact.

The political context

Many commentators on the 2005 election suggested it was of great importance, it was Labour's chance to seize an unprecedented full third term in government, it was to be a referendum on New Labour politics and was also likely to be dominated by the issue of trust post-Iraq and the debacle over weapons of mass destruction. Yet at the same time the campaign was talked about as a non-event. Labour's dominance in the polls indicated a reduced majority but that the result was still highly predictable – an easy Labour win. In the year preceding the election being called neither the Conservatives under Howard nor Kennedy's Liberal Democrats had dented Labour's lead in the polls substantially; furthermore the economy was strong, historically a key indicator that the government was unlikely to change hands. This did not mean, however, that the media and the parties did not attempt to sell the contest as being unpredictable. For example, throughout the 1980s the media asked whether the SDP/Liberal Alliance would replace the Labour Party. Now, with the Liberal Democrats' infamous 'decapitation strategy' of the Conservative Party leadership, the focus was on the future of the Tories. So for this election a mixed set of cues were being sent to the electorate by the media – watch closely or go on holiday and forget it! The latter view meant that some efforts had to be made simply to gain the attention of the electorate about the event itself above and beyond trying to convince them to support a particular party.

The media framed the election as a potential indictment of the Blair premiership, as well as a ballot on Michael Howard's performance as Conservative leader since the ousting of Ian Duncan Smith in October 2003. There are a number of issues that were predicted to be factors. Predominating was the issue of trust, which, though low for politicians generally, plummeted in the aftermath of the war on Iraq, the releasing of what became dubbed as the 'dodgy dossier' claiming Iraq had the capability of launching weapons of mass destruction in forty-five minutes, and the subsequent lack of said weapons following the removal of Saddam Hussein from power. The Hutton inquiry, following the suicide of government expert Dr David Kelly, who had claimed that the 'dodgy dossier' had been 'sexed up' by BBC journalist Andrew Gilligan, absolved Blair of blame. However, the inquiry was discredited within the media owing to the narrow remit and blame being laid totally at the door of the BBC. Liberal Democrats consistently called for an inquiry into the legality of the war, calls rejected by the government which may have led many to assume it had something to hide. Second, but related, was opposition to the war itself, a mood the Liberal Democrats should have been able to capitalise on through promoting themselves as the only party to oppose the war throughout. However, despite ongoing reports of unrest in Iraq and the unpopularity of the occupation, all reinforcing the feeling that little good would come of the adventure, it remained a low public priority and did not appear to have a significant impact on the campaign as a whole. More prominent, but perhaps not unrelated, was a less nebulous dissatisfaction, the feeling that Blair had not delivered on many of his promises and that key domestic policies were a failure. It was the record of the government that the Conservatives spent most of their efforts attacking; however, the question that voters were asked to consider was: could the Conservatives do better?

The media coverage was less ubiquitous than in previous years but remained transfixed by talk about the political battle itself, with reports on how the campaign was being planned and executed and much commentary about the opinion polls. As the campaign developed a subtext to media coverage was the relationship between Blair and Brown. Ever since the 2001 General Election the media reported numerous arguments, splits and disagreements between the Blairites and Brownites. The 2005 campaign seemed, initially, to follow this pattern, and then suddenly Labour were presenting a picture of the two Labour leaders as 'bosum chums', always together. The result of this strategy was that the political position of Gordon Brown was significantly enhanced. Engagement also featured heavily in the media too, with concern expressed in many quarters about a lack of interest in the election among much of the electorate. A rather ironic situation occurred where people were being asked to watch news reports about their lack of interest in the subject being covered!

The campaign itself was one of the most personally negative in British history, and this tone was quickly picked up by the media. While Labour attempted to control the agenda, and lead on their economic record, the Conservatives' attacks on health, with the 'war of Margaret's shoulder' – using the case of sixty-nine-year-old pensioner Margaret Dixon, whose hospital operation had been cancelled seven times – as well as the increased risk of catching 'superbugs' during a stay in hospital, often saw Labour on the back foot. This could all be used as inferential evidence for a managerial approach. Competence and trust appeared to be foregrounded; little suggested that the parties were attempting to offer some form of better society. Although there were comments on multiculturalism, and visions of the UK by all three major parties, these were in the context of a debate on immigration that was negative and to some appeared to border on racism. Clearly, because Labour had governed for eight years, competence had to be an issue. But was this foregrounding of 'how we govern' above 'why we should govern' a normal part of electioneering or a feature of a marketised political system? It remained largely presidential in style, though Labour's use of the Tony and Gordon team caused some diversionary commentary on the leader-in-waiting. Nevertheless the party leaders spearheaded most of the big set-piece events.

In the end it seemed that Labour's managerialist approach was the most successful, though coupled with a war on the ground that saw more localisation of campaigning than ever before. The Conservatives had small but highly significant victories, the Liberal Democrats failed to make the impact that they had predicted. It seemed that the localised campaigning had a greater impact, with constituencies not conforming to any definite pattern in line with predictions of national swings. There was also a sense of boredom with the campaign, and with politics in general. This was in some sense spearheaded by the tabloids (as Gaber notes in Chapter 6 of this book), but also evidenced in the low turnout and low interest shown in election news. The task we have is to explore the extent to which marketing enhanced or weakened participation and to understand the impact of party strategy and communication on the political consumers in the UK during the 2005 election campaigns.

Party marketing strategy in 2005: an overview

In essence it seemed that parties were trying to present themselves as distinct entities, each with its own unique selling point. Labour were the party of government, with a track record of maintaining economic stability. Despite the debacle over Iraq they argued they could still be trusted and reproduced the pledge card which detailed promises to the electorate (Figure 1.1). The Conservatives' position was the tried and tested traditional approach of Her Majesty's official Opposition, to attack Labour's record in government. Using a series of heuristics linked by the overarching theme 'Are you thinking what we are thinking?', party communications questioned Labour's custodianship of the health service, and in particular the prevalence of the MRSA superbug in hospitals, immigration policy and law and order. Attacking the perception that Labour had failed to deliver, they produced a 'timetable for action' against which a Conservative government could be held to account. The leaflet's main promises are reproduced in Figure 1.2.

The Conservatives' key problem throughout was that their slogan was constantly undermined, no more so than via the Internet. One Web site (www.deadbrain.co.uk/election2005/galleries/toryposters/) continually mocked the Conservative campaign, reinforcing concern that the party was not telling the truth about its economics and that there were racist undertones in the discourse on immigration. Two interesting examples are shown in Figure 1.3.

Our pledge to ensure a better life for you and your family

Your family better off
Your child achieving more
Your children with the best start
Your family treated better and faster
Your community safer
Your country's borders protected

Figure 1.1   Labour's 2005 pledges

MORE POLICE	We will recruit an extra 5,000 police officers each year. This will help restore discipline and respect to our society.
CLEANER HOSPITALS	In our first week we will make it possible for people to have access to information about hospital infection rates. This will give hospitals an incentive to clean up their act.
SCHOOL DISCIPLINE	On our first day we will set out plans to give head teachers the power to expel disruptive pupils. This will restore discipline to Britain's classrooms.
LOWER TAXES	In our first month, a Conservative Budget will stop Labour's next round of stealth taxes, give taxpayers value for money and cut taxes.
CONTROLLED IMMIGRATION	In our first month we will present plans for Parliament to set an annual limit on the number of people who can settle in Britain. This will substantially reduce immigration.

Figure 1.2 The five priorities from the Conservative Party Timetable for Action

The Liberal Democrats had carved themselves a niche through their opposition to the war on Iraq, which both Labour and the Conservatives supported, thus presenting themselves as 'the real alternative'. Their promise to replace Council Tax with a means-related local income tax and to scrap university student tuition fees gave them a distinctiveness; however, problems with articulating policy as well as fears that the tax reforms would hit many middle-income earners, coupled with their inexperience in power, meant they failed to make a national impact. Instead they were able to capitalise in areas where there was deep disillusionment with Labour and dislike of Conservative politics: this was evidenced in Manchester Withington. While they made advances in terms of support in areas where they had an incumbent MP or a strong local presence, they remained marginal, despite being seen as a threat by both parties during the campaign's early stages.

Advances certainly appeared to have been made in the way that the election campaign was 'professional' and used a scientific approach to gaining voter attention and garnering votes. This led to, in essence, three distinct campaigns. The first was the traditional mass communication campaign, using billboards, advertising, election broadcasts and news management. Second, in the marginal constituencies the candidates fought a campaign aimed at winning over floating voters and mobilising their voters. Third, the parties targeted individuals in marginal seats with tailored literature. Implicitly this meant that parties

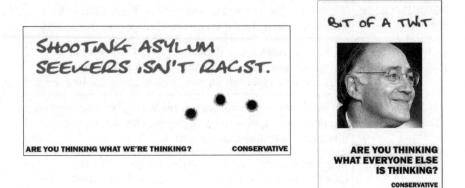

Figure 1.3   Anti-Conservative humour on the Web
Source: Reproduced by permission of
www.deadbrain.co.uk/election2005/galleries/toryposters

used a high degree of segmentation and attempted to adopt a post-modern approach to their communication.

This approach was facilitated by the use of ICT to identify voters with a propensity to be undecided, who would have key interests in areas of policy and who might be susceptible to certain kinds of message. The Conservatives employed Voter Vault, a system that provided in-depth socio-demographic data about voters in key constituencies. Similar to Labour's Experian Mosaic, such programmes were crucial because the parties believed, in the words of Conservative leader Michael Howard, 'if you know what people's social characteristics are, it is not difficult to identify how they will vote' (Watt and Borger 2004). This identification of key voters allowed direct communication to come of age. Running parallel to the mass communication campaign was a narrowcast campaign that directed party messages at voters. Labour used their ten separate paid-for mail-outs mainly to advertise the achievements of the Blair government since 1997, but to admit that the leadership recognised there was 'more work to do' and so they were the best choice for government. Letters from Brown talked up Tony Blair, encouraging the public to trust him, while a less formal letter from Deputy Prime Minister John Prescott detailed the dangers of not registering a vote for the government and 'waking up with Michael Howard'. These letters were targeted chiefly at Labour supporters disillusioned with Blair in the aftermath of the Iraq war and subsequent Hutton inquiry but who were unlikely to vote for Howard and so could either vote for a minority party that had little chance of winning or abstain from voting altogether.

The Conservatives used their mail-outs to attack the government, especially on issues of trust, in constituencies where the fight was against a Labour candidate; to defeat the Liberal Democrat decapitation strategy they highlighted the risks of electing Charles Kennedy as Prime Minister. Particularly effective was the leaflet distributed to undecided voters in Conservative/Liberal Democrat swing seats that highlighted the increases in tax for those earning over £20,000 per annum, the fear that Liberal Democrats would scrap mandatory life sentences for murderers and that they would be soft on immigrants. This leaflet directed voters to a specially created Web site, www.libdempolicy.org, a site the Conservatives had registered to undermine their chief opponent in much of the south of England but which was branded in the black and yellow synonymous with the Liberal Democrat party.

Examples such as www.libdempolicy.org, as well as the use of Web logs by candidates, a variety of spoof blogs, or blogs with uncertain credentials such as one detailing Alastair Campbell's thinking throughout the campaign, suggested that narrowcasting was also going on via the Internet. Much e-communication was directed at members; however, the use of the Web to promote or deride election candidates using humour added a new dimension to UK politics. It was here that the public mood often appeared to be captured, and definitely the message was consistent with the agenda of the tabloids.

The professional approach to the campaign suggests that the parties were trying much harder, and using every technique at their disposal, to reach the political consumer; what is less clear is the extent to which a marketing philosophy permeated the parties' thinking. Equally, and despite calls for politics to be made more entertaining, it is hard to judge how all this information was received, if at all. Thus while an overview of the campaign may suggest a high level of market orientation, given our stricter definition of marketing we are justified in scepticism at this stage of analysis. Our studies analyse the complexities of party behaviour in order to assess whether marketing was employed, how and with what effect in the 2005 UK General Election.

The studies

The book is divided into three parts: first, the political offering or more simply the product; second, we focus on the communication strategies and tools used, and finally we canvass the view from the electorate. Each part contains three chapters focusing on an element of the part's theme.

Part I introduces the notion of a market- or marketing-oriented party and enquires whether the main political parties in the UK have adopted such a strategy through a thorough assessment of both the process undertaken to determine their offering and the nature of the product offered to the electorate. This will be approached from three distinct directions: first, a study of the link between public opinion and policy development; second, the focus shifts to the parties' use of branding; and finally we study the core or unique selling point by focusing on the extent to which ideology featured in the parties' offerings.

Chapter 2 (Ormrod and Henneberg) searches for the influence of a political market orientation on offering development and positioning. Using two different but complementary models to examine the parties' election manifesto, and therefore their main policy promises, this qualitative content analysis of the offering characteristics of the party, as extrapolated from the three main parties' manifestoes, tests the extent to which parties were selling themselves or were informed by a marketing philosophy.

Chapter 3 (Lloyd), starts with the definition of a 'brand' as those attributes associated with a political party that differentiate it from its competitors, taking into account that both controllable and uncontrollable factors impact upon the way that consumers perceive political parties and that consumers themselves play a role in the construction of brand meaning (Firat and Dholakia 1998; Ozanne and Murray 1995). Using the multidimensional construct identified by de Chernatony and Dall'Olmo Riley (1998), this chapter analyses the way that the main UK political parties worked to create their brands within the context of the 2005 General Election. It examines the contribution that physical representation and controllable media make to the creation of the political 'brand' and the impact that the 'uncontrollable' media have upon consistency of brand message. The chapter outlines the way that political parties create what Lock and Harris term an 'overall packaged concept' (1996: 15) to simplify the complexity of the political brand offering. It then observes the extent to which the political 'brand' acts as a unifying force within the party itself, and the effect this has on the uniform communication of brand messages and their reception.

Chapter 4 (Savigny) considers the role of ideology in contemporary 'market driven' electoral campaigning. A key issue for Savigny is the extent to which market research, rather than 'political values', informs party behaviour and policy proposals. The analysis asks whether there is room for ideology in modern election campaigning, or do parties consider marketing is all that is really necessary? Are parties following a purely electoral professional model, as discussed by Downs (1957) and

Panebianco (1988), or is there a necessity to have a core ethos that is central to the party's brand? The role of ideology through this election campaign is informed by a consideration of the discourse of the election campaign. This chapter then turns to consider the compatibility of ideology and marketing in a political context.

Part II covers how political parties promoted their products to the voter during the 2005 election campaign. It considers whether political marketing tools represent a transient selling approach to campaigning, or alternatively whether they aim to build long-term relationships. Each chapter evaluates the use, nature and impact of key marketing techniques in order to see whether it is possible to determine a market orientation through the nature of the parties' communications, and if so what we can determine about the main parties' approaches.

Chapter 5 (Dermody and Hanmer-Lloyd) notes that despite politicians having a long track record of communicating direct with the electorate through public meetings, the rise of mass communications has significantly altered the way politicians communicate with their audiences (Negrine 1996; Scammell 1995). This chapter concentrates on one form of direct communication – advertising – offering an in-depth evaluation of the advertising employed by the Conservative, Labour and Liberal Democrat parties in the 2005 election. Some argue that political advertising has become one of the few ways a political party can reach a large audience with little or no mediation of its intended message (Wring 2000). The most recent Electoral Commission report, *Political advertising 2004*, advocates a strong role for this form of political communication, particularly in relation to informing and engaging parts of the electorate which might otherwise have little knowledge of or interest in politics. This analysis investigates how and to what extent the main parties addressed these issues in their advertising through the gathering of data from the parties' advertising agencies, coupled with a content analysis of a sample of the advertising used (party election broadcasts and poster advertising). The chapter concludes with an assessment of each of the parties' advertising campaigns: how market-oriented they were, and whether they responded to competitor communications.

Chapter 6 (Gaber) starts with the premise that, historically, for the vast majority of the electorate the campaign has been principally experienced as audience members of mass media – the press, radio and television. Hence parties devote considerable resources and energy to campaigning through the media; indeed, the parties' overall campaign strategies, and their media campaign strategies, are inextricably linked. Gaber studies how parties have, in the past, used the media to campaign and, with reference to the 2005 campaign, studies how that is now changing with the growth of twenty-four-hour news, the rise of direct marketing techniques and the increasing lack of political interest or party allegiance being demonstrated by the electorate. The chapter notes that in part a significant shift has been away from a single campaign and to two discrete campaigns: a mediated 'air' war and a locally based 'ground' war. This, Gaber notes, has had an effect on the parties' overall media campaigns, their strategies of media promotion, attack and defence, their use of the daily press conference, the leaders' tours, party election broadcasts and crisis management techniques. The discussion is contextualised within the overall marketing strategy of the parties.

Chapter 7 (Jackson) argues that political parties have traditionally used a transactional marketing approach to secure votes (Mauser 1983; Lees-Marshment 2001; Wring 2001). However, relationship marketing (Berry 1983; Gronroos 2004; Gummesson 2002) provides political parties with an alternative strategy for contesting elections. Regular, targeted communication that seeks to build long-term relationships with voters can, potentially, mobilise both core and floating voters (Dean and Croft 2001; Bannon 2003; Bowers-Brown 2003). Owing to the greater access to information, relationship marketing is considered more achievable online (Krol 1999; Wang *et al* 2000). Although the Internet played a limited role in the 2001 general election, the rapid increase in access to the Internet suggests that it should have played a much more important role in 2005 (Coleman 2001). This chapter considers whether parties did conduct an e-relationship marketing strategy, through a study of the use of Web sites and e-newsletters. Data collected through interviews with national party campaign strategists, and content analysis of Web sites and e-newsletters are measured against a five-point framework to assess whether the parties conducted an online relationship marketing approach.

Part III focuses on the 'audience' or targets for the product and its attendant communication, in psephological terms those we describe as the electorate (though this may mean not that they actually take part but that they are able to do so). The part studies the electorate's shape and composition, the ground war waged by the parties and the electorate's response to the local and national campaigns.

Chapter 8 (Scullion) takes an innovative approach in order to investigate the electorate at a micro-level. He starts with the premise that most of those who can be described as 'the electorate' are more likely to consider themselves primarily as consumers, or at least to think in a consumerist way. In other words their daily lives are taken up with being a consumer and all that that involves. Occasionally, and mainly during election periods, they are labelled electors, or even citizens, and are expected to see themselves as such, but do they? The chapter's purpose is to gain an understanding of where politics and more specifically the election fitted in people's overall lives. Was it conceptualised as just another burdensome choice they had to make? Were the choices presented during the election seen in a similar way to those encountered in other spheres (i.e. supermarket shopping or E-bay browsing)? Did their sense of empowerment as consumers impact on how they engaged with the election? Scullion offers a market-oriented context in which to view the election by exploring the meanings attributed to it through a consumerist lens. Using a series of in-depth interviews with a purposive sample of the electorate made up of those people who (via the use of filter questions) are considered what might be called 'late modern consumers' in the sense outlined by Campbell (2004), voters who have a positive predisposition towards being active consumers and through consumption 'discover who they are' Campbell (2004: 35), we find an alternative view of how electoral choice is perceived.

Chapter 9 (Lilleker) contrasts the traditional view of elections as a nationally orchestrated affair with the brand, the leader and the key messages as the determining factors in voter choices. Research suggests politicians segment the market along socio-economic lines (Cui and Choudray 2002), but the campaign remained national rather than local. The effectiveness of the national campaign, however, has been questioned, often starting with the overused aphorism 'All politics is local'. It is increasingly found that the energy and resources invested in the local campaign had a significant effect in terms of voter choice and turnout (Denver and Hands 2001; Denver *et al.* 2003; Johnston and Pattie 2003). Some of these factors are due to the service provided by the incumbent (Butler and Collins 1999); others, however, are related to candidates making political messages relevant to the lives of local people in the same way as local outlets translate brand values into a community (Lilleker and Negrine 2006). This chapter, using survey and focus group data, empirically tests the extent to which local factors and an integrated, but locally focused, marketing campaign play a role in voter choice selection, and assesses whether the local campaign can be a truer expression of a market orientation and acceptance of a marketing philosophy (Kotler 1991) throughout the organisation.

In Chapter 10 (Dean) notes that there has been extensive discussion in the literature of the loss of trust in politicians and the link with a reduction in turnout (Furnham and Gunter 1987; Heath and Park 1997; Park 1995, 1999). In the 2004 US presidential campaign there was a polarisation of voting intentions (Meyerson 2004) due to the contest being perceived either as a referendum on the presidency of George W. Bush or his actions in the 'war on terrorism'. The opinion polls monitoring voting intentions showed it would be a close contest, which according to Downs (1957) would suggest that turnout should actually increase. Was the same a feature of the UK, with trust in Tony Blair in the context of the Iraq war being a salient factor? Earlier studies have demonstrated that political campaigns may have an effect upon the electoral decision making but, rather than changing attitudes, campaigns merely reinforce existing opinions (Blumler and McQuail 1968; Ansolabehere and Iyengar 1995). However, as many voters have not decided on their voting intentions, Denver and Hands (1990) argue that voters may be more open to influence. This chapter reviews the political campaigns holistically through the eyes of young voters disengaged from politics. It will examine what (if any) information they took from the political communication campaigns, the reasons for their lack of engagement and the implications for political marketing.

The conclusion will reflect the arguments developed in each chapter to construct an analysis of the 2005 election, assessing whether it was a watershed in the use of marketing. We will question the extent to which a market orientation was evidenced in the creation of the products offered by each party. Was the communication that worthy of a slick public limited company or more of an amateur affair, and did it appeal to the political consumers or did the campaign offer only what was perceived as a series of lacklustre products that were left on the shelf? The aim will be to assess the impact of political marketing, the implications, and to offer some thoughts for future elections.

References

Aaker, J. L. (1997), 'Dimensions of brand personality', *Journal of Marketing Research* 34: 347.

Ansolabehere, S. D. and Iyengar, S. (1995), *Going Negative: How Political Advertisements Shrink and Polarize the Electorate*, New York: Free Press.

Bannon, D. P. (2003), 'Relationship Marketing and the Political Process', paper presented at the Political Marketing Conference 2003, Middlesex University, September.

Berry, L. (1983), 'Relationship marketing' in L. Berry, G. Shostack and G. Upak (eds), *Perspectives on Services*, Chicago: American Marketing Association.

Blumler, J. and Kavanagh, D. (1995), *The Crisis of Public Communication*, London: Routledge.

Blumler, J. and McQuail, D. (1968), *Television in Politics: its Uses and Influence*, London: Faber.

Bowers-Brown, J. (2003), 'A marriage made in cyberspace? Political marketing and UK party websites', in R. Gibson, P. Nixon and S. Ward (eds), *Political Parties and the Internet: Net Gain?* London: Routledge.

Bowler, S. and Farrell, M. (1992), 'The study of election campaigning', in S. Bowler and M. Farrell, *Election Strategies and Political Marketing*, Basingstoke: Macmillan.

Burkett, H. (2005), article posted on mad.co.uk, www.mad.co.uk/electionspecial/print.aspx?uid=5cc9ad6b-3db1-4877-bc47-9380704ec732, accessed 3 September 2005.

Butler, P. and Collins, N. (1994), 'Political marketing: structures and process', *European Journal of Marketing* 28: 19–34.

Butler, P. and Collins, N. (1999), 'A conceptual framework for political marketing', in B. Newman (ed.), *Handbook of Political Marketing*, Thousand Oaks CA: Sage.

Butler, P. and Collins, N. (2001), 'Payment on delivery: recognising constituency service as political marketing', *European Journal of Marketing* 35 (9–10): 1026–37.

Campbell, C. (2004), 'I shop, therefore I know that I am: the metaphysical basis of modern consumption', in K. Ekstrom and H. Brembeck (eds), *Elusive Consumption*, Oxford: Berg.

Christopher, M., Payne, A. and Ballantyne, D. (1991), *Relationship Marketing*, Oxford: Butterworth-Heinemann.

Clarke, H., Sander, D., Stewart, M. and Whiteley, P. (2004), *Political Choice in Britain*, Oxford: Oxford University Press.

Coleman, S. (2001), *Elections in the Age of the Internet: Lessons from the United States*, London: Hansard Society.

Coleman, S. (2003), *A Tale of Two Houses: The House of Commons, the Big Brother House and the People at Home*, London: Hansard Society/Channel 4.

Coleman, S. and Rowe, C. (2005), *Remixing Citizenship: Democracy and Young People's Use of the Internet*, Dunfermline: Carnegie United Kingdom Trust.

Cui, G. and Choudray, P. (2002), 'Marketplace diversity and cost-effective marketing strategies', *Journal of Consumer Marketing*, 19 (1): 54–73.

de Chernatony, L. and Dall'Olmo Riley, F. (1998), 'Defining a "brand": beyond the literature with experts' interpretations', *Journal of Marketing Management* 14: 417–43.

Dean, D. and Croft, R. (2001), 'Friends and relations: long-term approaches to political campaigning', *European Journal of Marketing* 35 (11–12): 1197–216.

Denver, D. and Hands, G. (1990), 'Issues, principles or ideology? How young people decide', *Electoral Studies* 9 (1): 19–36.

Denver, D. and Hands, G. (1997), *Modern Constituency Electioneering: Local Campaigning in the 1992 General Election*, London: Frank Cass.

Denver, D. and Hands, G. (2001), 'The fall and rise of constituency campaigning', in J. Bartle and D. Griffiths (eds), *Political Communications Transformed: From Morrison to Mandelson*, Basingstoke: Palgrave Macmillan.

Denver, D., Hands, G. and MacAllister, I. (2003), 'Constituency marginality and turnout in Britain revisited', in C. Rallings, R. Scully, J. Tonge and P. Webb (eds), *British Elections and Parties Review* XIII, London: Frank Cass.

Dermody, J. and Scullion, R. (2005), 'Young people's attitudes towards British political advertising: nurturing or impeding voter engagement?' *Journal of Non-profit and Public Sector Marketing*, special edition on political marketing.

Downs, A. (1957), *An Economic Theory of Democracy*, New York: Harper & Row.

Firat, A. and Dholakia, N. (1998), *Consuming People: From Political Economy to Theatres of Consumption*, London: Routledge.

Fournier, S. (1998), 'Consumers and their brands: developing relationship theory in consumer research', *Journal of Consumer Research* 24 (4): 343–64.

Furnham, A. and Gunter, B. (1989), *The Anatomy of Adolescence: Young People's Social Attitudes in Britain*, London: Routledge.

Gabriel, Y. and Lang, T. (1995), *The Unmanageable Consumer*, London: Sage.

Gould, P. (1998), *The Unfinished Revolution: How the Modernisers Saved the Labour Party*, London: Little Brown.

Gronroos, C. (1994), 'From marketing mix to relationship marketing: towards a paradigm shift in marketing', *Management Decision*, 34 (3): 5–14.

Gummesson, E. (2002), *Total Relationship Marketing*, Oxford: Butterworth-Heinemann.

Heath, A., Jowell, R. and Curtice, J. (2001), *The Rise of New Labour: Party Policies and Voter Choices*, Oxford: Oxford University Press.

Heath, A. and Park, A. (1997), 'Thatcher's children?' in R. Jowell, J. Curtice, A. Park, I. Brook and K. Thomson (eds), *British Social Attitudes: The Fourteenth Report. The End of Conservative Values?* Aldershot: Gower.

Holt, D. (2002), 'Why do brands cause trouble? A dialectical theory of consumer culture and branding', *Journal of Consumer Research* 29: 70–90.

Houston, F. S. (1986), 'The marketing concept: what it is and what it is not', *European Journal of Marketing* 50: 81–7.

Jackson, N. A. (2004), 'Party e-newsletters in the UK: a return to direct political communication?' *Journal of E-government* 1 (4): 39–62.

Johnston, R. and Pattie, C. (2003), 'Do canvassing and campaigning work? Evidence from the 2001 General Election in England', in C. Rallings, R. Scully, J. Tonge and P. Webb (eds), *British Elections and Parties Review* XIII, London: Frank Cass.

Knuckey, J. and Lees-Marshment, J. (2005), 'American political marketing: George W. Bush and the Republican Party', in D. G. Lilleker and J. Lees-Marshment (eds), *Political Marketing in Comparative Perspective*, Manchester: Manchester University Press.

Kohli, A. K., Jaworski, B. J. and Kumar, A. (1993), 'MARKOR: a measure of market orientation', *Journal of Marketing Research* 30: 467–77.

Kotler, P. (1991), *Marketing Management: Analysis, Planning, Implementation and Control*, 7th edn, Upper Saddle River NJ: Prentice Hall.

Kotler, P. and Armstrong, G. (2001), *Principles of Marketing*, 9th edn, Englewood Cliffs NJ: Prentice Hall.

Krol, C. (1999), 'Web becomes crucial to relationship efforts: Miller/Huber's new clientele formalises its interactive capabilities', *Advertising Age*, 24 May: 52.

Lees-Marshment, J. (2001), *Political Marketing and British Political Parties*, Manchester: Manchester University Press.

Lees-Marshment, J. (2004), *The Political Marketing Revolution*, Manchester: Manchester University Press.

Lees-Marshment, J. and Lilleker, D. (2005), 'Political marketing in the UK: a positive start but an uncertain future', in D. G. Lilleker and J. Lees-Marshment, *Political Marketing in Comparative Perspective*, Manchester: Manchester University Press

Lewis, J., Inthorn, S. and Wahl-Jorgensen, K. (2005), *Citizens or Consumers: What the Media tell us about Political Participation*, Maidenhead: Open University Press.

Lilleker, D. G. (2005a), 'The impact of political marketing on internal party democracy', *Parliamentary Affairs* 58 (3): 570–84.

Lilleker, D. G. (2005b), 'Political marketing: the cause of a democratic deficit?' *Journal of Non-profit and Public Sector Marketing* 14(1/2): 5–26.

Lilleker, D. G. and Lees-Marshment, J. (2005), 'Conclusion: towards a comparative model of party marketing', in D. G Lilleker and J. Lees-Marshment, *Political Marketing in Comparative Perspective*, Manchester: Manchester University Press.

Lilleker, D. G. and Negrine, R. (2003), 'Not big brand names but corner shops: marketing politics to a disengaged electorate', *Journal of Political Marketing* 2 (1): 55–75.

Lilleker, D. G. and Negrine, R. (2006), 'Mapping a market orientation: can we only detect political marketing through the lens of hindsight?' in P. J. Davies and B. I. Newman (eds), *Winning Elections with Political Marketing*, New York: Haworth.

Lock, A. and Harris, P. (1996), 'Political marketing: *vive la différence*', *European Journal of Marketing* 30 (10–11): 14–24.

Marland, A. (2005), 'Canadian political parties: market-oriented or ideological slagbrains?' in D. G. Lilleker and J. Lees-Marshment (eds), *Political Marketing in Comparative Perspective*, Manchester: Manchester University Press.

Mattey, S. (2005), article posted on mad.co.uk, www.mad.co.uk/electionspecial/print.aspx?uid=7261458d-f86a-46e2-924a-705f37809776, accessed 9 June 2005.

Mauser, G. (1983), *Political Marketing: An Approach to Campaign Strategy*, New York: Praeger.

McGee, L.W. and Spiro, R. L. (1988), 'The marketing concept in perspective', *Business Horizons* 31 (3): 40–5.

Mercer, G. (2005), article posted on mad.co.uk, www.mad.co.uk/electionspecial/story.aspx?uid=b44cbb3a-05d5-410c-912c-7fd8dfbe2a36, accessed 9 June 2005.

Meyerson, F. A. B. (2004), 'Policy view: immigration, population policy, and the Sierra Club', *Population and Environment* 26 (1): 61–9.

Miller, D. (1997), *Capitalism; An Ethnographic Approach*, New York: Berg.

Moloney, K. (2004), 'The Sceptical Case for Political Marketing', paper presented at the Political Studies Association annual meeting, University of Lincoln, 6–8 April.

Narver, J. and Slater, S. (1990), 'The effect of market orientation on business profitability', *Journal of Marketing* 54: 20–35.

Negrine, R. (1996), *The Communication of Politics*, London: Sage.

Negrine, R. and Lilleker, D. (2003), 'The professionalisation of media-based campaigning in Britain, 1966–2001: the rise of a proactive media strategy', *Journalism Studies* 4 (2): 199–211.

Newman, B. I. (1999), *The Mass Marketing of Politics*, Thousand Oaks CA: Sage.

Norris, P., Curtice, J., Sanders, D., Scammell, M. and Semetko, H. (1999), *On Message: Communicating the Campaign*, London: Sage.

Ormrod, R. (2005), 'A critique of the Lees-Marshment market-oriented party model', *Politics*, forthcoming.

O'Shaughnessy, J. (1990), *The Phenomenon of Political Marketing*, London: Macmillan.

Ozanne, J. and Murray, J. (1995), 'Uniting critical theory and public policy to create the reflexively defiant consumer', *American Behavioural Scientist* 38: 516–25.

Panebianco, A. (1988), *Political Parties: Organisation and Power*, Cambridge: Cambridge University Press.

Park, A. (1995), 'Teenagers and their politics', in R. Jowell, J. Curtice and A. Park, *British Social Attitudes: Twelfth Report*, Aldershot: Dartmouth.

Park, A. (1999), 'Young people and political apathy', in R. Jowell, J. Curtice, A. Park, K. Thompson and L. Jarvis (eds), *British Social Attitudes: The Sixteenth Report*, Aldershot: Ashgate.

Popkin, S. (1994), *The Reasoning Voter: Communication and Persuasion in Presidential Campaigns*, Chicago: University of Chicago Press.

Rudd, C. (2005), 'Marketing the message or the messenger? The New Zealand Labour Party, 1990–2003', in D. G. Lilleker and J. Lees-Marshment (eds), *Political Marketing in Comparative Perspective*, Manchester: Manchester University Press.

Savigny, H. (2005), 'Labour, political marketing and the 2005 election: a campaign of two halves', *Journal of Marketing Management*, forthcoming.

Scammell, M. (1995), *Designer Politics*, Basingstoke: St Martin's Press.

Scammell, M. (1999), 'Political marketing: lessons for political science', *Political Studies* 47: 718–39.

Shama, A. (1976), 'The marketing of political candidates', *Journal of the Academy of Marketing Science* 4 (4): 767–77.

Wang, F., Head, M. and Archer, N. (2000), 'A relationship-building model for the Web retail marketplace', *Internet Research: Electronic Networking Applications and Polic,* 10 (5): 374–84.

Watt, N. and Borger, J. (2004), 'Tories reveal secret weapon to target voters', *Guardian*, 9 October.

Wernick, A. (1991), *Promotional Culture*, London: Sage.

Whiteley, P., Clarke, H., Sanders, D. and Stewart, M. (2001), 'Turnout', *Parliamentary Affairs* 54 (4): 775–88.

Wring, D. (2000), 'Machiavellian communication: the role of spin doctors and image makers in early and late twentieth-century British politics', in P. Harris, A. Lock and P. Rees (eds), *Machiavelli, Marketing and Management*, London: Routledge.

Wring, D. (2001), 'Selling socialism', *European Journal of Marketing* 35 (9–10): 1038–47.

Wring, D. (2002), 'Images of Labour: the progression and politics of party campaigning in Britain', *Journal of Political Marketing* 1 (1): 23–37.

Wring, D. (2005), *The Politics of Marketing the Labour Party*, Basingstoke: Palgrave.

Part I

The product

At the heart of much marketing exchange is a product. It is the reason why the buyer and seller come together. For many the quality of the product on offer becomes the ultimate test of whether an organisation deserves to survive and prosper. If insufficient people prefer one offering to other compatible offerings then it is usually necessary to make changes to the product. If this premise has any truth in it, and it is applicable to a political context, then it becomes clear why it is vital first to investigate the organisation's products in a full and critical manner.

So what is a political product? Service marketing is relevant in our context, given that the nature of the political product is largely characterised as a service rather than a physical product. This means we are talking about something intangible, making it hard to judge *before* we decide which product to buy; thus actual experience becomes critical. However, some tangible items are produced that allow us to research the political product. An important representation of the product is contained in the party manifesto, the subject, in part, of Chapter 2. This recognises that the political product is in part created as a result of customers' (electors) direct contact with the providers (political party) rather than some pre-packaged item we select from a shelf. The clichéed analogy with selling baked beans has some, but only crude and limited, substance. Consequently the political product is hard to standardise, as aspects are perceptual and individual, and indeed trying to do so may not be very desirable. That said, some attempts to create a constant and consistent political product can be seen when we look at the parties, branding, the subject of Chapter 3.

Products are often described as a layered concept, suggesting products are composed of a core, a peripheral, an augmented and a potential element. One way of applying this to the context of a political party might be to see a set of strongly held views about how society *should* be ordered at its core: its programme of promises sometimes referred to as its ideological roots. This element may now be less pronounced than once was the case and is again a subject picked up in Chapter 4.

Facets of the party's organisation, including its leading personalities and branding strategy, may contribute to the peripheral layer: how is it going to implement the plan and who are the lead figures? These issues are investigated in Chapter 3. Augmented elements may include style, aesthetic and how it communicates. Some of the pertinent issues here are covered in Part II. A political product's potential lies, to an extent, in the perceptions held about its record of competence, its ability to succeed and its future intentions. The book explores this further, whilst exploring the consumer's perspective of the election in Part III.

Any brief discussion about the importance of understating the product needs to embrace the notion that offerings are strategically managed. That is to say, the offering is created and developed in part with the intention of placing it in a specific 'position' *vis-à-vis* its competitors. Here 'position' refers to a perceptual space in the minds of relevant stakeholders, including party members, supporters, journalists and opponents. In any competitive setting some form of differentiation over other offerings is vital. This requirement is particularly acute during election periods, when each party is trying to persuade as many people as possible to demonstrate support for it at the ballot box. There are of course many ways to achieve a differentiated positioning. Part I focuses on those most closely associated with the product itself: ideology, strategic posture and branding. An emerging theme that seems particularly relevant to the British political party market place is the apparent convergence of the offerings: all three main political parties talk about occupying the deified 'middle ground'. We are not making any claims here that such circumstances are right or wrong, just that they are less evident, and certainly rarely commented on, in most other market places.

If, at the heart of much marketing exchange, we can still see the product, it is worthy of being our starting point for our marketing analysis of the British General Election of 2005.

2

'Are you thinking what we're thinking?' or 'Are we thinking what you're thinking?' An exploratory analysis of the market orientation of the UK parties

Robert P. Ormrod and Stefan C. M. Henneberg

Understanding how political players such as parties or candidates inter-act with voters, citizens, and other political stakeholders in the electoral sphere is at the heart of research on political marketing. The analysis of political campaigns is now a well researched aspect of political market-ing theory (Butler and Collins 1996; Kotler and Kotler 1999; O'Cass 2001; Lees-Marshment 2001a, 2003; Smith 2001; Smith and Hirst 2001; Wring 2002; Baines *et al.* 2002; Newman 2002), but as well as the 'how' of political exchanges, there is also the question of the 'what'. What is the political product or, better, the 'political offering' that polit-ical actors create in order to facilitate exchanges by creating mutual value (Henneberg 2002)? And how do exchange and value come about? The way the offering of electoral policies is developed, i.e. the promises about general and specific political issues, is an important element of a party or candidate's orientation towards political marketing manage-ment. Analysing how parties or candidates relate to other political stake-holders, especially voters and citizens, through the development of electoral policies enables a deeper insight into their 'market orientation' as well as their 'strategic posture' as part of political marketing man-agement. Manifestoes are the codified and most direct exemplifications of these electoral policies, i.e. the core offering of parties and candidates.

Therefore, the Conservative slogan for the 2005 UK General Election, 'Are you thinking what we're thinking?' (Conservative Party 2005a, b; Scottish Conservative Party 2005), may already indicate a specific way of relating to voters. Note that the slogan does not state 'We are thinking what you are thinking'. That would indicate an orientation of understanding, i.e. listening to the needs and opinions of the voters, something that is commonly attributed to a Voter or Market Orientation, and analogous to a 'consumer orientation' in commercial marketing. However, the Conservatives chose to turn it around, starting with their own convictions and asking people to align themselves with these convictions: 'Are you thinking what we're thinking?'

The semantic difference between these two possible slogans may be no more than that, a semantic difference, without pointing towards some more general, underlying orientation of the party regarding its electoral offering. However, in order to assess these issues in a more analytical fashion, we will employ several concepts from marketing theory to foster a better understanding of how the main political parties in the UK relate to other actors in the political sphere, and more specifically their core offering of the election manifesto. For this purpose, we introduce and operationalise two different political marketing concepts, that of Political Market Orientation (Ormrod 2005) and that of Strategic Political Postures (Henneberg 2006a). Both are directly developed out of the rich theoretical and empirical literature on market orientation in commercial marketing that has become the focus of strategic marketing concepts since its introduction at the beginning of the 1990s (Kohli and Jaworski 1990; Narver and Slater 1990). Therefore, the aim of this chapter is twofold: first, we will provide a discussion of the market orientation of the main UK parties in the 2005 General Election through an exploratory content analysis. In order to achieve this, we are focusing on the content of the party political offering as exemplified by the different manifestoes. This analysis is informed by two different conceptual aspects of market orientation. Through such an analysis, we will gain analytical insight into whether the 2005 UK General Election was a 'political marketing election'.

Specifically, we are going to focus on two research questions with regard to the party political offering:

1 How 'voter and market-oriented' are the three major British political parties in the 2005 General Election?
2 What are the key differences in voter and market orientation between the parties?

Both research questions will be analysed using the British and regional main electoral party manifestoes of the Conservative Party, the Liberal Democrat Party, and the Labour Party as examples of their offering. This chapter will be structured as follows. We commence by providing a discussion of the political offering, with special emphasis on the issue of the party political manifesto. Following on from this, a conceptual grounding is provided by briefly introducing the framework of market orientation. Two examples of the use of this concept in political marketing research are discussed (Political Market Orientation by Ormrod 2005 and Strategic Political Postures by Henneberg 2006a) and an operationalisation framework is developed. After a discussion of our research methodology, a section on the findings of our analysis will address our research questions. We will conclude with a discussion of the results of this study, as well as with an outline of the general implications.

The manifesto as a political offering

The political exchange process (as the core *explanandum* of political marketing theory) is characterised by a complexity that sets it apart from most of the commercial exchange processes (Henneberg 2004). Briefly stated, certain aspects of this exchange can be clearly identified. First, many different stakeholder groups are involved in political exchanges. This has been characterised as the interplay between 'high politics' (i.e. electoral and governmental political exchanges) and 'low politics', i.e. interest-based and non-electoral political exchanges (Henneberg 2002). Second, this is further complicated by the fact that the core (electoral and governmental) exchanges are made up of many actors; unlike a commercial situation with a buyer and a seller, here the exchange is diffused and multi-phased; moreover, the electorate exchanges with parties/candidates then merge into government or executive power, which implements certain policies for the citizens. Third, because mostly 'public goods' are exchanged in politics, the electoral decision making is not direct and individual but indirect and aggregated (Wortmann 1989; Newman 1994).

These political exchange characteristics have an impact on the fabric of the 'political offering'. In this chapter, the political offering is posited to be the electoral promise on which candidates and parties can expect to garner support, and which voters use to differentiate between different options in the electoral market. As such, the political offering is a multi-faceted concept (Reid 1988; Butler and Collins 1999; Wring 2002), dependent on voters' idiosyncratic decision-making processes and contextual variables of the election campaign (Sniderman *et al.* 1991; Popkin 1994). Therefore the political offering is much more complex and bundled than any analogy of 'politics being sold like soap' would imply. Also, the political offering does not show product characteristics but is inherently a service-equivalent offering (O'Shaughnessy and Holbrook 1988; Harrop 1990; Newman 1994; Scammell 1999; Lloyd 2003). As such, it consists of tangible as well as non-tangible aspects (promise and expectation-based) (Lock and Harris 1996). Furthermore, services are delivered mainly by interaction between people (service providers as well as customers). Therefore, an assessment of the people aspect of the offering is crucial for an overall evaluation. With regard to the political offering, it has been suggested that a focus on issue policies, as embedded mainly in the election manifesto, does not cover the whole political offering. The candidate characteristics (Kavanagh 1995; Kotler and Kotler 1999; Smith 2001; Lloyd, 2003) and also the overall party image and history are crucial variables that complete the multi-faceted offering concept underlying political marketing theory.

In our study we will focus on the 2005 election manifestoes of the three main UK parties for our analysis of their market orientation. Our focus on text for the analysis of market orientation (in contrast with, for example, an interview-based enquiry) was determined by our aim of identifying 'actual' strategic positions of the parties and not 'intended' or 'perceived' ones (Kohli and Jaworski 1990). The manifesto is seen as a *pars pro toto* of the whole offering, i.e. it best reflects the strategic position of the political parties, and provides what Dermody and Scullion (2000) call the signification and representation function of political exchange. We posit that this is due to the manifesto being the main element of the offering, and that it does not change significantly during the duration of the election campaign. Furthermore, the manifesto is disseminated in a relatively coherent and undifferentiated way, while other offering characteristics are used in a targeted and tailored way as part of political marketing activities. One caveat to this is constituted by the fact that, in recent years, manifestoes have become themselves somewhat targeted, mainly with regard to the mass media and their representation of the manifestoes. However, manifestoes can still be seen as 'framing' campaigns to some extent. These characteristics allow us to research the strategic aspects which are embedded in a market orientation without contamination by the tactics present in all electioneering activities.

Before the different manifestoes are analysed, it is necessary to discuss the conceptual grounding of our study. Therefore, the next section will briefly introduce the concept of market orientation, which is of great importance to contemporary marketing theory. We will also discuss two different applications and the operationalisation of this concept for political marketing.

Conceptual grounding: market orientation

Market orientation, strategic postures, and marketing theory

Although there have been various conceptualisations of the constituent elements of a commercial market orientation, Lafferty and Hult (2001) reviewed the literature and identified two general approaches that characterised the vast majority of research in this area. Kohli and Jaworski (1990) conceptualised a market orientation as a set of *managerial behaviours* that centred on the ability of the organisation to generate, disseminate, and act upon market intelligence. This goes beyond a mere 'customer orientation' because it becomes a holistic, company-wide, perspective that is oriented towards competitors and other stakeholders, as well as customers. At the same time, Narver and Slater (1990) emphasised the *organisational culture* that has to be in place in order for a market orientation to exist. This was conceptualised as a focus on customers, competitors, and the way in which the different departments of the business worked together. These two fundamental approaches, a behavioural and an organisational culture approach, have formed the basis of most of the subsequent research in the commercial marketing literature (see Deshpandé 1999 for an overview; Lafferty and Hult 2001). It is posited that a higher degree of market orientation enhances organisational performance (and while this is generally true, Kohli and Jaworski (1990) discuss some contextual issues). As such, market orientation is an important application of the resource-based and competence-based view of the firm from the strategy literature within marketing theory (Hunt and Lambe 2000).

While the concept of market orientation has been widely used in theoretical and empirical research in marketing (Morgan and Strong 1998), the literature on political marketing has not yet adopted the full potential of this concept. Whilst research in political marketing has mainly conceptualised a Political Market Orientation as being synonymous with a Voter Orientation (O'Cass 1996, 2001; Lees-Marshment 2001a, b; Lilleker and Lees-Marshment 2005), the marketing literature makes an important distinction between being market-oriented and customer-oriented (or customer-led) (Slater and Narver 1998) when focusing on the positioning strategy that a business can adopt. A business that follows a customer-led philosophy will place more importance on gaining information from product users in order to facilitate a gradual evolution of the offering; it *follows* the market. On the other hand, the market-oriented philosophy can also attempt to anticipate customers' future needs and wants, by creating novel offerings that are unexpressed; it *leads* the market (Slater and Narver 1999). As such, the balance between leading and following is represented in the strategic posture of an organisation with regard to offering development (Connor 1999).

In the following, we will therefore drive the conceptual development of Political Market Orientation further by, first, discussing a concept that incorporates behavioural as well as cultural and attitudinal aspects required to operationalise Political Market Orientation. Second, the distinction between party political postures, i.e. leading and following voters in developing a political offering, is introduced to provide a second facet of Political Market Orientation in our analysis.

A conceptual model of Political Market Orientation

The conceptual model of Political Market Orientation that we will use in the following (Ormrod 2004, 2005) draws upon commercial marketing research in this field (Kohli and Jaworski 1990; Narver and Slater 1990; Harrison-Walker 2001), and includes Lafferty and Hult's (2001) synthesis of the dimensions of market orientation, emphasis on the customer, the importance of information, inter-functional co-ordination and taking action. The model also expands on the various conceptualisations in the commercial marketing literature by including an explicit reference to the importance of relationship development with actors in society that are not voters or competing parties, i.e. incorporating the complex 'market' situation of political exchanges. The market-oriented political party is said to exist when 'its members are sensitive to the attitudes, needs and wants of both external and internal stakeholders, and [use] this information within limits imposed by all stakeholder groups in order to develop policies and programmes that enable the party to reach its aims' (Ormrod 2005: 51).

The conceptual model of Political Market Orientation is built up around eight constructs. The four behavioural constructs capture the way in which the party gains information on the external and internal stakeholders, passes this information on, includes it in policy and strategy development and then implements these in a consistent fashion. The four behavioural constructs are arranged in a chain that maps the process of information through the party; this does not, however, imply capability dependence, as it is possible for large amounts of information on, for example, voter preferences to be produced, but little of this is passed on to other party members (Ormrod 2005). The remaining four constructs represent the attitudes of party members to four distinct stakeholder groups, namely voters, competitors, party members and other external stakeholder groups, such as the media, interest groups and lobby groups. Whilst voters and competitors are present in the commercial market orientation literature, as well as to some extent a focus on internal members (Narver and Slater 1990), Ormrod's model (2005) emphasises the importance of other actors in society owing to their ability to affect policy development through, for example, agenda setting (Dean and Croft 2001; O'Cass 2001; Henneberg 2002). The four stakeholder groups impact upon each stage of the behavioural 'chain'; for example, the behaviour of the media may be discussed widely throughout the party but have no real effect on how consistently the strategy is implemented.

In order to analyse the 2005 election manifestoes, the content of each of the dimensions of the construct of Political Market Orientation must be made explicit through an operationalisation. However, the operationalisation used for this study focuses on the cultural and attitudinal aspects of a Political Market Orientation. This is due to the fact that these aspects directly manifest themselves in the electoral policies and their description, while the behavioural aspects, that is, the way in which party members generate information, disseminate it throughout the party, etc., in order to produce the manifestoes, cannot be gauged from the electoral offerings themselves.

Table 2.1 lists the four attitudinal variables as the second-level constructs, their definitions (Ormrod 2004, 2005), and a content description with sub-variables as first-level constructs for the operationalisation of a content analysis. The first construct, Internal Orientation, concentrates on references to party members in the offerings. These can be the party elite (e.g. incumbent politicians at Westminster, party professionals), elected members in other legislative bodies or the party rank and file, and evidence will be sought as to the extent to which these are named, involved, and valued. The content of the Voter Orientation construct looks for indications that the party has empathy with and knowledge of the opinions of the electorate and the extent to which they are considered to be important. This should not be understood as if the party exclusively follows voter opinion, as it is possible for the party to listen to voters and yet consider other factors to be more relevant when making a decision. The third construct, Competitor Orientation, examines the extent to which the party in question accepts that it may be necessary to co-operate with competing parties or other organisations to attain the party's own long-term aims; again, the party does not have to co-operate, it is simply the acknowledgement that this is a possibility which is important. An emphasis on being aware of competitors' policy positions is important for this construct. Finally, the External Orientation construct concerns the perception by the party of the existence and importance of stakeholders in society that are not voters, competitors or party members.

Table 2.1 The attitudinal constructs of Political Market orientation

Attitudinal constructs (second-level construct)	*Definition (Ormrod 2005)*	*Construct dimension for analysis (first-level construct)*
Internal Orientation	'the party-wide awareness and acceptance of the value of other members' opinions, irrespective of position in the party'	• Inclusiveness of the party • Acknowledgement of the importance of other party members • Acknowledgement of the existence of other party members
Voter Orientation	'the party-wide awareness of voter needs and wants and an acknowledgement of the importance of knowing these'	• Acknowledging the importance of current voters • Acknowledging the importance of future voters • Awareness of voter opinions
Competitor Orientation	'the party-wide awareness of other parties' attitudes and behaviours and an acknowledgement that co-operation with other parties may be necessary to attain the party's long-term objectives'	• Attitudes to long-term co-operation with competing parties • Attitudes to long-term co-operation with competing parties • Awareness of the positions of other political parties
External Orientation	'the party-wide acknowledgment of the existence and importance of stakeholders in society that are not voters or competitors'	• Macro-level stakeholders (the media) • Meso-level stakeholders (lobby and interest groups) • Public-sector employees • Micro-level stakeholders (local/community) organisations)

Source: adapted from Ormrod 2004.

Evidence of this will be looked for via the extent to which other groups are mentioned in the manifestoes.

A conceptual model of Strategic Postures of Political Marketing Management

The basic orientation of a party with regard to customer and market orientation, as well as offering development, is called its Strategic Posture. This posture 'to a large extent dictates the implementation of marketing through elements of the marketing mix' (Hooley *et al.* 2001: 503). The following conceptual discussion is mainly based on Henneberg (2006a, b).

Fundamentally, political parties have two different dimensions to choose from:

1 They can try to lead, i.e. know that their political concept (i.e. political product, ideology) is essentially right. This means that political marketing management is a tactical means to fulfil a certain mission. Leading essentially consists of trying to actively convince others (party members, voters, other constituencies) of the beneficial nature of a political offer. Leading means influencing others to achieve a behavioural reaction (e.g. provide resources, vote for the party) to realise their political aims.
2 Conversely, a party can choose to follow, i.e. it can guess, anticipate, or analyse the wishes of its specific constituency and then create a political offering that best integrates and articulates the wishes of the greatest possible number of constituency members. In this case, political marketing is not only a managerial tool to execute strategies but consists of the strategy itself to develop a political offering.

By having to decide their strategic orientation, political parties and candidates face the same decisions and trade-offs as commercial and non-commercial organisations with regard to their approach to marketing and customer orientation. Whilst most marketing literature identifies these concepts as mainly anticipating and analysing customer demands and, consequently, fulfilling them (Davis and Manrodt 1996), this description reveals only half the story. It represents the market-driven approach: based on extensive market research for profitable sub-segments, new products or product positions are based on what customers really want. In effect, this approach of following customers (or voters) leads to a policy of frequent incremental improvements. In marketing theory this is often called a customer-led philosophy (Slater and Narver 1998).

However, another expression of marketing and customer orientation is also discussed in the theoretical literature, namely a creative approach to offering development, i.e. a market-driving approach (McDonald and Wilson 2002; Hellensen 2003), leading to a new and revolutionary offering that fulfils latent (and often unexpressed) demands hitherto unknown to companies and customers alike (Kotler 2003). Slater and Narver (1998) call this the 'market-oriented philosophy'. The approach of leading is based on conviction (even in the face of contradictory evidence) and long-term commitment to understanding exchange partners (like customers or voters), but also requires empathy with one's key constituents. However, it must be based on pragmatic knowledge of what is possible and achievable; leading without gaining a following is not really leading. Leading has always been an important positive attribute of politicians. Herrmann and Huber (1996) show in a conjoint-based study of attributes of political candidates that the ability to lead is one of the three main factors in positive perception by voters (the others being social competence and integrity).

However, one caveat needs to be applied to the explanations above. Although leading and following, i.e. driving the market or being driven by it, are seemingly antagonistic concepts on a continuum, this is not the case when discussing a Political Market Orientation. Therefore, the balance with which both dimensions are applied simultaneously constitutes the specific strategic posture a political party or candidate holds. Leading and following can happen simultaneously as part of political marketing management; such a supposition is in line with the approach found in the strategic marketing literature (Connor 1999; Slater and Narver 1999).

In order to analyse the main party manifestoes, the concept of strategic postures needs to be detailed for empirical clarity. However, aspects of leading and following have not been widely operationalised in the (political) marketing literature. While Henneberg (2006b) introduces a quantitative perspective of operationalisation in a longitudinal analysis of Tony Blair's political postures between 2003 and 2004 as perceived by voters and political experts, our operationalisation in this chapter is analogously structured to the qualitative attitudinal first and second level constructs of Political Market Orientation (as outlined in Table 2.1).

Table 2.2 lists four attitudinal orientations as the second-level constructs, indicating different political postures together with content descriptions and sub-variables as first-level constructs for the operationalisation in a content analysis. The first construct of Ideology Orientation studies the impact that an ideology, in the sense of a

Table 2.2 Constructs of Strategic Political Postures

Attitudinal constructs (second-level construct)	Definition	Construct dimension for analysis (first-level construct)
Ideology Orientation	'The degree to which a guiding ideology determines or mediates policy and offering development and implementation'	• Needs and wants analysis of voters (and other actors) • Ideology centrality • Policy justification and integration • Rationale policy conflict resolution
Dialogue Orientation	'Ability to interact in meaningful exchanges with changing agenda-setting function with all main exchange constituencies'	• Communication channels and policy development sources • Empathy and understanding of perceptions of other actors • Indication of feedback from voters (and other actors) • Multiple/complex agendas, instigated by multiple actors
Stakeholder Orientation	'Degree of consideration of and interaction with a wide range of relevant actors within the electoral, governmental, and other non-traditional political markets'	• Evidence of coverage of electoral actors • Evidence of coverage of governmental actors • Evidence of coverage of 'low politics' actors • Evidence of coverage of intermediary actors
Temporal Orientation	'Ability to sustain a forward-looking posture in comparison to a backward-looking rationalisation; degree of election campaign versus permanent campaign'	• Policy offering is prospective-oriented (future projection) • Policy offering is historically developed (future extrapolation) • Offering focus on campaign, election period or longer term

relatively rigid frame of overarching value judgements, has on offering development and conflict resolution. A very central position of ideology (indicating a leading posture) can be mediated by a deep and proactive understanding of voter needs and wants (indicating more of a following posture). Crucial indicators of this second-level construct are also the justification for stands on policies and issues in the manifesto or any rationale given for resolving conflicting policy positions or stakeholder demands. The Dialogue Orientation (Varey and Ballentine 2005) of the party refers to evidence that a dialogue, through interaction, has been used as part of policy development and conflict resolution (i.e. more of a following posture) or policy communication (more typical for a leading posture). It also refers to signs of a deep understanding of a variety of exchange partners in the political market as well as opportunities for them to participate in policy considerations (e.g. via feedback loops and agenda-setting prerogatives). The third attitudinal construct, Stakeholder Orientation, refers to the specific coverage of multiple actors and actor groups as part of offering considerations. A strict Voter Orientation (a following posture) would mainly see voters as priorities, while a leading posture would be focused on governmental actors; a more market-oriented approach would balance both aspects and enrich the interaction frame by other secondary actors, e.g. single-interest groups, donors, the media (Henneberg 2002). The Temporal Orientation is an attitudinal indicator linked to a prevailing outlook in policy development: is it based on and derived from assumptions on likely future scenarios (e.g. of the economy, social changes, international developments) or is the outlook historically determined and therefore just an extrapolation of existing measures fitting existing phenomena? In addition, the Temporal Orientation is concerned with regard to the main focus of the proposed issues and policies, i.e. whether they are specifically addressing campaign and short-term issues (which would indicate more of a following posture), whether they focus also on the whole election period of office, or if they are indeed long-term and independent of election or legislation periods (indicating more of a leading posture).

Using the qualitative and exploratory operationalisation of the two facets of market orientation as introduced above, we will now continue to describe the research methods employed and how the analysis was designed and structured.

Methodology

The methodology of this chapter follows a collective case study framework (Huberman and Miles 1994; Stake 2000) and employs content analysis methods. This type of exploratory investigation was chosen owing to the nature of the models used (Yin 2003a). Both the conceptual model of Political Market Orientation and the leader/follower strategic dimensions of political marketing management have their origins in the commercial market orientation literature (Kohli and Jaworski 1990; Narver and Slater 1990; Slater and Narver 1998; Lafferty and Hult 2001). Also, the common conceptual foundation underpinning the results of the case studies carried out had the same empirical data, allowing comparisons and generalisations to be made on the ability of each model to describe phenomena and to delimit the explanatory boundaries (Yin 2003b). The content of the dimensions of the two conceptual models (first-level constructs) was explicated in order to facilitate the analysis, and then used as a framework with which to investigate each of the manifestoes.

We used content analysis techniques to overlay our constructs (components) over the analysed texts (Hodder 1994; Krippendorff 2004; Manning and Cullum-Swan 1994). Abductive inferences are used to link our research questions and the construct operationalisation with the manifesto text. Using reflexive contrast and comparison techniques as well as multi-rater assessments (Altheide and Johnson 1994; Hodder 1994; Huberman and Miles 1994) allows us to reduce the data and present our findings as 'linguistic re-presentations', e.g. exemplified in quotes from the manifestoes, synthesis and juxtaposition tables (Krippendorff 2004).

The sample chosen for analysis consisted of the 2005 General Election manifestoes of the three main parties, the Labour Party, the Conservative Party, and the Liberal Democrats. Regional parties such as Plaid Cymru (Wales) and the Scottish Nationalist Party (Scotland), minor parties such as the United Kingdom Independence Party and the British Nationalist Party, and Independents standing in only one constituency, were not selected for analysis as we intended to focus on the competitive Political Marketplace for governmental power. Only the three chosen parties position themselves strategically relative to each other, while other parties can be seen as niche players (Butler and Collins 1996). Furthermore, we also discarded 'mini-manifestoes' by the three main parties that were launched during the campaign, as they did not provide further insight and were more of a tactical campaign instrument. The choice of sample not only reflects the focus of the current work, but also provides clear-cut boundaries to the collective case design (Stake 2000), enables tentative generalisations to be made regarding market orientation and 'catch-all' parties (Kirchheimer 1966; Henneberg and Eghbalian 2002), i.e. those that appeal to a varied electorate with multiple 'segments', and which allows analysis of the regional differences that exist in each of the parties.

The Labour Party published two election manifestoes (Labour Party 2005; Scottish Labour Party 2005) for the General Election of May

2005, one that can be considered to be a 'general' example of its offering and one that was fundamentally the same but altered to reflect those policy offerings that were specific to Scotland. Both election manifestoes are 112 pages long and contain details of the achievements of the Labour government over the previous two terms, together with legislative aims for the next parliamentary period. The three Conservative Party manifestoes, one each for Britain (Conservative Party 2005), Scotland (Scottish Conservative Party 2005) and Wales (Welsh Conservative Party 2005), are very different in style from those of the Labour Party, being each only twenty-eight pages in length and concentrating on giving a more succinct overview of the party's plans for the following parliamentary period. Finally, the Liberal Democrats published four manifestoes of varying length, one each for Britain (Liberal Democrats 2005), Scotland (Scottish Liberal Democrats 2005) and Wales (Welsh Liberal Democrats 2005), and a further 'Scottish Supplement' (Scottish Liberal Democrats 2005) that detailed how the party would use the additional funds allocated to the Scottish Executive should it form the government at Westminster.

Market orientation and the main parties

In the following, we will provide analysis of each party manifesto with regard to the two explanatory constructs of market orientation used for this study, together with a visual representation of a 'grading' of first-level constructs (from 'not developed' to 'highly developed') which will summarise the level of Political Market Orientation and Strategic Political Postures for each of the parties relative to the other two. Thus providing a picture of the situation that was particular to the General Election of 2005. We will allude to the constructs as outlined in the previous section on operationalisation (see Tables 2.1–2). Furthermore, we will discuss whether and how differences in regional manifestoes impact on these aspects of market orientation.

Our operationalisation (using QSR NVivo) related aspects of first-level constructs to 'events' in the manifesto text, i.e. number of occurrences, strength of occurrence, relationship of occurrence with other related events (Strauss and Corbin 1998; Krippendorff 2004). From this we derived a relative positioning of each party for each first and second-level construct, which allowed an overall assessment of the Political Market Orientation and the Political Postures as described below. As such, this operationalisation needs to be seen as a relative snapshot of the three parties in comparison with each other in the context of the 2005 General Election, and not as an absolute score of market orientation as part of a longitudinal analysis. However, this positioning (see Figures 2.1–2) is only an expression of the 'extent' that a certain orientation or construct is present (e.g. a party is influenced significantly by a 'conflict resolution rationale'). This information needs to be supplemented by 'content' interpretations (e.g. the 'conflict resolution' is done mainly by referring to values or an ideology) in order to provide insight into a strategic political posture (in other words, second-level constructs depend on the 'extent' *and* the 'content' of the first-level constructs).

A comparison of political market orientations

The Labour Party

Explicit references to Labour's party members were restricted to those elected to the European Parliament, although there were many references to 'we' when describing the aims of the party; it was, however, unclear as to whether this should be understood as the rank and file and/or the party elite. The opposite level of attention was afforded to voters, where not only Labour's own voters but also the population in general – including young adults and children – were considered to be of importance, with consultation occurring nationally (a referendum on e.g. adopting the euro as the national currency) and at individual policy levels. There were also references to the needs and wants of voters, although there was no indication of the source from which this information was gained. The Labour manifestoes also emphasised accountability to the general public as an important characteristic of public services and the government, and to a lesser extent the party itself.

Whilst the Labour Party demonstrated a detailed knowledge of the Conservative Party's policies, the Liberal Democrat Party was not mentioned, and the only reference to co-operation with other parties was determined by the effects of the external environment on the policy area, rather than an internal willingness on the part of the party: 'because of the long-term nature of transport planning, we will seek political consensus in tackling congestion' (Labour Party 2005: 25). Finally, the Labour manifesto acknowledged the existence of external stakeholders that operate at the supranational and national level. The importance of public-sector employees was emphasised, along with the interesting finding of allowing communities autonomous control over some local assets previously administered by government authorities and thus under some form of party control. All in all, the Labour Party demonstrated a high level of Political Market Orientation on the dimensions of the Voter and External Orientation constructs, whilst this was

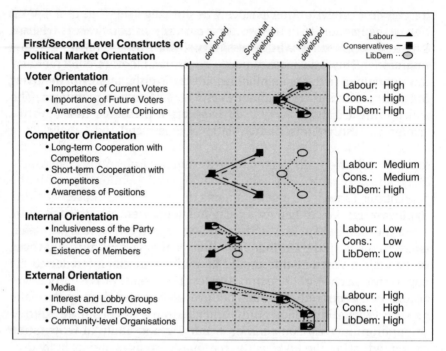

Figure 2.1   Levels of Political Marketing Orientation of the three parties

low on the Competitor and Internal Orientation constructs. This is represented graphically in Figure 2.1.

The Conservative Party

The primary slogan of the Conservative Party, 'Are you thinking what we're thinking?', demonstrates that the offering aims to inform the reader of the party's unity; however, whilst the manifestoes contain references to both 'we' and 'conservatives', it is not possible to determine whether this should be understood as referring to party members or those in the population who hold similar beliefs. All voters, however, were accorded a high level of importance, the manifesto explicitly stating that 'A Conservative government will govern in the interests of everyone in our society' (Conservative Party 2005a: 1). The Conservative Party was aware of the opinions of voters in a similar way to the Labour Party in that it primarily consisted of referenda and increasing the accountability of public services. The three manifestoes also stated knowledge of voter needs and wants on particular areas of policy, although no source was provided for this information.

Co-operation with other parties was not ruled out, but in a similar way to the Labour Party this would occur only on policy areas where a long-term perspective was necessitated by the nature of the external environment, such as infrastructure. Whilst the Liberal Democrat Party was not named in the main manifesto or the Welsh manifesto, the party was connected with the Labour Party in the Scottish manifesto. The policies of the Labour Party itself were often presented in a negative fashion to justify Conservative Party policies, and the Labour Party leader and Prime Minister, Tony Blair, was referred to as 'Mr Blair', dissociating him from his party and governmental positions of responsibility and, arguably, implying an impersonal relationship with the population. There were also comments that the Prime Minister wielded significant influence over other cabinet ministers, as emphasised by using the phrase 'Mr Blair's government'. Finally, the external stakeholders named in the Conservative Party's manifestoes mirrored those in the Labour Party manifestoes, again with a special reference to the importance of the public sector. As such, the Conservative Party manifestoes demonstrated a similar pattern of market orientation to the Labour Party's: high on the dimensions of Voter and External Orientation, low on Competitor Orientation and Internal Orientation (see Figure 2.1).

The Liberal Democrats

As with the Conservative Party, both 'we' and 'Liberal Democrats' were named as having particular beliefs as to the optimal direction of societal development and the policies that should be implemented, although it was never specified as to whether this was to be understood as referring to the sympathetic population in general or to party members in particular. The Liberal Democrat manifestoes went to great lengths to demonstrate the successes of the elected members of the Scottish Parliament that functioned as ministers in the Scottish Executive ('We can point with pride to the example of Scotland, where Liberal Democrat government ministers have already delivered', Welsh Liberal Democrats 2005: 2). There were, however, no other references to party members in general. Unlike the other two parties there were no references to *all* the population, although the Liberal Democrat Party was the only one to explicitly state that it would not forget its voters. The pattern of using referenda to gain knowledge of voter opinions on major questions was continued, together with increasing accountability of primarily public services rather than the party in particular. As with the Labour Party, the Liberal Democrat Party explicitly singled out the young as a stakeholder group of importance.

Unlike the other two parties, the Liberal Democrat Party emphasised its willingness to co-operate with other parties, especially the Labour Party in Scotland, underlining that this enabled the party to pass legislation that it had committed to in its manifesto for the Scottish Parliament elections. In all four of the party's manifestoes there were references to the Labour and Conservative Parties, and in the Scottish Supplement there was even a reference to the Scottish National Party (SNP); these references, except when emphasising the party's willingness to co-operate, were phrased negatively and as a justification for their own policies. Again, the public sector was singled out as an important external stakeholder group, with the characteristics of the remaining groups following the pattern discovered in the Labour and Conservative Parties' manifestoes. A significant difference, however, was the use of endorsements in the manifestoes for each policy area, where an individual with knowledge in that field was quoted as giving their support to the Liberal Democrat Party. The Liberal Democrat Party is arguably the most market-oriented of the three parties, in that whilst it had similar levels on the dimensions of the Voter and External Orientation constructs (high) and the Internal Orientation construct (low), evidence was found that indicated a high level of market orientation on the dimensions of the Competitor Orientation construct (see Figure 2.1).

As can be deduced from the analysis, the manifestoes of the three parties were fundamentally similar in the topics that were addressed and the way in which these were offered – high levels of Political Market Orientation on the dimensions of the Voter and External Orientation constructs, lower levels on Competitor Orientation and negligible on Internal Orientation. The only major difference was between the Labour and Conservative Parties on the one hand, and the Liberal Democrats on the other with regard to the dimensions of the Competitor Orientation construct, where the latter party emphasised the positive aspects of its co-operation with the Labour Party in the Scottish Executive. This could indicate that there is a marketplace-determined 'gravitational centre' to the level and structure of each party's Political Market Orientation where the structure of the offering is limited by the nature of the manifesto as a communicative tool, the party's political environment, and the nature of political competition.

A comparison of party political postures

Certain elements of the analysis of a market orientation and of party political postures overlap conceptually (e.g. Voter Orientation as a second-level construct of market orientation and as a first-level construct operationalisation of Ideology Orientation within party political postures). Therefore, in presenting the analysis of party political postures, emphasis is given to the distinguishing aspects of both concepts.

The Labour Party

Throughout the manifesto, the Labour Party shows some concern with the needs and wants of voters. However, other actors are only implicitly acknowledged. This can be juxtaposed with a strong but mediated focus on ideology. Although this is represented in a veiled manner and mostly expressed in terms of 'our values', it permeates the whole logic of the manifesto. Together with this runs a strong tendency to justify previous actions (as would be expected of an incumbent party): the 'New Labour record' leads each of the nine policy chapters in the manifesto. Inherent friction points between different policy stances are not acknowledged, neither is there a clear rationale (apart from somewhat opaque values such as 'provide opportunity and security for all in a changing world', Labour Party 2005: 5). While this indicated a medium Ideology Orientation, the Dialogue Orientation can be assessed as high: willingness to 'listen' and being empathetic is evident throughout. Feedback mechanisms, especially from voters, are hinted at (without detail) and specific segment policy agendas are explicitly discussed. Regarding a Stakeholder Orientation, the fact that Labour is the incumbent party increased its score on this issue. However, while governmental issues were clearly embedded in the presentation and discussion of the party manifesto, this is not the case for intermediate actors or 'low politics' groups. Their Temporal Orientation, however, can be seen as high, as they are retrospective (policy justification) as well as prospective (detailed policy and implementation outline with specific and sometimes extremely detailed and quantified targets) in their outlook. Compared with the other two parties, the manifesto is characterised by less of a campaign focus. Figure 2.2 summarises the construct scores for the Labour Party.

The Conservative Party

Whilst acknowledging voters and other actors, the Conservative manifesto focuses on axiomatic expressions ('It's not racist to impose limits on immigration', Conservative Party 2005: 18) and shows a frequent reference to ideology throughout. This starts with Michael Howard's leading essay 'The British Dream', leading on his personal credo: 'I believe . . .'. Policy is justified exclusively by reference not to pragmatic issues but to values. On the other hand, the Dialogue Orientation is relatively low: not many policy development channels are described; in

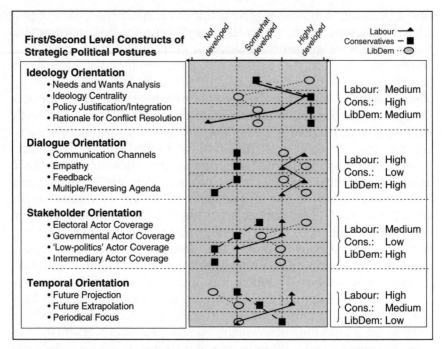

Figure 2.2   Levels of Party Political Postures of the three parties

general an emotional alignment of voter opinion with the party line is implied. Agenda complexity is suppressed. This is to some extent mirrored in the Conservatives' Stakeholder Orientation. However, their Temporal Orientation shows a campaign and historical focus: policy issues are introduced by criticising Labour's performance and by providing 'catchy' solutions. However, these are generally rhetorical and provide no implementation guidance. For example, the section on the NHS ('I mean, how hard is it to keep a hospital clean?', Conservative Party 2005: 10) is about 400 words long (of which half is a description of the current situation). The main policy promises are 'More investment in local hospitals; shorter waiting times and cleaner wards; health professionals freed from Whitehall interference; more choice for patients; support for family doctors' (Conservative Party 2005: 13). The detail is extremely low and vague, the appeal mainly at the emotional level. Again, Figure 2.2 summarises and juxtaposes the overall assessment.

The Liberal Democrats
In terms of the Ideology Orientation, it is noteworthy that the main rationale for the policy suggestions has to do with pragmatic solutions

and a link with 'real people'. The manifesto is sprinkled with 'testimonials' by citizens, activists, experts, as well as senior party figures. This is linked with a high degree of Dialogue Orientation that is embedded in the discussions as well as the presentation of the manifesto. While mostly printed in extremely small print, the policy discussions (clearly distinguished by topic) provide multiple viewpoints, policy discussions, as well as implementation suggestions, including the involvement of citizens and multiple actor groups. The association of the LibDem manifesto with many non-electoral bodies and individuals (top managers from industry, patient/consumer associations, Royal Commissions, single-issue campaigners like the Campaign to Protect Rural England) furthermore shows a highly developed Stakeholder Orientation. However, the Temporal Orientation is somewhat unclear. The presentation does not give the impression of a 'campaign-oriented' manifesto. However, while there is evidence of a future projection of policy offerings, the implementation remains underdeveloped. Compared with the Labour manifesto with its 'managerial' focus and the Conservative manifesto with its 'emotional' focus, the Liberal Democrat manifesto does not show clear momentum.

In contrast with the operationalisation of a Political Market Orientation, the analysis of the party manifestoes using Strategic Political Postures shows significant distinctions. Figure 2.2 shows that the parties are differentiated by the first-level constructs. Furthermore, it also shows that the first-level constructs for each party differentiate clearly discrete political postures. While Labour overall represents more of a 'follower' stance which is oriented to interactions with many different actors and a managerial and 'technocratic' approach to policy development and implementation, the Conservatives clearly put their own convictions first. Their 'emotional' interpretation of values and ideology means that they are more inward-focused and unspecific, in line with a follower posture. The Liberal Democrats mirror Labour to some extent in their stance. However, their low Temporal Orientation and the unspecific nature of their policy implementations mean that their 'follower' stance is less developed. This may hint at the possibility of their being perceived as 'political lightweights' (Henneberg 2006b), i.e. a non-differentiated and difficult to comprehend stance in the eyes of other political actors.

A final point concerns the intra-party regional differences. This mainly concerns adjusting the text of each of the manifestoes to increase their relevance to each region. Having said this, only the Liberal Democrat Party explicitly stated the reason for publishing regionally targeted manifestoes, explaining its motive as 'reflecting the different choices, priorities and circumstances, and often the influence of Liberal Democrats in

Government' (Liberal Democrats 2005: 3). The adjustment of the text can be illustrated by an example from the Conservative Party:

> Rising council tax bills, which are up by 76 per cent since Labour came to power. (Conservative Party 2005: 4)
> Rising council tax bills, which are up by 55 per cent since Labour came to power (Scottish Conservative Party 2005: 4)

These changes varied in length, from individual sentences (Labour Party) to adding an extra page ('Our contract with Scotland', Scottish Conservative Party 2005: inside cover) and producing a separate document, the Liberal Democrat Party's 'Manifesto Scottish Supplement', that made explicit how the extra funds promised to the Scottish Executive following a Liberal Democrat victory in the General Election would be used. Whilst the latter on first inspection may appear to represent a large regional difference (there are no equivalents to the English or Welsh manifestoes), the 'Manifesto Scottish Supplement' is just that – an addendum designed to detail plans that were not relevant to the other parts of Britain.

As such, the regional differences reflect an attempt by the parties to raise the level of Voter Orientation and Dialogue Orientation respectively, thus making it easier for the electorate to relate to a differentiated regional offering. The opposite was the case with the dimensions of the Internal, Competitor, and External Orientation constructs and the relevant constructs of Strategic Party Postures, none of which demonstrated significant regional differences. Therefore, a tentative hypothesis from our case analysis is that both constructs, Political Market Orientation and Strategic Party Posture, are stable with regard to regional offering differences.

Conclusion and implications

Our qualitative and exploratory conceptualisation of two distinct but overlapping aspects of a Political Market Orientation has shown that the derived first-level constructs can be used to analyse political offerings such as party manifestoes. The different dimensions show discriminatory power with regard to different parties as well as between dimensions. Furthermore, the different results of both constructs reinforce our conviction that there are different facets of a market orientation, as hinted at in the theoretical discussion of the marketing theory antecedents, as previously discussed, and that our initial operationalisation and exploratory results of the investigation can provide a benchmark for further quantitative studies of this facet of political marketing.

As can clearly be seen in the graphical representation in Figure 2.1, the Voter Orientation, Internal Orientation and External Orientation constructs display a consistent pattern across the three main parties, indicating that these may represent a fundamental characteristic of the manifesto as a political offering. Voters are considered the prime target group for the message contained in the manifesto, and so are afforded a central role, along with the majority of the stakeholder groups that make up the External Orientation construct. The only construct where there was evidence of differentiation was in the elements of a Competitor Orientation, but the pattern of the data indicates that this is more likely to represent the nature of competition, the *Realpolitik*, than a factor that can be adjusted in the context of an election campaign.

However, the overall party political stance that was communicated, i.e. the Strategic Posture, comprehensively distinguished the three parties. That indicates that there is room for differentiation within a marketplace-determined structure (Figure 2.2). It can be posited that Labour's programme showed evidence of a 'follower' mentality, with high Dialogue and comprehensive Temporal Orientation (Butler and Collins 1996; Henneberg 2006a). This is to some extent interesting, as at the same time Tony Blair was perceived by voters generally as having shifted from a 'follower' to a 'leader' stance in the context of policy decisions related to the Iraq war (Henneberg 2006b). The Conservatives provided the 'real alternative' (this was in fact the Liberal Democrat slogan), at least when it came to the chosen strategic posture: they were using emotional appeals, based on values that stood for a clear Ideology Orientation, i.e. a 'leader' stance. It means that their slogan 'Are you thinking what we're thinking?', if ultimately not successful, nevertheless represented their political stance very well. On the other hand, the Liberal Democrats' did not show a clear posture, in the course of the campaign allowing the other parties to attack them for 'sitting on the fence'.

The investigation may also demonstrate evidence of two more fundamental characteristics of manifestoes as a political offering, the 'gravitational centre effect' and the 'incumbent effect'. The results of the analysis of the manifestoes using the Political Market Orientation constructs tentatively point to the existence of a marketplace-determined 'gravitational centre', impacting on the level and structure of each party's Political Market Orientation, and reflecting a long-term change dynamic. Therefore, aspects of Political Market Orientation may be determined or strongly mediated by structural variables embedded in the party system, competitive constellation, or societal structure. At the same time there appears to be an 'incumbent effect', where the party in power up to the election senses a need to justify its past deeds. This 'incumbent effect' may not be restricted to the past; whilst it is not possible to investigate this using the sample selected for this analysis, it could be hypothesised that this effect also exists into the future, dependent on whether (for example) opinion polls point to a clear winner of the election far enough in the future to be taken into consideration when designing the manifesto.

Despite the exploratory nature of this investigation, the two theoretical hypotheses that emerge from the analysis of the manifestoes have important practical implications. First, the characteristics of the four Political Market Orientation constructs, a long-term dynamic with some form of 'gravitational centre', may indicate that practitioners could use the elements of the constructs in order to create a fundamental framework for the election manifesto. In order to differentiate the manifesto from the competition and take into account the idiosyncratic context of each election, the elements of the Strategic Political Postures, characterised by a short-term dynamic and an 'incumbent effect', could then be used to create a political offering that distinguished itself and the party from the competition. In this way, existing voter cognitive structures used to attend to the manifesto – the manifesto 'style' – could be appealed to, whilst the party's election message – the manifesto 'content' – could then be tailored to suit the party's strategic posture.

In conclusion, the question set out in the introduction to this book concerns whether the General Election of 2005 could be described as being a 'political marketing election'. In this chapter, the authors have analysed a core element of the election environment, the party manifesto as a main political offering component, using constructs that have been developed from the commercial marketing literature to take the idiosyncrasies of the political market place into account. In the commercial marketing literature, these constructs have formed the backbone of much work during the last fifteen years, and the evidence gained from analysing the party manifestoes in 2005 indicates that elements of all constructs to a greater or lesser extent are present in the offerings. If it is accepted that fundamental concepts from the realm of commercial marketing can be used to explain phenomena in the political market place, then we would answer 'Yes . . . but' to the question posed in the introduction: the General Election of 2005 was indeed a political marketing election (in terms of core offering arrangement and presentation) *but* it was also characterised by a cautious approach to the full-scale adoption of a Political Market Orientation (parties focused mainly on voters and external players and neglected especially the 'internal marketing' aspects). Whilst the fundamental nature of manifestoes, and their use of rhetoric, and the context of an election campaign may dictate a particular structure, it is not impossible to change the political offering and thus escape historical inertia. However, with regard to the strategic use of political marketing as analysed in the specific relative postures, the marketing aspect of differentiation was clearly employed by the parties (especially between Conservatives and Labour, i.e. a 'leader' versus 'follower' constellation).

References

Altheide, D. L. and Johnson, J. M. (1994), 'Criteria for assessing interpretive validity in qualitative research', in N. K. Denzin and Y. S. Lincoln (eds), *Handbook of Qualitative Research*, Thousand Oaks CA: Sage .

Baines, P. R. (1999), 'Voter segmentation and candidate positioning', in B. I. Newman (ed.), *Handbook of Political Marketing*, Thousand Oaks CA: Sage .

Baines, P. R., Harris, P. and Lewis, B. R. (2002), 'The political marketing planning process: improving image and message in strategic target areas', *Marketing Intelligence and Planning* 20 (1): 6–14.

Butler, P. and Collins, N. (1996), 'Strategic analysis in political markets', *European Journal of Marketing* 30 (10–11): 25–36.

Butler, P. and Collins, N. (1999), 'A conceptual framework for political marketing', in B. I. Newman (ed.), *Handbook of Political Marketing*, Thousand Oakes CA: Sage.

Connor, T. (1999), 'Customer-led and market-oriented: a matter of balance', *Strategic Management Journal* 20: 1157–63.

Conservative Party (2005a), *Are You Thinking What We're Thinking? It's Time for Action*, election manifesto for the 2005 General Election, London: Conservative Party.

Conservative Party (2005b), *Are You Thinking What We're Thinking? It's Time for Action*, election manifesto for the 2005 General Election (Wales), London: Conservative Party.

Davis, F. W. and Manrodt, K. B. (1996), *Customer-responsive Management*, Oxford: Blackwell

Dean, D. and Croft, R. (2001), 'Friends and relations: long-term approaches to political campaigning', *European Journal of Marketing* 35 (11–12): 1197–216.

Dermody, J. and Scullion, R. (2000), 'Delusions of grandeur? Marketing's contribution to "meaningful" Western political consumption', *European Journal of Marketing* 35 (9–10): 1085–98.

Deshpande, R. (1999), *Developing a Market Orientation*, Thousand Oaks CA: Sage.

Harrison-Walker, L. J. (2001), 'The measurement of a market orientation and its impact on business performance', *Journal of Quality Management* 6: 139–72.

Harrop, M. (1990), 'Political marketing', *Parliamentary Affairs* 43: 277–91.

Hellensen, S. (2003), *Marketing Management*, Harlow: Prentice Hall.

Henneberg, S. C. (2002), 'Understanding political marketing', in N. J. O'Shaughnessy and S. C. Henneberg (eds), *The Idea of Political Marketing*, Westport CT: Praeger .

Henneberg, S. C. (2004), 'The views of an *advocatus Dei*: political marketing and its critics', *Journal of Public Affairs* 4 (3): 225–43.

Henneberg, S. C. (2006a), 'Leading or following? A theoretical analysis of political marketing postures', *Journal of Political Marketing*, forthcoming.

Henneberg, S. C. (2006b), 'Strategic postures of political marketing: an exploratory operationalisation', *Journal of Public Affairs*, forthcoming.

Henneberg, S. C. and Egbalian, S. (2002), 'Kirchheimer's catch-all party: a reinterpretation in marketing terms', in N. O'Shaughnessy and S. Henneberg (eds), *The Idea of Political Marketing*, Westport CT: Praeger.

Herrmann, A. and Huber, F. (1996), 'Candidate-positioning via Customer-orientation: an empirical study using conjoint analysis', in S. Henneberg, N. O'Shaughnessy and S. Egbalian (eds), Proceedings of the Second Conference on Political Marketing, Cambridge.

Hodder, I. (1994), 'The interpretation of documents and material culture', in N. Denzin and Y. Lincoln (eds), *Handbook of Qualitative Research*, Thousand Oaks CA: Sage.

Hooley, G., Greenley, G., Fahy, J. and Cadogan, J. (2001), 'Market-focused resources, competitive positioning and firm performance', *Journal of Marketing Management* 17: 503–20.

Huberman, A. M. and Miles, M. B. (1994), 'Data management and analysis method', in N. Denzin, and Y. Lincoln (eds), *Handbook of Qualitative Research*, Thousand Oaks CA: Sage.

Hunt, S. D. and Lambe, C. J. (2000), 'Marketing's contribution to business strategy: market orientation, relationship marketing and resource–advantage theory', *International Journal of Management Reviews* 2 (1): 17–43.

Kaid, L. L. (2002), 'Trends in political advertising', *Journal of Political Marketing* 1 (1): 207–10.

Kavanagh, D. (1995), *Election Campaigning: The New Marketing of Politics*, Oxford: Blackwell.

Kirchheimer, O. (1966), 'The transformation of the Western European party systems', in J. LaPalombara and M. Wiener (eds), *Political Parties and Political Development*, Princeton NJ: Princeton University Press.

Kohli, A. K. and Jaworski, B. J. (1990), 'Market orientation: the construct, research propositions, and managerial implications', *Journal of Marketing* 54: 1–18.

Kotler, P. (2003), *Marketing Management*, Englewood Cliffs NJ: Pearson.

Kotler, P. and Kotler, N. (1999), 'Political marketing', in B. I. Newman (ed.), *Handbook of Political Marketing*, Thousand Oaks CA: Sage.

Krippendorff, K. (2004), *Content Analysis*, Thousand Oaks CA: Sage.

Labour Party (2005), *The Labour Party Manifesto 2005*, election manifesto for the 2005 General Election, London: Labour Party.

Lafferty, B. A. and Hult, G. T. (2001), 'A synthesis of contemporary market orientation perspectives', *European Journal of Marketing* 35 (1): 92–109.

Lees-Marshment, J. (2001a), 'The product, sales and market-oriented party', *European Journal of Marketing* 35 (9–10): 1074–84.

Lees-Marshment, J. (2001b), *Political Marketing and British Political Parties*, Manchester: Manchester University Press.

Lees-Marshment, J. (2003), 'Political marketing: how to reach that pot of gold', *Journal of Political Marketing* 2 (1): 1–32.

Liberal Democrats (2005), *The REAL Alternative*, election manifesto for the 2005 General Election, London: Liberal Democrats.

Lilleker, D. G. and Lees-Marshment, J. (2005), *Political Marketing: A Comparative Perspective*, Manchester: Manchester University Press.

Lloyd, J. (2003), 'Square peg, round hole? Can marketing-based concepts such as 'product' and the 'marketing mix' have a useful rote in the political arena?', paper presented to the Political Studies Association Conference, University of Leicester, April.

Lock, A. and Harris, P. (1996), 'Political marketing – *vive la différence*', *European Journal of Marketing* 30 (10–11): 14–24.

Manning, P. K. and Cullum-Swan, B. (1994), 'Narrative, content, and semiotic analysis', in N. Denzin and Y. Lincoln (eds), *Handbook of Qualitative Research*, Thousand Oaks CA: Sage.

McDonald, M. and Wilson, H. (2002), *The New Marketing*, Oxford: Butterworth-Heinemann.

Morgan, R. E. and Strong, C. A. (1998), 'Market orientation and dimensions of strategic orientation', *European Journal of Marketing* 32 (11–12): 1051–73.

Narver, J. and Slater, S. (1990), 'The effect of market orientation on business profitability', *Journal of Marketing* 54: 20–35.

Newman, B. I. (1994), *The Marketing of the President*, Thousand Oaks CA: Sage.

Newman, B. I. (1999), *The Mass Marketing of Politics*, Thousand Oaks CA: Sage.

Newman, B. I. (2001a), 'Image-manufacturing in the USA: recent US presidential elections and beyond', *European Journal of Marketing* 35 (9–10): 966–70.

Newman, B. I. (2001b), 'An assessment of the 2000 US presidential election: a set of political marketing guidelines', *Journal of Public Affairs* 1 (3): 210–16.

Newman, B. I. (2002), 'The role of marketing in politics', *Journal of Political Marketing* 1 (1): 1–5.

O'Cass, A. (1996), 'Political marketing and the marketing concept', *European Journal of Marketing* 30 (10–11): 45–61.

O'Cass, A. (2001), 'Political marketing', *European Journal of Marketing* 35 (9–10): 1003–25.

Ormrod, R. P. (2004), *Operationalising the Conceptual Model of Political Market Orientation*, Report Series on Political Communication 14, Washington DC: Institute for Democratic Communication.

Ormrod, R. P. (2005), 'A conceptual model of Political Market Orientation', *Journal of Nonprofit and Public Sector Marketing*, forthcoming.

O'Shaughnessy, N. J. and Holbrook, M. B. (1988), 'What US businesses can learn from political marketing', *Journal of Applied Business Research* 4 (3): 98–109.

Popkin, S. L. (1994), *The Reasoning Voter*, Chicago: University of Chicago Press.

Reid, D. M. (1988), 'Marketing the political product', *European Journal of Marketing* 22 (9): 34–47.

Scammell, M. (1999), 'Political marketing: lessons for political science', *Political Studies* 47: 718–39.

Scottish Conservative Party (2005), *Are You Thinking What We're Thinking? It's Time for Action*, election manifesto for the 2005 General Election, Edinburgh: Scottish Conservative Party.

Scottish Labour Party (2005), *The Labour Party Manifesto 2005*, election manifesto for the 2005 General Election, Glasgow: Scottish Labour Party.

Scottish Liberal Democrats (2005), *The REAL Alternative*, election manifesto for the 2005 General Election, London: Liberal Democrats.

Slater, S. F. and Narver, J. C. (1998), 'Customer-led and market-oriented: let's not confuse the two', *Strategic Management Journal* 19: 1001–6.

Slater, S. F. and Narver, J. C. (1999), 'Market-oriented is more than being customer-led', *Strategic Management Journal* 20: 1165–8.

Smith, G. (2001), 'The 2001 General Election: factors influencing the brand image of political parties and their leaders', *Journal of Marketing Management* 17: 989–1006.

Smith, G. and Hirst, A. (2001), 'Strategic political segmentation', *European Journal of Marketing* 35 (9–10): 1058–73.

Sniderman, P. M., Brody, R. A. and Tetlock, P. E. (1991), *Reasoning and Choice: Explorations in Political Psychology*, Cambridge: Cambridge University Press.

Sparrow, N. and Turner, J. (2001), 'The permanent campaign', *European Journal of Marketing* 35 (9–10): 984–1002.

Stake, R. E. (2000), 'Case studies', in N. Denzin and Y. Lincoln (eds), *The Handbook of Qualitative Research*, Thousand Oaks CA: Sage.

Strauss, A. and Corbin, J. (1998), *Basics of Qualitative Research*, Thousand Oaks CA: Sage.

Varey, R. J. and Ballantyne, D. (2005), 'Relationship marketing and the challenge of dialogical interaction', *Journal of Relationship Marketing* 4 (3–4): 13–30.

Welsh Liberal Democrats (2005), *The REAL Alternative*, election manifesto for the 2005 General Election, Cardiff: Liberal Democrats.

Wortmann, M. (1989), 'Political Marketing: A Modern Party Strategy', unpublished Ph.D. dissertation, Florence: European University Institute.

Wring, D. (2001), 'Selling socialism', *European Journal of Marketing* 35 (9–10): 1038–46.

Wring, D. (2002), 'Conceptualising political marketing: a framework for election-campaign analysis, in N. O'Shaughnessy and S. Henneberg (eds), *The Idea of Political Marketing*, Westport CT: Praeger.

Yin, R. K. (2003a), *Applications of Case Study Research*, Thousand Oaks CA: Sage.

Yin, R. K. (2003b), *Case Study Research*, Thousand Oaks CA: Sage.

3

The 2005 General Election and the emergence of the 'negative brand'

Jenny Lloyd

On Tuesday 5 April 2005, Prime Minister Tony Blair emerged from Buckingham Palace to announce the dissolution of Parliament and, with this act, signalled the 'official' start of the 2005 General Election campaign. However, the political landscape that greeted the political contenders at this point was a treacherous one, as they faced a backdrop of increased voter apathy, dissatisfaction and distrust (Gosschalk *et al.* 2002; Marshall 2005). Their challenge, therefore, was not only to persuade the electorate that their brand of politics was superior to that offered by their rivals, but that it was actually worth making the effort to vote for. However, what actually happened was that the two foremost UK political brands undertook election campaign strategies that not only undermined themselves as brands, but ultimately damaged the political 'product sector' as a whole.

The political brand

The concept of branding is one that is central to commercial marketing and offers significant scope as an analytical tool in the field of politics. In general, the concept of a 'brand' might be seen to be distinct from that of a 'product' in that 'A product is something with a functional purpose. A brand offers something in addition to its functional purpose. All brands are products . . . but not all products are brands' (Jones 1986: 29).

As with the marketing concept, there are a plethora of definitions of a 'brand', and because of their commercial origins they are generally commercial in nature. However, Smith (2003) cites Aaker's (1991) definition of a brand as having particular relevance to the political market: 'A brand is a distinguishing name and/or symbol (such as a logo) intended to identify the goods or services of either one seller or a group of sellers and to differentiate those goods or services from those of competitors' (Aaker 1991: 7).

The product

Figure 3.1   Examples of the political parties' logos

Certainly political parties in Great Britain have long had associations with colours (red for Labour, blue for Conservative and yellow for Liberal) and also with symbols such as the red rose (Labour), the 'bird of freedom' (Liberal Democrat) or the torch (Conservative) (see Figure 3.1). In this way, logos function as 'signs' which convey meaning to consumers. This is done through a form of 'code' which takes the form of words, pictures, or a combination of the two (Fiske 2002; Hall 1996; Watson 2003).

Linked to the concept of the brand as 'logo' is the idea that a central function of a brand is the way that it performs as an identity system (de Chernatony and Dall'Olmo Riley 1998). According to Nandan (2005), 'brand identity' may be defined as the vehicle that a brand uses to convey its individuality and uniqueness to its various publics. Unlike a logo, which simply delineates one brand from the next, identity is a multi-faceted entity which comprises such diverse components as vision, culture, positioning, personality, relationships and presentations (de Chernatony 1999; Harris and de Chernatony 2001).

At the basic level of the proprietary logo there is little dispute as to the applicability of the concept of the 'brand'. However, when considered in its fullest sense there has been disagreement as to its relevance to the field of politics. Yet, despite this, there have been some interesting similarities in the descriptors used by the different fields. For example, in their criticism of the applicability of marketing concepts to the political arena, Lock and Harris suggest that it is the complexity of the political candidate or party that make the two fields such uncomfortable bedfellows. They state that 'The political party or candidate is a complex intangible product which the voter cannot unbundle. As a consequence most voters have to judge on the overall packaged concept or message' (Lock and Harris 1996: 22).

Kapferer's (1992) description of a brand holds echos of Lock and Harris's (1996) description. He identifies a brand as being a complex entity whose meaning and direction are constructed through its component parts. This is also a proposition supported by de Chernatony and Dall'Olmo Riley (1998), who suggest that, far from being two-dimensional, the 'brand' is a multi-dimensional construct whose sum is greater that its constituent parts. From this perspective it becomes clear that in the construction of a political brand, far from being a onesided activity on the part of the brand owner, it is also the result of efforts on the part of the consumer. This proposition is supported by Firat and Venkatesh (1995) and Ozanne and Murray (1995), who suggest that, whilst management may generate elaborate brand constructions, consumers themselves play an important and active part in the construction of a brand, and, therefore, brands perform important functions for consumers themselves.

These functions, which may be as important to consumers as to the brand owner (Kellner 2003; Aaker 1991) might be referred to as the 'added value'. This, as Hirschman and Holbrook (1982) suggest, is the consumer's value concept attached to the brand that is subjective and has emotional significance. Added value is seen as a process 'whereby consumers imbue a product with a subjective meaning in addition to the functional characteristics it possesses' (de Chernatony and Dall'Olmo Riley 1998: 423). Doyle too adopts a consumer focus in his definition of 'added value', in which it is 'not what the producer puts in but what the consumer gets out' (1989: 78). Therefore, consumer value might be seen as benefits generated by a particular brand that a consumer recognises as having the potential to fulfil a need, either functional or emotional.

From a functional perspective, brands act to simplify the analytical processes employed by consumers within a potential choice situation. They do so by acting as a form of 'shorthand' for all its characteristics, thereby generating 'short cuts' which spare the consumer the time and effort of seeking out and reprocessing large and complex amounts of information every time they have to make a decision pertaining to a brand. In this way they are reflective of the concept of 'heuristics': mental short cuts or 'rules of thumb' that facilitate a consumer's decision-making processes (Solomon *et al.* 2002). Interestingly, however, there appear to be distinct differences between the field of marketing and the field of politics in the understanding of how and why heuristics are used.

Within the field of marketing it has largely been assumed that heuristics were employed as a way of distilling a vast array of consumers' knowledge of a brand into an easily processed form. In contrast, within the field of politics, heuristics are seen as rules that are largely employed by voters who are in possession of limited knowledge, either as a result of their inability to process information or simply because they are not fully informed (Cutler 2002). Berelson *et al.* (1954) propose that the use of heuristics is simply 'an irrational last resort of the ill-informed' (Cutler 2002: 466). Yet Dolan (1998) refutes this proposition and suggests that even the better-educated voters take demographic heuristics into consideration but to a much lesser degree. Her rebuttal is supported by empirical evidence from the United States which suggests 'more sophisticated voters do not transcend the use of short cuts such as their affective orientations to parties – they simply combine more decision criteria in a broader and deeper net than the less well informed' (Cutler 2002: 483),

In addition to the provision of functional value to consumers, brands have the ability to generate emotional value as well (Kellner 2003), which can take a number of forms. If, as is often stated, political parties in the UK are converging on the ideological middle ground, then other factors than policy must be seen as a differentiator. These factors might take the form of a 'relationship' (Fournier 1998) with a politician, a party or with a community, virtual or real, that supports that party (Muniz and O'Guinn 2001; Schouten and McAlexander 1995). Alternatively, affiliation with a specific party may provide more of a symbolic benefit to an individual in their attempt to establish their identity (Belk 1988) or their place in society (Bourdieu 1984).

Yet, most important, a clearly branded political party offers the 'added value' of acting as a risk reducer in the minds of voters. Bauer (1960) identifies that when consumers make a choice between products and services they perceive a degree of risk. Solomon *et al.* (2002) identify five kinds of risk faced by consumers; monetary risk, functional risk, physical risk, social risk and psychological risk. A political party or candidate functioning as a brand can reassure voters that their economic status, their personal security or their social position will be secure if they are elected. New Labour successfully capitalised upon the desire for risk reduction in the 1997 General Election and sought to do so again in the 2005 election with the use of pledge cards which they handed out to the general public. In 1997 pledges addressed every type of risk, either directly ('We will be tough on crime, tough on the causes of crime') or indirectly ('We will give Britain the leadership in Europe which Britain and Europe need'). However, whilst in the 2005 election the approach was entirely indirect ('Your family better off', 'Your child achieving more') the intention was the same as in the 1997 election; to address voters' underlying concerns and thereby offer them a safe choice when casting their votes.

Therefore, it is possible to analyse political parties' use of branding within the 2005 General Election context, but such an analysis would be incomplete without the inclusion of the consumer perspective.

Methodology

In order to understand the material from which voters were able to draw their conceptualisations, over five weeks prior to the 2005 General Election date of 5 May, the researcher monitored the political brands' presence across the popular media. All the major broadsheets and tabloids were reviewed on a daily basis together with the output of television and radio news programmes. Direct output from the political brands such as party election broadcasts, posters, leaflets, together with special events such as the one-to-one Paxman interviews on BBC TV with the main party leaders were also scrutinised for brand symbolism.

In addition, twelve 'life history' depth interviews were undertaken. A research method utilising an interpretivist approach was selected in line with the research objective of understanding the way that political brands informed consumers' conceptualisations within the context of a General Election. As an epistemology it was thought most appropriate because it embraces a wide variety of philosophical and social thought in an attempt to explain the social world from the point of view of the actors within it (Schwandt 2000; Silverman 2001).

From a practical perspective, the 'life history' approach is the method that most closely relates to the unique characteristics of the political brands and the political market. As identified in previous work (Lloyd 2003), unlike almost any other type of product, the political product is universally consumed, but to varying degrees, and consumers 'consume' it holistically or in bite-size chunks (for example, the economy, the National Health Service, education, etc.) both passively and actively from the moment they are conceived until the day they die. The 'life history' approach allows the researcher to probe the nature and extent of their personal experiences together with those consumed vicariously through relations and friends. Further, by adopting a broader, 'lifetime' focus it enabled the researcher to explore the extent to which consumers' conceptualisations were influenced by 2005 election-specific material as well as that to which they had been previously exposed.

Mariampolski (2001) advocates the use of life histories as especially useful for studies exploring brand imagery and product positioning. This is particularly useful when seeking to understand how consumers visualise political parties and how they understand their relative ideological positions. Further, she highlights that it is a useful tool in understanding external influences upon brand perception and the dynamics of perceptual change.

A process of theoretical sampling was used as, within the time constraints imposed by the election campaign period, it was seen as a highly

effective and efficient way of obtaining detailed data. Unlike more prob-
abilistic methods of sampling, which might allow a researcher only
limited access to a particular phenomenon, theoretical sampling allows
the researcher to pursue an emerging concept through focused recruitment of individuals and groups with specific characteristics (Goulding
1998; Charmaz 2000). Through probability sampling, one would have
to recruit a much larger sample to gain access to a similar-size group
with the desired characteristics. The sample size itself was determined
by two factors. First it was determined there could be a point of 'satu-
ration' at which the researcher deemed that little additional useful information might be gleamed (Goulding 2002; Mariampolski 2001). Also,
the limited time frame of the General Election campaign restricted the
number of interviews that could be conducted, transcribed and then
analysed effectively enough to inform the recruitment of the next
participant.

The interviews were undertaken in the participants' own homes and
lasted for between twenty-five minutes and three hours. The participants were invited to talk about their lives from the point of their earli-
est memories and reflect upon the various political parties and
politicians that were present throughout. The slight narrowing of the
focus of the life-history approach to that of a 'political life history' is one
that is advocated by Chicchi, who suggests that it is a neat way of sur-
mounting a problem that he labels 'the impasse of the [biographical]
approach' (2000: 16). Such a strategy, he claims, gets over the problem
of too great a volume of information by choosing not to collect every
biographical detail. Such an approach, he claims, still generates a huge
amount of rich data, but that which is collected has much greater relevance to the topic in hand.

The interviews were audio-taped and transcribed as soon as possible
after the event. In addition notes were taken throughout by the
researcher to record any physical reactions and other nuances that might
have occurred during the course of the interview but might otherwise
not have been apparent on an audio recording. Analysis and interpretation of the data were an ongoing and continuous process that started
from the commencement of the first interview. Key themes were noted
as they emerged and, in line with the tenets of theoretical sampling,
were used to inform the selection of further participants.

Brands as differentiators

Over the course of all the interviews it became clear that, in particular,
the colours associated with the main three political parties fulfilled their

function as pure differentiators between the political brands. All but two of the participants mentioned the colours repeatedly over the course of the interviews and there was no suggestion from any of them of confusion between the parties themselves. This therefore suggests that, in its proprietary sense, the use of colour has been particularly successful in the creation of strong and enduring brand associations.

This is particularly interesting in the light of the patchy nature of the branding strategy employed by two of the main parties: New Labour and the Conservative Party. In the main, almost all the Liberal Democrat broadcasts and campaign material were strongly branded, right down to the presence of Charles Kennedy's yellow tie. However, in contrast to the Liberal Democrats, New Labour and the Conservative Party took a much less consistent approach to the use of colour and form and there appeared to be little consistency between their local and national branding strategies. Whilst, locally, small posters and boards bearing local candidates' names in the parties' colours and sporting the parties' logos were visible at the roadside throughout the course of the election, nationally there was little evidence of the traditional colours and logos on the larger billboards. Indeed, where they did appear they were usually relegated to the bottom corner of the poster and lacked integration into the overall content of the message (see also Dermody and Hanmer-Lloyd in Chapter 5 of this volume).

Similarly, branding in its proprietary sense was also very low-key in prominent party documents such as the New Labour and Conservative Party election manifestoes. The traditional colours appeared only as 'accents' and whilst the Labour's 'rose' logo made an understated appearance at the bottom of the page on the inside of the document, the Conservative 'torch' did not appear at all. This difference was also observable in the broadcast media, where the presence of the Conservative and Labour Party logos was relatively low-key during press conferences and party election broadcasts in comparison with that of the Liberal Democrats.

Yet what also became apparent was that many of the associations made by voters were not purely proprietary and that, in the main, they were linked not just with the political brands participating in the 2005 election, but with the parties in all their previous incarnations. For example, the term 'blue' was often expressed in conjunction with very positive associations such as constancy and patriotism (e.g. 'true blue') and were most often used by participants when they referred back to the ex-Conservative Prime Minister, Margaret Thatcher. This was despite the fact that many of the participants expressed a dislike either of her policies or of her personally. In contrast however, when recounting their thoughts on New Labour, the term 'red' was often used as a derogatory term for individuals linked with the party whom they felt to be particularly radical or militant (e.g. 'Red Ken').

These strong historical links also generated some confusion, particularly with regard to the move from the Labour Party to New Labour, as many of the associations no longer seemed to apply and, as a result, the participants were no longer sure what they currently stood for. In the words of one participant:

> New Labour . . . when it came in . . . I don't know . . . it seemed to be that shift where it was called Labour, had the look of Labour, had the rose and the red colour and everything, but it was like . . . when it came down to it, I don't think they were really interested in things like trade unions.

A further problem associated with the clear identification associated with successful proprietary colours and logos is that they proffer the opportunity for the recipient of party literature to discriminate against it before it is fully read. One participant described her reaction to the election material that had been posted through her letter box: 'As soon as I see that it's from a political party I chuck it in the bin'.

This reaction was typical of most of the participants in this study and reflects the very poor standing of the political sector in the eyes of the potential electorate. It appears that communications received directly from all the political parties possessed very low levels of credibility, largely based upon the perceived failure in previous elections of governments to fulfil their election promises. This was not restricted to direct mail but included all formal broadcast communications, for example party political broadcasts, which in most of the participants' households were seen as an opportunity to make a cup of tea. Indeed, even first-time voters, who possessed only limited experience of the field, expressed similar sentiments, suggesting that these beliefs had established themselves as a cultural fact, as one of the eighteen-year-old participants demonstrated when she said, 'They're like slimy salesmen. They'll just say anything to get you to vote for them.' The question therefore arises as to what the brands truly stand for in the mind of the voters and, in the face of the low levels of credibility attached to their promises, how do they go about choosing between them?

'The best of a bad bunch'

When talking about the political brands, a phrase that was used by a quarter of the participants was that it was a matter of finding 'the best of a bad bunch'. In light of the poor overall standing of the political sector, and the lack of credibility assigned to any communications issued from the political brands themselves, a further question arises as to how the participants actually obtained their conceptualisations of political brands?

From the perspective of the participants, this appeared to happen in two stages. First, information about political brands was treated seriously only if it emanated from sources that were considered credible. All said that their primary source of information about political parties was gained through the media and other third-party sources uncontrolled by the political brands. BBC television programmes were cited most often by participants as having source credibility, together with the broadsheet newspapers, as they were generally seen as more objective and less sensationalist than the commercial stations and tabloids. In particular, programmes that had apparently uncontrolled content were seen as particularly good sources; the most frequently cited was Jeremy Paxman's series of one-to-one interviews with the three main party leaders. These were seen as credible sources because, on the whole, it was felt that the politicians would be forced to answer the difficult questions that were never satisfactorily answered elsewhere.

The participants also said that they preferred 'uncontrolled' media vehicles because they felt that they exposed the politicians for who they really were and what they really stood for. In this way it allowed the participants to proceed to the second stage, where they used heuristics to generate their conceptualisations of the respective political brands. The most influential of these heuristics were those relating to 'likeness' and 'otherness'. 'Likeness' may be defined as the conformity of a subject to the accepted norms and ideals of a particular individual or group whereas conversely 'otherness' relates to nonconformity (Bullock and Trombley 2000).

The heuristics of likeness versus otherness

When talking about the various political brands contesting the 2005 General Election, a comment that was frequently made by participants was that their policies were so similar that it didn't really matter for whom one voted. Therefore, when considering the relative merits of the brands, heuristics associated with 'likeness' and 'otherness' were used as the main basis upon which they conceptualised the relative brand offerings. Further, these judgements tended to be based upon the characteristics of the party leaders rather than the party as a whole because, as leaders, not only did they tend to receive the most media coverage, but also their position inferred that they were the best example of what the brand had to offer.

Participants who were able to positively express a preference for one political brand over another generally did so because they were able to identify or aspire to some aspect of the party leader. The heuristics employed by the participants related to the belief that the greater the 'likeness' of the party leader the more likely he was going to understand the participant's priorities and address them. For example, those participants who had young families were more positive towards Tony Blair and Charles Kennedy, whose new baby, Donald James, was born during the course of the campaign. Similarly, older participants facing retirement were more positive towards Michael Howard because they felt that he was more likely to understand their concerns than his relatively youthful competitors.

However, it became apparent during the course of the interviews that the participants often found themselves more able to articulate which brands they didn't identify with than those that they did. This was often because the participant felt that he or she was working from a point of no knowledge and was unable to make any positive judgement about the brands. This phenomenon was apparent in the comment made by one participant when she said, 'I don't know much about politics but I know who I don't like.' Frequently, rather than positively commit themselves to the support one specific party, the participants would ally themselves against another by offering comments such as 'I've never been a red [Labour supporter]' or, in the case of another participant, 'I think I would have to go for Labour because I would rather cut off my hands than have the Tory Party back in power.'

As with 'likeness', aspects of 'otherness' often related to the very personal characteristics of the party leaders. This was commonly exhibited in a participant's dislike of a politician on the basis of his or her physical appearance or personal characteristics. For example, as with his Labour Party predecessor Neil Kinnock, a number of the participants ridiculed Charles Kennedy for his red hair. Geographical prejudices also came to bear as five of the participants objected to Michael Howard's 'Welshness', although interestingly there did not appear to be the same prejudice over the Scots.

In addition to apparent differences in personal characteristics, any deviance in terms of what was considered acceptable behavioural norms was also ridiculed. The norms associated with integrity and truthfulness meant that suspicions that Tony Blair had misled the electorate over the motives for the Iraq war coloured the way that many of the participants conceptualised the whole New Labour brand. Similarly, Charles Kennedy's past history of appearing on humorous television shows made it difficult for many of the participants to take the Liberal Democrats seriously, with two dismissing them as a 'joke party'.

The overall negativity towards the political sector and the difficulty in discerning between political brands appeared to have a major impact upon the way that younger participants in particular regarded the idea of participation in the political process. Of the four participants under twenty-five years of age, only one was certain that she would vote. The others said that they preferred to lend their support to organisations that would have greater impact upon their locality. Membership of organisations such as Friends of the Earth, involvement in local recycling schemes and participation in the Make Poverty History campaigns were all seen as preferable to participation in electoral politics. As one participant said, 'It took the anti-war march in London to show that politicians just don't listen and they couldn't care less. I prefer to spend my time doing something that you can see has real benefit – *here*.'

In this context it is possible to conclude that at the 2005 General Election political brands functioned very efficiently in the proprietary sense, acting as a physical differentiator between competing political brands. The absence of what the participants perceived to be concrete ideological differences between the parties and cynicism on their part towards any direct communications meant that the cues used to conceptualise political brands were instead based upon the degree to which the party leaders reflected or differed from the participants' own backgrounds, personal characteristics, values and norms. Further, these cues were likely to have been derived from media that have their own agenda and may, at times, have borne only a scant resemblance to the truth. The result of this was that some voters turned away from conventional elective brands towards less conventional, non-elective ones which they felt might be responsive to their needs and have more impact upon their immediate environment.

Discussion

One possible reason behind the difference between the Liberal Democrats' strongly branded campaign and that of New Labour and the Conservative Party is their central objective of being seen as a credible alternative for government. For any brand trying to establish its credentials in a market, it is essential that a clear and coherent message is conveyed through all brand-based materials. In the case of the Conservative Party and New Labour, the situation was that, having previously been parties of government, they may have had no need to establish their credentials. Instead, their move away from the use of traditional symbols may well be seen to be related to a desire to distance themselves from their past. Therefore, by either minimising or avoiding the use of established logos, the parties are effectively distancing themselves from the negative associations that they might possess for voters.

The resulting focus upon the party leader reflects a phenomenon that has long been present in the United States, known as the 'personalisation of politics' (Harris 2001), in which the 'the party leader is at the centre of its brand image' (Lock and Harris 1996: 17). The political concept of 'personalisation' bears some resemblance to the marketing concept of 'brand personality', which Aaker defines as 'the set of human characteristics associated with a brand' (1997: 348). In this way the human characteristics of those individuals most closely associated with the various brands become inextricably intertwined with them in the minds of voters – a proposition that is supported by both Aaker (1997) and McCracken (1989).

Over the course of the 2005 General Election period it became clear that the various parties were very much aware of the important role that their leader's personality played in voter conceptualisations of the various political brands and worked hard to capitalise on it. First, the leaders of the main parties, or, in the case of New Labour, the leader and the Chancellor of the Exchequer, were central to all the party's broadcast communications. Either they were seen to deliver a personal message on behalf of their party or, alternatively, the broadcast focused upon the personal characteristics with which the voters could personally identify. Equally, in the Liberal Democrat party election broadcast 'A Political Journey' there was a strong focus on the party leader, Charles Kennedy's 'middle income' background, including rosy images of his new family. Similarly, the Conservative Party broadcast 'Values' focused upon aspects of Michael Howard's attendance of a state school, and his experience with public services, most particularly the loss of his mother-in-law to the MRSA virus. Moreover, wherever possible, the party leaders spoke in terms of personal messages, pledges and promises that closely identified them with their respective political brands such as that to be found in the preface to the New Labour election manifesto. Next to a smiling picture of himself Tony Blair concludes his overview of the manifesto with the line 'This preface is my personal message'.

Following the outcome of this research, one might think that the political brands' focus upon these controlled communications is a fruitless exercise because of the likely disregard by a cynical electorate. However, whilst the voters might not have received these communications directly, the fact that they were reviewed and thereby communicated by media that possessed greater credibility meant that, in the main, they were not totally lost. Indeed, on occasion, briefings to launch the various posters and other materials often resulted in much greater coverage when the media focused upon an area of contention such as was seen with New Labour's infamous proposed, but abandoned, 'flying pigs' and 'hypnotist' posters that were branded as potentially antisemitic.

Yet whilst a strategy of brand personalisation provides neat and easily comparable entities for the voters upon which they can use their heuristics, it is not without significant danger for the political brands themselves, both in the short and in the long term. First, the sustained and positive focus upon the leadership risks building them up to too great an extent. Voters' expectations can be raised to an unrealistic level and, as the leader is only human, any flaws that might be exposed not only become glaring but are also transposed on to the party as a whole. This became particularly apparent over the course of the election campaign as the opposition parties repeatedly targeted Tony Blair with accusations of untruthfulness following questions regarding his justification for the Iraq war. Accusations appeared not only in posters, the press and in the party election broadcasts of both opposing parties, but were also reported and commented upon across a variety of media.

A second danger relates to the fact that a party leader is only a transitory figure and at some point is likely to step down. Therefore the danger arises that by focusing too heavily upon the leader of a party in the creation of a brand concept, when that leader retires, all those values attached to them might also disappear in the minds of the voting public. This has become extremely pertinent as both the leader of New Labour, Tony Blair, and also the leader of the Conservative Party, Michael Howard, each expressed a desire to step down. For New Labour, this may not to prove too much of a hurdle, as Gordon Brown, the Chancellor of the Exchequer and one of the architects of the New Labour project (Rawnsley 2001) has long been touted in the media as a suitable successor . However, this is likely to provide a more serious issue for the Conservative Party, as, in the run-up to the election it expended significant effort in promoting Michael Howard as the best man for the job, the subtext being that anyone else might be considered second-best. In addition, yet another leadership contest has the potential to destroy the veneer of unity restored to the party by reopening old wounds over Europe and thereby exposing any fragmentation or conflict that might still exist within the party.[1]

A further area of concern relates to the way that the focus on individual personality offers clear targets for negative campaigns. Negative campaigning, the generation of personal attacks upon a particular individual (Kotler and Kotler 1999), was a common occurrence on the part

Figure 3.2   Example of a New Labour poster

of New Labour and the Conservative Party throughout the whole of the 2005 election campaign. The aim of communications such as the Conservatives' 'Take that look off your face' cinema ad and New Labour's ironic use of the Conservatives' own slogan 'Are you thinking what we're thinking?' (Figure 3.2) was simply to undermine the opposition without the provision of any positive brand message of their own.

Kotler and Kotler (1999) highlight the fact that a negative approach in campaigning can be highly effective in that it plants a seed of doubt in the minds of the voters and also keeps its opponents engaged as they spend time rebutting attacks that might otherwise have been spent spreading a positive message about their brand. However, whilst this might be perceived as an effective tactic, as a strategy it can only end in failure, as it reinforces voters' already negative perceptions of the political arena as a whole and of political brands in particular. In the 2005 General Election, where both the main brands engaged in negative campaigning, the outcome of such a mutually destructive strategy was the generation of what might be termed 'negative brands'.

A 'negative brand' is one whose proposition is not based upon what the brand stands for, instead it is based upon the fact that it is not the competition. Therefore, such a brand cannot be viewed in isolation, as it relies upon the 'other' brand to justify its position. Because of the focus upon negativity at the expense of the promotion of its own positive brand proposition, when viewed in isolation, the electorate has very little that is tangible upon which to make their judgements.

The impact of negative brands

Whilst there was a marginal increase in turnout over the 2001 General Election, the 61% achieved in the 2005 General Election (MORI, 16 May 2005) suggests that the negative tendencies associated with the campaign did nothing to seize the hearts and minds of the electorate in a meaningful way. This is hardly surprising, as this research showed that the participants saw little to separate the two main political brands, and, with both focusing strongly upon negative campaigning techniques, they gave them very little material with which to do so. Further, when negative campaigning becomes the dominant force in an election, as it appeared in 2005, not only do consumers become negative toward the brands involved, but they are also likely to become negative towards the sector as a whole.

This negativity is not only dangerous for the political brands themselves but is in danger of infecting institutions outside the immediate environment of Westminster. Mortimore (2003) suggests that negativity towards political brands and the political system has the potential to extend to any institution that is perceived, or might be perceived, as having links with the political process. In this way, any unelected body attached to the political process, such as the civil service, local authorities and public utilities, are also regarded with suspicion and their work is ultimately undermined by the climate of negativity originated by political brands.

The increasing popularity of non-conventional political brands

Disillusionment with the political system and the negative perception attached to the major political brands means it is hardly surprising that participants turned to other non-elective political movements such as the 'Make Poverty History' campaign. Led by the film director Richard Curtis and the musicians Bob Geldof and Bono, the 'Make Poverty History' campaign is the result of a coalition of more than 500 charities, trade unions and other campaigning groups which aim to alleviate poverty in some of the world's poorest countries by influencing international governments in three key areas: trade, debt and aid (source: www.makepovertyhistory.org).

It is not difficult to see why these single-issue parties and campaigning organisations such as Make Poverty History hold greater appeal than conventional elective political brands. Their brand concept stems from a clear, simple message with an outcome that would be laudable according to most people's beliefs, values and behavioural norms. In addition, those involved are seen to be acting out of motives of not personal gain but commitment to a specific purpose that they feel will ultimately be to the benefit of a particular group of people. In this way they are seen as 'authentic', which, according to Kellner (2004), is the key to political success. He states that the public want 'real people, thinking real thoughts, giving their real views, making real promises that will yield real improvements – not plastic, on-message politicians in thrall to dogmas, spin doctors, control freaks or tribal passions' (Kellner 2004: 840).

Moreover, unlike conventional elective political brands, movements such as Make Poverty History offer 'added value' to the individuals who choose to support their cause. Not only do they have the opportunity to participate in activities such as the Live 8 concert that offers a real, positive outcome, they also offer the chance to become an identifiable member of an aspirational community. The easily identifiable device of the white wristband allowed the wearers to make a simple statement whilst at the same time identifying with other high-profile supporters of the cause such as Liam Neeson, Brad Pitt and Kate Moss. In this way, non-elective brands now might be seen to offer the electorate the sort of camaraderie and sense of purpose that was once the province of the grass-roots movements of the conventional political brands.

Conclusion

In the context of the political market the voting public have, time after time, been subject to negative associations produced both unintentionally and intentionally by the sector. Poor expectation management on the part of the political brands has resulted in the electorate repeatedly being disappointed with governments' ability to meet their election promises whilst allegations of 'sleaze' and dishonesty do nothing to improve their impression of the political sector as a whole.

Because the majority of voters still feel some obligation to vote, elections offer the opportunity for political brands to build positive values in the minds of voters not only with regard to their brands but also with regard to the political sector as a whole. However, whilst the original intention was to understand the role of a political brand within the context of a time frame such as that imposed by a General Election campaign, it soon became clear that the participants' conceptualisations spanned a much greater time frame, thus bearing out Gardner and Levy's proposition that it is 'a body of associations it has built up and acquired as a public object over a period of time' (1955: 35).

It may be as a result of the main parties' appreciation of this fact that the Liberal Democrats adopted such a strongly branded approach whilst New Labour and the Conservative Party did not choose to physically brand their campaign in any coherent fashion. With the aim of being perceived as 'the real alternative' to the other main parties, the appearance of a professional and coherent approach was essential for the Liberal Democrats. Anything less was likely to have been torn apart by aggressive media in search of new angles in the reportage of the parties' campaigns. This appeared less important to the Conservative Party and New Labour, whose credentials for government were already established by way of first-hand experience. That there was little need to reinforce the physical branding of the parties as an identification device was also apparent, as the participants appeared to possess very clear associations as to which colour and logo belonged with which party.

However, whilst the participants were able to physically distinguish between the main brands, they were less clear as to what they stood for. This was further compounded by the lack of positive action within the election context by the two main brands. The parties' strategy of negative campaigning appeared to do little other than cancel each other out in the minds of voters, leaving nothing to judge them upon other than heuristics associated with the personal characteristics of the party leaders. Whilst these 'tried and tested' rules of thumb might be satisfactory short-term for the voters themselves, they bode ill for the future of British party politics, and possibly the future of parliamentary democracy as a whole, on a number of counts.

First, if voters are unable to differentiate between the main political brands using anything other than personal heuristics, the government is likely to be selected on the basis of appearance over substance. This may well mean that gifted individuals, lacking in presentational skills, who might otherwise have made a valuable contribution to the process of government may be lost to the political sector in place of people who, though less gifted, are perceived as more attractive. Indeed, some might argue that this has already been the case in the US with George Bush's victory over Al Gore and, in the UK, with Tony Blair's victory over William Hague. In addition, such superficial criteria are in danger of leaving the door open for a charismatic personality with dubious motives or potentially harmful policies to find a place in government.

Second, the use of 'otherness' as a distinguishing factor between parties, particularly with regard to the personal characteristics of candidates, highlights the lack of 'likeness' and authenticity in electoral politics. Whilst it is possible to take a Saussurian perspective and say that such an approach is simply another way of creating meaning, the results of this research concur with the proposition by Derrida (1972) that the generation of an 'other' is not a valueless distinction between entities. Across all the participants, the 'other' was seen as a lesser entity, materially, physically, socially or morally. This distinction concurs with the supposition of Du Gay *et al.* (1997) in that, with the creation of a classificatory system, there is also likely to be a hierarchical one. In a post-9/11 environment that struggles to reconcile the concepts of equality, multiculturalism and integration, any judgement that places one individual above or below another on purely personal characteristics is potentially divisive, as it encourages individuals to look for 'otherness' where it would not otherwise have existed.

Third, there are serious issues associated with the lack of constructive discussion and debate that is a consequence of negative campaigning. Unless voters have read party manifestoes or literature they can have no deep understanding of the various party propositions other than those which are provided through media interpretation. This then leaves the voters subject to messages tempered by external motives and, in the case of less assiduous media, sensationalism. Further, if the electorate are not sure about the platforms upon which respective political brands stand, once elected, they struggle to hold them to account. Moreover, claims by political brands over the fulfilment of their election promises will potentially lack credibility in the eyes of the electorate if they did not really understand or register what they were at the outset.

Finally, if political brands themselves, or the political sector as a whole, continue to be seen as negative and ineffective, then electors may continue to abstain from the process or seek alternative product areas or brands. What became clear during the course of the interview process was that the participants were disengaged not from political brands but from the parliamentary system and the brands that support it. In contrast, they show strong levels of engagement with unconventional political brands that offer them not only tangible life benefits but also the added value of feeling that they are contributing to the well-being of others and the wider global community.

Yet whilst such negativity within the UK political system may appear depressing, there is also significant hope. The fact that over 61% of the electorate still chose to participate in the electoral system, in spite of their apparent dissatisfaction with it, is a very positive indicator. Following the 2005 General Election, the challenge must now be for the political brands within the existing system to provide a positive proposition that energises the electorate not only in relation to the brands themselves but also towards the political system as a whole. Without a positive perspective such as this, interest and engagement on the part of the electors will simply shift to brands that satisfy their needs in other ways, with major implications for the legitimacy of Parliament.

Note

1 Though, at the time of going to press, the differences between the two main contenders, David Davis and David Cameron, were more ones of style than ones which could create deep ideological divisions within the party, this seems unfounded following Cameron's victory and partial rebranding of the party and leader.

References

Aaker, D. A. (1991), *Managing Brand Equity*, London: Free Press.

Aaker, J. L. (1997), 'Dimensions of brand personality', *Journal of Marketing Research* 34: 347–57.

Ansolabehere, S. and Iyengar, S. (1994), 'Does attack advertising demobilize the electorate?' *American Political Science Review* 88: 829–39.

Bauer, R. (1960) 'Consumer behaviour as risk taking', in Hanckok, Robert S., *Dynamic Marketing for a Changing World*, Chicago: American Marketing Association.

Bauer, H. H., Huber, F. and Herrmann, A. (1996), 'Political marketing: an infor- mation-economic analysis', *European Journal of Marketing* 30: 152–65.

Belk, R. (1988), 'Possessions and the extended self', *Journal of Consumer Research* 15: 139–69.

Berelson, B. R., Lazarsfeld, P. F. and McPhee, W. N. (1954), *Voting*, Chicago: University of Chicago Press.

Bourdieu, P. (1984), *Distinction: A Social Critique of the Judgment of Taste*, trans. R. Nice, London: Routledge.

Bullock, A. and Trombley, S. (2000) *The New Fontana Dictionary of Modern Thought*, London: HarperCollins.

Charmaz, K. (2000), 'Grounded theory: objectivist and constructivist methods', in N. K. Denzin and Y. S. Lincoln (eds), *Handbook of Qualitative Research*, London: Sage.

Chicchi, F. (2000), 'Grounded theory and the biographical approach: an attempt at an integrated heuristic strategy', *International Review of Sociology* 10: 5–23.

Cutler, F. (2002), 'The simplest short cut of all: socio-demographic characteris- tics and electoral choice', *Journal of Politics* 64: 466–90.

de Chernatony, L. (1999), ' Brand management through narrowing the gap between brand identity and brand reputation', *Journal of Marketing Management* 15: 157–79.

de Chernatony, L. and Dall'Olmo Riley, F. (1998), 'Defining a "brand": beyond the literature with experts' interpretations', *Journal of Marketing Management* 14: 417–43.

Derrida, J. (1972), *Positions*, Chicago: University of Chicago Press.

Dolan, K. (1998), 'Voting for women in the "Year of the Woman"', *American Journal of Political Science* 42: 272–3.

Doyle, P. (1989), 'Building successful brands: the strategic objectives', *Journal of Marketing Management* 5: 77–95.

Du Gay, P., Hall, S., Janes, S., Mackay, H. and Gegus, K. (1997), 'Doing Cultural Studies: the story of the Sony Walkman', London: Sage/Open University.

Firat, A. F. and Venkatesh, A. (1995), 'Liberatory postmodernism and the reen- chantment of consumption', *Journal of Consumer Research* 22: 239–67.

Fiske, J. (2002), *Introduction to Communication Studies*, London: Routledge.

Fournier, S. (1998), 'Consumers and their brands: developing relationship theory in consumer research', *Journal of Consumer Research* 24 (4): 343–64.

Gardner, B. B. and Levy, S. J. (1955), 'The product and the brand', *Harvard Business Review* 33: 33–9.

Gosschalk, B., Marshall, B. and Kaur-Ballagan, K. (2002) 'Non-voters, political disconnection and parliamentary democracy', *Parliamentary Affairs* 55: 715–30.

Goulding, C. (1999), 'Consumer research, interpretive paradigms and methodological ambiguities', *European Journal of Marketing* 33: 859.

Goulding, C. (2002), *Grounded Theory: A Practical Guide for Management, Business and Market Researchers*, London: Sage.

Grayson, K. (2002), 'Telling the difference: consumer evaluations of authentic and inauthentic market offerings', *Advances in Consumer Research* 29: 44–5.

Hall, S. (1996), 'Encoding, decoding', in S. Hall, D. Hobson, A. Lowe and P. Willis (eds), *Culture, Media, Language*, London: Routledge.

Harris, F. and de Chernatony, L. (2001), 'Corporate branding and corporate brand performance', *European Journal of Marketing* 35: 441–56.

Harris, P. (2001), 'To spin or not to spin, that is the question: the emergence of modern political marketing', *Marketing Review*, 2: 35–53.

Hirschman, E. C. and Holbrook, M. B. (1980), *Symbolic Consumer Behaviour*, Ann Arbor MI: Association for Consumer Research.

Hirschman, E. and Holbrook, M. (1982) 'Hedonic consumption: emerging concepts, methods and propositions', *Journal of Marketing* 46 (3): 92–101.

Holt, D. (2002), 'Why do brands cause trouble? A dialectical theory of consumer culture and branding', *Journal of Consumer Research* 29: 70–90.

Jones, J. P. (1986) 'What's in a name? Advertising and the concept of brands', Lexington MA: D. C. Heath.

Jones, T. (2000), 'Old Clause IV to New Clause IV', in B. Brivati and R. Hefferman (eds) *The Labour Party: A Centenary History*, Basingstoke: Macmillan.

Kapferer, J-N. (1992), *Strategic Brand Management*, London: Kogan Page.

Keller, K. L. (2003) 'Brand synthesis: the multidimensionality of brand knowledge', *Journal of Consumer Research* 29: 595–600.

Kellner, P. (2004), 'Britain's culture of detachment', *Parliamentary Affairs* 57: 830–43.

Kotler, P. and Levy, S. J. (1969), 'Broadening the concept of marketing', *Journal of Marketing* 33: 10–15.

Kotler, P. and Kotler, N. (1999), 'Generating effective candidates, campaigns and causes', in B. Newman (ed.), *Handbook of Political Marketing*, Thousand Oaks CA: Sage.

Lloyd, J. (2003), 'Square peg, round hole? Can marketing-based concepts such as the "product" and the "marketing mix" have a useful role in the political arena?' Paper presented at the Political Studies Association annual meeting, University of Leicester, April.

Lock, A. and Harris, P. (1996), 'Political marketing: *vive la différence!*' *European Journal of Marketing* 30: 14–24.

Luck, D. J. 'Broadening the concept of marketing – too far', *Journal of Marketing* 33: 53–5.

Mariampolski, H. (2001), *Qualitative Market Research: A Comprehensive Guide*, London: Sage.

Marshall, B. (2005), 'Getting the Public Involved in Politics', paper presented to the Political Studies Association Political Marketing Group conference, London, 24–5 February.

McCracken, G. (1989) 'Who is the celebrity endorser? Cultural foundations of the endorsement process', *Journal of Consumer Research* 16 (3): 310

McCracken, G. (1990) *Culture and Consumption: New Approaches to the Symbolic Character of Consumer Goods and Activities* (Midland Book edition), Indianapolis IN: Indiana Press.

MORI (2005), General Election 2005, www.mori.com/election2005/index.shtml, accessed 1 September 2005

Mortimore, R. (2003), 'Why politics needs marketing', *Journal of Nonprofit and Voluntary Sector Marketing* 8 (2): 107–21.

Muniz, A. M., Jr and O'Guinn, T. C. (2001) 'Brand community', *Journal of Consumer Research* 27, 412–33.

Nandan, S. (2005), 'An exploration of the brand identity–brand image linkage: a communications perspective', *Brand Management* 12: 264–78.

Newman, B. I. and Sheth, J. N. (1985), 'A model of primary voter behaviour', *Journal of Consumer Research* 12, 178–87.

O'Shaughnessy, N. (2001), 'The marketing of political marketing', *European Journal of Marketing* 35: 1047–57.

Ozanne, J. and Murray, J. (1995), 'Uniting critical theory and public policy to create the reflexively defiant consumer', *American Behavioural Scientist* 38: 516–25.

Rawnsley, A. (2001), *Servants of the People: The Inside Story of New Labour*, London: Penguin.

Riley, R. (1996), 'Revealing socially constructed knowledge through quasi-structured interviews and grounded theory analysis', *Journal of Travel and Tourism Marketing* 5 (1–2): 21–40.

Schouten, J. W. and McAlexander, J. H. (1995), 'Subcultures of consumption: an ethnography of new bikers', *Journal of Consumer Research* 2: 43–61.

Schwandt, T. A. (2000), 'Three epistemological stances for qualitatitive enquiry', in N. Denzin and Y. Lincoln (eds), *Handbook of Qualitative Research*, London: Sage.

Sears, D. O. (1969), 'Political behavior', in G. Lindzey and E. Aronson (eds), *The Handbook of Social Psychology*, Reading MA: Addison Wesley.

Silverman, D. (2001), *Interpreting Qualitative Data: Methods for Analysing Talk, Text and Interaction*, London: Sage.

Smith, G. (2003), 'Assessing Brand Personality of UK Political Parties: An Empirical Approach', paper presented to the Academy of Marketing Political Marketing conference, London, September.

Solomon, M., Bamossy, G. and Askegaard, S. (2002) *Consumer Behaviour: A European Perspective*, Hemel Hempstead: Prentice Hall.

Watson, J. (2003), *Media Communication: An Introduction to Theory and Process*, Basingstoke: Palgrave Macmillan.

Web sites

www.makepovertyhistory.com, accessed on 5 September 2005.
www.mori.co.uk, accessed on 5 September 2005.

4

Political marketing and the 2005 election: what's ideology got to do with it?

Heather Savigny

On 6 May 2005 Tony Blair led Labour to a historic third successive term in office. This was following highly marketised campaigns run by both the Labour and Conservative parties. The Liberal Democrats made significant electoral inroads; both Labour and the Conservatives lost seats to them. While the Liberal Democrats represented a challenge to the dominance of the two main parties, they did little, however, to alter the balance of electoral competition. Given the increasingly sophisticated nature of marketing employed by the two main parties, this chapter considers the campaign strategies pursued by both Labour and the Conservatives and reflects upon the role of ideology in contemporary 'market driven' campaigning. What does the use of marketing materials reveal? To what extent do marketing techniques and ideology, rather than political ideologies, inform party behaviour? Is there room for political ideology in electoral campaigning, or do political actors consider marketing all that is necessary? This chapter considers the extent to which marketing itself has become the driving ideology in politics, which is reflected upon through a discussion of the campaigning strategies of both the Conservatives and Labour; and the context in which they operated. It examines the extent to which the employment of marketing materials and strategies reveals an underlying ideological commitment to neo-liberalism, and the primacy of the market over and above a commitment to democratic debate and party competition. This chapter will proceed by giving an overview of the context of the campaign, highlight the theoretical discussion on adopting a marketing approach and the role of ideology, and explore the extent to which there has been continuity and change from previous elections. The final section of this chapter then assesses what the use of marketing reveals about the ideological commitments of the two main parties.

The product

The campaign context

The 2005 election campaign was conducted in the context of the highly unpopular decision by Blair to support the US in the Iraq conflict. Party strategists (particularly in the Labour camp, who were most likely to be affected by this) raised concerns over potential low voter turnout. This was coupled with the notion that perceptions of Conservative incompetence in the 1990s were thought to be fading from voters' minds, particularly given that the Conservative Party was presenting itself as united behind Michael Howard. While there was again limited distance in policy agendas, these contextual factors meant that the election was a much closer contest than in 1997 and 2001. Both parties continued to be engaged in extensive marketing, and were advised by marketing professionals and campaign strategists from the UK, Australia and the US.

Marketing, as this volume suggests, plays an increasingly significant role in the political process. Election campaigns are inconceivable events without the use of marketing (Newman 1994: 21) and as has been widely acknowledged 'the problem of getting elected is a marketing one' (Reid 1988). The British general election of 2005 was no different. As will be noted below, both parties ran highly generic national-level campaigns, distinguished by differences in style rather than substantive distinctions in policy. The lack of debate at national level, in the context of a stable economy and both parties appealing to a relatively prosperous middle class, meant that parties clearly perceived campaign resources better focused elsewhere. The peculiarities of the electoral system also meant that it was key voters in marginal seats who would determine the outcome of the election. While this is nothing new, what was different in this campaign was the extent to which sophisticated marketing strategies and technologies meant that both Conservatives and Labour could, first, bypass the traditional media and, second, identify these voters and personalise the campaign message. This happened to an unprecedented degree: the real campaign was focused on the floating voters. In 2005 they comprised 2% of the electorate (Wintour 2005), and throughout the campaign marketing was the driving process. In that sense, this chapter reflects upon the way in which beliefs of political parties as to the role of marketing in the process of politics can be considered through the extent to which marketing informed their campaign strategies. This chapter proceeds by considering the role of ideology within a market-oriented strategy, and what the use of marketing as a guiding principle reveals about the ideological commitments of both main parties.

Theoretical framework: the role of ideology

Political marketing is premised upon an analogy: the analogy is that parties behave as businesses, voters as consumers, all operating in a political market place. Located in the managerialist school of thinking, the marketing that informs political marketing is underpinned by neo-classical economics. The Downsian underpinnings of this literature has been broadly accepted by political marketing scholars (Mauser 1983; Scammell 1999; Lees-Marshment 2001; a critique developed in more detail elsewhere: see Savigny 2004). Ideology plays a significant role in the political process; indeed, the role of values, and beliefs about the proper distribution of resources, and what a society should look like, underpins the notion of politics. In political marketing models a brand is considered to provide a function similar to ideology. In economic models, ideology is comprised of policy bundles as a cost-saving device for voters (Downs 1957). In the contemporary environment the domi-nant bundling package is that of marketing. In the 2005 campaign (building upon previous campaigns), ideas and beliefs about the utility of marketing dominated and drove the electioneering process. And while the use of marketing at election time is nothing new (see, for example, Wring 1996, 2005), as Kotler notes, what has changed is its reach and sophistication (1982: 461–2). Both Conservatives and Labour now rely extensively on techniques and processes of marketing, as is demonstrated below.

Marketing models note the restrictive nature of ideology (Scott 1970: 57). As a consequence of the adoption of marketing, Lees-Marshment describes the changing nature of party behaviour, stating that parties 'no longer pursue grand ideologies, fervently arguing for what they believe in and trying to persuade the masses to follow them. They increasingly follow the people' (2001: 1). For her this is a positive benefit, suggest-ing the successful implementation of the marketing concept, which locates the consumer at the centre of the process (Keith 1960; Kotler and Levy 1969), means that political actors are more responsive to the demands of consumers (Scammell 1995; O'Cass 1996; Lees-Marshment 2001). This responsiveness, however, is only in order that the organisa-tion can achieve its goals (Wring 1997; Sackman 1992). As such this is not the equal relationship that is first implied. Not all consumer prefer-ences are identified and responded to. Only those necessary for the polit-ical actor to achieve his/her/their goal: win the election. In the UK this means that political parties are responsive to floating voters, in key mar-ginal seats. In 2005 they were 2% of the population (Wintour 2005; Worcester 2005) which undermines notions of equality among voters;

rather a minority of the populace are responded to and the political 'product' is personalised to fit their expressed preferences. This suggests that the package in which this is presented is fluid, implying that ideology can be adapted to suit the packaging. Ideology becomes a tool within the marketing process, something that can be altered in response to changing demands and preferences. As such, the ideological underpinnings of political marketing are, within much of the political marketing literature and practice, empirical questions in relation to the proper extent and use of marketing in politics, rather than a political vision of what society should be.

The use of marketing has in itself become an ideological act, and, as Harris and Wring note, 'managerialism has to some extent replaced traditional forms of ideology as the driving force within modern politics' (2001: 909). It is also argued that this, in part, has been facilitated by the context within which political actors are operating, and the ideas actors hold of their context. It is suggested that the 2005 campaign cannot be fully understood without recourse to this context. British politics is conducted in a media-saturated environment. Technological developments have both impacted upon and been exploited by politicians. The media industry itself can be argued to have been complicit in the changing nature of the political process, given, for example, the twenty-four-hour demand for news stories. This context has also been characterised by the changing social base of the electorate: voter dealignment has been widely accepted; class and partisan loyalty are no longer thought to structure the vote. Marketisation has led to parties and marketers discursively constructing voters as consumers. This is also in the context of the fundamental acceptance, by the main parties, of neo-liberalism, which emphasises markets as the primary ordering mechanism in society. The extent to which markets are regulated is the concern of contemporary political actors, rather than whether markets have a proper role in the activity of politics.

This dominance of market thinking has permeated into electoral campaigning. Indeed, marketing scholars positively advocate this, arguing that, for marketing to be successful, it must be adopted as a mind set (Kotler and Andreasen 1996: 37), a philosophy or an orientation (O'Cass 1996; Lees-Marshment 2001). Economic analyses highlight the need for parties to be 'ideologically adaptable' in order to take advantage of 'strategic opportunities' (Scott 1970: 57). Ideology as a concept associated with political values, then becomes malleable in the marketing process. To this end, it is suggested that the role of ideology in political marketing, in this instance with a particular focus upon the 2005 election campaign, reveals a limited role for political ideologies and a consolidation and primacy of neo-liberalism and marketing as a guiding philosophy for political actors.

The marketing campaign and ideology

This section explores the twofold approach of both parties to the election campaign. This is underpinned by a reflection on the questions: What marketing strategies were used? What do they reveal about the ideology of the parties? It is suggested that exploration of the strategies adopted by the two main parties indicates an underlying ideological belief in, and commitment to, the utility of marketing. Both Labour and the Conservatives adopted similar strategies, broad campaigns at national level and, at the local level, campaigns focused, targeted and personalised towards the floating voters. National-level campaigning focused upon immediate and short-term issues. Both parties promoted similar populist visions, albeit to slightly differing degrees, and there was consensus over the bigger issues, for example, the proper role and function of the state.

Evidence suggests that the degree to which these parties engaged in campaign strategy indicates a real philosophical commitment to marketing rather than political debate. This also implies a level of internalisation of the belief in the utility of marketing (consistent with those advocates of this approach, as noted above). As such it is contended that it is managerialist thinking which was driving the campaign process rather than traditionally considered 'political' views and ideologies. At national level, both parties engaged in extensive advertising and image management. At local level, segmentation and targeting were used to identify crucial voters. The following section highlights the national and local-level campaigns, arguing that this represented an overall strategic coherent marketing strategy on the part of both main parties, reflecting an ideological commitment to marketing which, in this campaign, preceded and informed political behaviour and beliefs.

The national level

The national-level campaigns by both parties were ideologically cohesive in their use of marketing. Both focused extensively on the pursuit of broad imagery. While the Conservatives' campaign was heavily populist, Labour's was broad, cursorily engaging with popular culture, yet both were seeking to appeal to the median voter. Labour began the campaign by seeking to focus attention on their economic success. This was done through the presentation of Tony Blair and Gordon Brown together, seeking to remind voters of the strength and stability of the economy, linking Blair with the success of Brown. This was highlighted in a soft-focus television advertisement, shot by Anthony Minghella, director of *The English Patient*, which emphasised the special relationship between Blair and Brown. Labour did, however, have difficulty capturing the media agenda during the first week of the campaign. In part it could be argued this was because its campaign focused upon the economy. A stable economy is not something that necessarily attracts media or voter attention, particularly in an environment where the middle classes are relatively economically stable. As research carried out at by the Communications Research Centre at Loughborough University indicated, the first week of the election campaign saw the media provide less coverage than in recent years (Gibson 2005). Moreover, when this coverage was provided more than half focused upon the process, campaign strategies, polls and prediction rather than issues. (Gibson 2005). The Conservatives took advantage of this and successfully dominated the national media campaign. Initially this was with their highly populist Saatchi-created 'Are you thinking what we're thinking?' campaign. Michael Howard then captured national media attention during the second week. Heavily advised by Australian strategist Lynton Crosby (known for his willingness to 'go negative'), the Conservatives continued their populist campaigning, focusing on immigration, implicitly challenging Labour to respond, which indeed it did. Blair symbolically made Labour's policy announcement in respect of immigration at Dover.

As noted above, this campaign was also being waged in the context of the highly unpopular Iraq war. The conflict had been supported by the Conservatives, leaving little room for campaign differences. Halfway through the campaign a document was leaked to and published in the *Mail on Sunday* which questioned the legality of the Iraq war. Despite Conservative support for the Iraq war, this document provided the Conservatives with the opportunity to continue the highly negative campaigning (which was being engaged in by both parties). Howard sought to draw attention to Blair's integrity. He focused campaign energies on publicly branding Blair a 'liar'. This highly personal and negative campaigning seemed, however, to have little impact upon the public. Labour's lead in the national polls remained consistent. And, despite Howard's claims, polls showed him to be less trusted by the public than Blair (www.mori.com).

Both parties engaged in highly negative campaigning throughout, with Labour warning of low turnout facilitating a Conservative victory 'by the back door'. This negativity was also seen in the advertising process. Labour again employed Trevor Beattie of TBWA (responsible for controversial FCUK and Wonderbra ads). His team created the highly contentious 'flying pigs' ad. While published only on Labour's Web site (rather than on national billboards, for example) this advert attracted extensive media coverage because of the criticism levelled at its negative imagery and messages.

The campaigning, at national level, was also characterised by minor stylistic differences, but little in terms of policy differentiation. There was fundamental agreement by both parties over basic issues that reached the agenda, such as the economy, health, crime and immigration (and also those that did not reach the agenda, for example Europe and environmental issues), suggesting that while there were many similarities at national level, with consensus on issues that would reach the campaign agenda, there was also agreement on those that wouldn't (cf. Bachrach and Baratz 1962). Further, in a move echoing Labour's modernisation strategies of the 1990s, the Conservatives agreed to retain key planks of Labour policy, including independence for the Bank of England, and a commitment to a minimum wage. The Conservatives decided to match Labour spending plans on health and education (Kaletsky 2005). In doing this the Conservatives' electoral strategy mirrored that of Labour in opposition through their process of modernisation.

Labour's modernisation process had been regarded by some as an attempt to 'change the party's instincts and values in accordance with [a] new political economy' (Kenny and Smith 1997, in Finlayson 2003: 66). This then is more than the acceptance of Thatcherism. It highlights the acceptance of changed social and economic conditions. In this sense, these conditions are characterised by managerialism and the rhetoric of the markets. The use of marketing and its discourse, then, has ideological implications. Its use can be regarded, in part, as a response to the environment in which both parties are operating; however, they also have the capacity to influence this environment. In pursuing such similar electoral strategies (in terms of agreement over spending plans, lack of debate as to the proper role and function of the state, and the techniques employed to attract electoral support) both parties acquiesced in – indeed, they endorsed – the managerialism that informed political practice.

The generality and similarity of their campaigning was evidenced again, for example, by both parties' appeal to a broad cross-section of the electorate with the use of phrases such as 'hard-working families'. This phrase was widely used by both parties (as was done by Kerry and Bush in the US election) and had been market tested in focus groups, although, as one Conservative strategist suggested, 'What family is going to think that they don't work hard?' (Freedland 2005). Both parties heavily relied on this style of nondescript rhetoric to characterise the kind of person that they were seeking to identify with. Yet, it could be argued, this represented a perception, held by the parties themselves, of the existence of very little ideological difference between them. Competition and discussion occurred around a narrow centre ground, given the limited issues on the agenda, and focused around the minutiae of policy. This election campaign, at national level, was about differences in imagery rather than substantive political/ideological distinctions.

Both parties also sought to promote a bland, voter-friendly image through extensive engagement with channels of popular culture. Blair appeared on *Richard and Judy's* 'You say, we pay', was interviewed by *Little Ant and Dec*, but was turned down for a cameo role in *Little Britain* (Conlan 2005). Leaders' wives were also part of this process of engaging with the public through non-traditional means. Sandra Howard appeared on the television chat show *Loose Women*; Cherie Blair extolled the virtues of knitting patterns in *Woman's Own* magazine. Again this was a deliberate strategy, pursued in order to try and identify with those who were perceived to be the less politicised among the electorate: to connect with the 'ordinary voter'.

The cross-over between popular culture and politics has been extensively noted (Street 1997), prompting the identification of a 'celebrity politician' keen to engage in entertainment media (Street 2004; Baum 2005). While some argue that this has led to a dumbing down of politics (Franklin 1994), in contrast it has been claimed that it enhances the opportunity for engagement, making politics available and accessible to a wider audience (Temple 2005). Norris (2000) suggests that those who are politically interested will engage in political information anyway, and that those who are politically disengaged will not engage – implying the media have little if no effect upon political behaviour or consciousness. In a similar vein, Prior (2005) argues that those who prefer to engage with entertainment, rather than serious or 'political' media, are less likely to engage in the activity of voting. While this debate as to the impact of the media upon voters, and political consciousness, ensues within academic circles (see also Newton and Brynin 2001), clearly politicians believe the media have some impact. Hence the extensive devotion of resources to image management, marketing and proactive media management strategies at both national and local level, both in previous election campaigns and to an unprecedented level of engagement with popular culture during this campaign. Labour's manifesto launch saw six key party members at podiums in a manner similar to that of the game show *The Weakest Link*. The style of the Conservatives' election campaign, with its emphasis upon ousting Blair from office over

Iraq, could also be regarded as akin to calling for eviction from the *Big Brother* house.

As well as engaging with the content of popular culture, politicians sought to continue to extend campaigning outside traditional media forms. While in 1997 and 2001 new technological developments facilitated extra campaigning by text message, during this election online blogging also became a campaign tool. Labour consulted the controversial US Democrat adviser Zack Exley about their online presence. Many candidates had online blogs, including Blair's ghost-written diary; Iain Dale (Conservative) from north Norfolk was mentioned on the satirical television quiz *Have I Got News for You* – proudly cited with the blog, as a result of his 'Are you drinking what I'm drinking?' blog diary entry. Sandra Howard recorded her campaign diary and her thoughts on her husband's campaign trail. Yet the content of these message boards was not serious policy debate, but rather 'chatty' personal diaries (Lawson 2005).

While the Conservatives ran a highly populist national-level campaign, producing its shortest manifesto to date, Labour ran a broad national-level campaign, seemingly not designed to capture the media's imagination. However, despite the Conservatives apparent success at attracting, and initially driving, the national-level media agenda, this made little difference to the national polls, which throughout predicted a Labour victory. The media also declared themselves bored with the election (Hames 2005) and complained about the lack of competition between the two (Marr 2005). National-level strategies had resulted in minor stylistic differences between the two parties, and the convergence of competition, as such attracting or exciting little national media attention. Policy played a minimal role. Race and immigration were perceived by the media as important issues (Miles 2005) and Iraq was regarded as the other significant issue at national level (Cowley 2005). Yet broad agreement by both main parties over issues that would reach the policy agenda produced centripetal competition. Differences between the parties at national level were stylistic rather than of any political substance. However, it could be argued this was a strategic move on the part of both parties, as this was not where the election was really being fought. The real election battles were occurring in 100 or so marginal seats. The peculiarity of the British electoral system means that elections are won or lost in a few key seats. Sophisticated marketing techniques and technologies meant that both parties could identify these voters individually and personally target the campaign message to them. It could be argued that the inability of Labour to dominate the media agenda was a consequence of strategic marketing. Labour had no need to promote anything nationally other than a broad image, reflecting the belief that this was not where the election was being fought. Both parties recognised that their resources needed to be targeted at the local level, bypassing traditional media channels of communication.

The local level

It has been argued elsewhere that the 2005 election was a campaign of two halves (Savigny, 2005). Unlike the elections of 1997 and 2001, this campaign was thought to have the potential to impact upon the result (*The Economist* 2005). While the national polls showed a consistent lead for Labour throughout, as noted above, the real battle occurred in the marginal seats. And it is here that election campaigning was considered to be crucial (Wintour and White 2005). Labour's lead was only a few points; the unpopularity of Blair's decision over Iraq, and the Conservatives' recovery, were sufficient to pose a real threat to Labour. Labour's narrow lead, and concern also in respect of low voter turnout, meant that both parties were aware that the election could be won or lost in around 100 key Labour/Conservative seats (Jones 2005). More narrowly than that, it would be decided by the floating voters within those marginal constituencies. Given the peculiarities of the British electoral system, marginal seats have greater influence over the election outcome; therefore resources tend to be targeted there. This is nothing new: historical analysis of the Labour Party shows the early use of stratified electioneering (Wring 2001). However, this campaign was unusual in that advances in technology and increasingly sophisticated marketing meant that voters could be personally targeted, with an individualised campaign message.

Both main parties had acquired computer software to support these high levels of segmentation and targeting. Labour had the labour.contact database, while the Conservatives acquired the VoterVault software from Republican strategist Karl Rove. These databanks were used to store information from a range of sources, in order to identify voters to be targeted. Both parties had also purchased a profile of every postcode in Britain from the marketing firm Experian Mosaic, which holds extensive profiles of consumer behaviour. This was then cross-checked against electoral data, the party's own records. In the year preceding the election both Labour and the Conservatives had set up call centres to establish and identify target voters and their preferences. This information was also cross-checked against credit histories in order to build up lifestyle pictures of target voters. This meant voters were no longer targeted by class, or even broad groups such as Mondeo man and Worcester woman, popularised during previous election campaigns. The Conservatives used the software to identify which party a voter supported, whether they were undecided or whether they were not going to vote. Candidates then focused their attention on 'V-sixes' (Tories, but reluctant voters), V-eights (undecideds who would definitely vote) and V-fives (undecideds, who might vote). The party thought this software was operating to a level of around 70% accuracy (*The Economist* 2005). Labour used the software to identify up to sixty new kinds of target categories, including groups such as 'symbols of success' or 'upscaling new owners' (Wintour 2005). The election campaign saw parties gain the ability to identify preferences and target personalised messages to houses with the same postcode. The aim then was to contact key voters in person, by mail shot and on the phone. This technology was also supported through the extensive use of call centres, to contact potential voters. The campaign message could then be highly personalised to the voter's profile.

Structural constraints on campaigning also paved the way for the employment of this technology. Parties are restricted by law to spending 40p per voter (*The Economist* 2005), so resources had to be targeted efficiently. Mail shots and phone calls have to be targeted where they might be effective, not where they may be 'wasted'. This localised and heavily individualised strategy, and technology, were premised upon the notion that consumer habits could be equated, or at least seen to be indicators of, political beliefs and potential voting behaviour. Consumption and commercial activity of voters were thought to be indicative of political beliefs, and as such establishing purchasing behaviour in the market place could be used to extrapolate a person's likely voting intentions. This reinforces the perception of linkage and overlap between marketing and political thinking. Indeed, it indicates again the extent to which beliefs about the significance and primacy of markets precede and inform the beliefs of political actors about the activity of politics.

Ideology in electoral competition?

This section assesses the above description of campaign behaviour and addresses the question: what does party behaviour reveal about parties' ideological commitment? Consistent with the rationale of this book, it also considers the extent to which there are continuity and change from previous election behaviour.

The extensive employment of marketing at both national and local level by both parties suggests belief in the primacy of marketing as a driving force in the political process. Indeed, Kotler and Andreasen suggest that in order for marketing to be successful it must be adopted as a mind set (1996). The behaviour of both parties suggests very much that their guiding philosophy, their mind set, in this campaign was a marketing one. This represents a continuation of strategies from previous elections. As noted, the use of marketing is nothing new. What has changed is the environment in which the actors operate. The last century saw the development of increasingly sophisticated targeting systems which politicians sought to harness. Social and political change has meant voters are dealigned from traditional cleavages that were previously thought to structure voting loyalty/behaviour. It is generally accepted that the mid-1980s saw the acceptance of the term 'marketing' by both parties, and over the last twenty years that marketing has been consolidated, and become increasingly significant to the extent that it now dominates political campaign thinking. It is argued that this most recent election campaign represented a continuation and consolidation of the belief in the utility of marketing in the political process, with managerialist thinking dominating the activity of campaigning.

The departure from previous election campaigns was that this technology and these strategies had become even more refined. For the first time this belief produced a highly personalised campaign targeted to a small segment of the electorate, a bland national image by Labour, and a broad populist image promoted by the Conservatives. This would suggest then that the perceptions that both parties held of the environment within which electoral competition was being conducted was characterised by the need for effective media management (given that for many voters the election is what is viewed through the media), an electoral system that produces disproportionate results, strengthening the influence of marginal seats; a changing social base; and a political and economic environment characterised by a commitment to neo-liberalism and market thinking. It is acknowledged that political actors have a greater capacity to shape/influence their environment than conventional business organisations (Wring 2005: 171); however, the Labour and Conservative campaigns were characterised by little desire to effect broader structural or ideational change. Instead, they were premised upon underlying acceptance of neo-liberalism, evidenced in the intensive use of marketing, and narrow competition around similar party policy platforms.

Clearly there are benefits to adopting a marketing approach to the study of politics. Contemporary election campaigning is heavily characterised by the use of marketing and therefore it is logical to use concepts and tools associated with marketing to undertake analysis. These frameworks provide the opportunity for rich description of contemporary political behaviour. It facilitates analysis and enables consideration of the implications of applying marketing to politics. However, as the above discussion on the relationship with ideology suggests, it is important to keep these tools and concepts analytically and ontologically distinct. Description of the strategies employed in the 2005 campaign reveals a conflation of marketing and politics, which has meant that the guiding ideology in political election campaigning is that of marketing, not political values and ideals. Marketing may provide a useful analytical tool, but that does not necessarily mean that it has a normative function and should replace political ideology in practice. While the notion of marketing can perform an analytical function, enabling the identification and description of a particular set of characteristics of the political product, this is distinct from ontologically defining a political process as a marketing activity. While ideology may perform a similar function to marketing (in that it provides an underlying guiding philosophy), there is a significant difference between a marketing philosophy and a political ideology. Marketing is concerned with evoking a response for organisational benefit. Political ideology is a set of guiding principles as to the manner in which society should be organised. Marketing and politics have fundamentally differing starting points, yet their conflation has led to the redefinition of political practice as a marketing activity.

The identification and description of the use of marketing during the 2005 election campaign revealed an underlying ontological and ideological commitment to the primacy of markets and marketing. Campaign resources were strategically focused, markets were segmented, individual voters identified and targeted personally. The strategies pursued by both parties, refined and employed in 2005, suggest that marketing has become the guiding philosophy for the activity of political campaigning. Moreover the eagerness of both parties to focus on marketing strategies and techniques at the expense of political debate, or the willingness to produce an informed citizenry, implies real problems for the political process. The increased emphasis by both parties on image management and marketing resulted in minor stylistic differences in the election campaign. These stylised differences meant there was little or no potential for political debate as policy platforms converged. Yet choice in electoral competition is the essence of democracy. The less the public are presented with a choice and engaged in democratic dialogue the greater the potential for disengagement.

What political marketing as an approach, a body of literature, or indeed a practice, has yet to consider is the impact that its use has on the electorate. With turnout reaching record low levels in 2001, and only marginally increasing in 2005, this is an area that political marketing needs to consider. Participation in the 2005 election, although slightly up on 2001, was still low. At 61.3% it was up only 2% from the previous election, and way below the average of 76% (Worcester 2005). Labour were returned to power on 35.2% of the UK votes cast, which comprised 22% of the total possible electorate, the lowest vote share for a governing party in modern times (Norris and Wlezien 2005: 2). While public action has occurred – for example, Live 8, protests against the war in Iraq, and foxhunting – voters have become less inclined to turn out at elections. This might suggest that, while the public are still prepared to mobilise around political values, they do not respond to marketing, as the parties appear to believe. Proving the link between the use of marketing and voter disengagement is beyond the remit of this chapter, but the link between the growth of marketing as a guiding and driving philosophy for the activity of politics, the marketisation of political parties and the decline in electoral turnout may be well worth considering. Citizens do have an interest in, and can be mobilised by, 'political issues'. In fact the success of the Liberal Democrats in stealing seats from Labour was widely regarded as a backlash against Blair's decision to go to war (Brannigan 2005). It could be argued that the increased belief in marketing at the level of elite political activity means that what is traditionally considered as 'political' action is occurring elsewhere. But it can be suggested that too much 'politics' outside the democratic political system can be destabilising; the November 2005 riots in French cities, instigated by members of ethnic communities who feel disenfranchised, may perhaps be cited as evidence.

Conclusion

The 2005 election saw a continuation and consolidation of the use of political marketing. It informed the behaviour and campaign strategies of both Labour and the Conservatives, and both parties have become adept at the implementation of marketing principles and strategies. This meant not only the production of highly stylised and sophisticated media management strategies, but also party campaign behaviour being increasingly informed by market research data. The parties' behaviour also revealed adherence to the fundamental principle that marketing needed to be internalised, adopted as a guiding principle, to be successful. The structure of the market in the 2005 election campaign produced tacit collusion between the two main actors. Both parties promoted broad images at national level, although Labour did not seek to court national media attention in the manner the Conservatives did. But both employed strategies that suggested the real campaign was being fought in marginal seats over floating voters. Increasingly sophisticated application of marketing strategies, supported by technological developments, meant the campaign was centred on a small area of the electorate. This kept costs low, and expected rewards (in terms of floating voters persuaded to vote) high.

The methods of marketing have been explored and employed to assess the underlying ideological commitments of the two main parties competing. It has been argued that the use of marketing exposes an internalisation of the assumptions that underpin marketing approaches. Politics in the 2005 campaign was driven by marketing ideals: an underlying ideological commitment to marketing, resulting in limited political debate and little democratic dialogue. While marketing in election campaigns is nothing new, the sophistication and personalisation of campaign techniques was unprecedented. Both parties engaged extensively with popular culture, promoting their leaders as celebrities. Differences between parties at national level were in bland imagery and marketing strategies, techniques and the ability to tap into populist sentiment. The consensual nature of the issues that did and did not reach the agenda meant that the 2005 campaign saw very little opportunity for public democratic debate. As a result of this seeming convergence around policy issues, and non-policy issues, commentators noted that the decision for voters, then, was to decide 'which campaign team had implemented the best marketing strategy' (Shakespeare 2005). The extensive use of marketing strategies reveals the underlying commitment by both main parties to market-led solutions to political issues; resources were targeted where they would matter in terms of electoral outcome, not in terms of democratic dialogue. This chapter has argued that the identification of the extensive use of marketing by both major parties in the 2005 election campaign reveals their ideological commitment to neo-liberalism and market ideals rather than political debate and the competition of ideas and ideologies.

References

Bachrach, P. and Baratz, M. S. (1962), 'Two faces of power', *American Political Science Review* 56: 947–52.

Baum, M. A. (2005), 'Talking the vote: why presidential candidates hit the talk show circuit', *American Journal of Political Science* 49 (2): 213–34.

Brannigan, T. (2005), 'Third force gains in town and country', *Guardian*, 6 May.

Conlan, T. (2005), 'Little Britain turns its back on Blair', *Guardian*, 1 March.

Cowley, D. (2005), 'A good campaign?' online at www.bbc.co.uk/news, 3 May.

Downs, A. (1957), *An Economic Theory of Democracy*, New York: Harper & Row.

The Economist (2005), 'Those lucky target voters', 7 April.

Finlayson, A. (2003), *Making Sense of New Labour*, London: Lawrence & Wishart.

Franklin, B. (1994), *Packaging Politics*, London: Edward Arnold.

Freedland, J. (2005), 'Something for everyone', *Guardian*, 23 April.

Gibson, O. (2005), 'Campaign fails to catch fire', *Guardian*, 18 April.

Hames, T. (2005), 'Zzzzzzz . . . Wake up, there. I've got this idea for making elections interesting', *The Times*, 25 April.

Harris, P. and Wring, D. (2001), 'Editorial. The marketing campaign: the 2001 British General Election', *Journal of Marketing Management* 17: 909–12.

Jones, G. (2005), 'Labour worries in marginals may just be a ploy', *The Telegraph*, 4 May.

Kaletsky, A. (2005), 'Why Blairism, not Thatcherism, may prove to be Britain's big idea', *The Times*, 24 March.

Keith, R. (1960), 'The marketing revolution', *Journal of Marketing*, January, pp. 35–43.

Kenny, M. and Smith, M. (1997), '(Mis)understanding Blair', *Political Quarterly* 68 (3): 220–30.

Kotler, P. (1982), 'Voter marketing: attracting votes', in P. Kotler (ed.), *Marketing for Nonprofit Organizations*, Englewood Cliffs NJ: Prentice Hall.

Kotler, P. and Andreasen, A. (1996), *Strategic Marketing for Nonprofit Organisations*, 5th edn, Englewood Cliffs NJ: Prentice Hall.

Kotler, P. and Levy, S. (1969), 'Broadening the concept of marketing', *Journal of Marketing* 33: 10–15.

Lawson, M. (2005), 'It's uncut, left-wing and Pooterish', *Guardian*, 23 April.

Lees-Marshment, J. (2001), *Political Marketing and British Political Parties: The Party's Just Begun*, Manchester: Manchester University Press.

Marr, A. (2005), 'All to play for at half-way stage'. BBC Television News, online at www.bbc.co.uk/news, 21 April.

Mauser, G. (1983), *Political Marketing*, New York: Praeger.

Miles, A. (2005), 'It's the race issue, stupid', *The Times*, 6 April.

Negrine, R. and Lilleker, D. (2003), 'The rise of a proactive local media strategy in British political communication: clear continuities and evolutionary change, 1966–2001', *Journalism Studies* 4 (2): 199–211.

Newman, B. (1994), *The Marketing of the President: Political Marketing as Campaign Strategy*, London: Sage.

Newton, K. and Brynin, M. (2001), 'The national press and party voting in the UK', *Political Studies* 49: 265–85.

Norris, P. (2000), *A Virtuous Circle*, Cambridge: Cambridge University Press.

Norris, P. and Wlezien, C. (2005), 'Introduction. The third Blair victory: how and why?' in P. Norris and C. Wlezien (eds), *Britain Votes, 2005*, Oxford: Oxford University Press.

O'Cass, A. (1996), 'Political marketing and the marketing concept', *European Journal of Marketing* 30 (10–11): 45–61.

Prior, M. (2005), 'News versus entertainment: how increasing media choice widens gaps in political knowledge and turnout', *American Journal of Political Science* 49 (3): 577–92.

Reid, D. M. (1988), 'Marketing the political product', *European Journal of Marketing* 22 (9): 34–47.

Sackman, A. (1992), 'The Marketing Organisation Model: Making Sense of Modern Campaigning in Britain', paper presented at the Political Studies Association annual conference, Belfast, April.

Savigny, H. (2004), 'Political marketing: a rational choice?' *Journal of Political Marketing* 3 (1): 21–38.

Savigny, H. (2005), 'Labour, political marketing and the 2005 election: a campaign of two halves', *Journal of Marketing Management*, 21(9–10): 925–42.

Scammell, M. (1995), *Designer Politics: How Elections are Won*, London: Macmillan.

Scammell, M. (1999), 'Political marketing: lessons for political science', *Political Studies* 47 (4): 718–39.

Scott, A. (1970), *Competition in American Politics*, New York: Holt Rinehart & Winston.

Shakespeare, S. (2005), 'They seem to be campaigning for the sake of it', *The Observer*, 17 April.

Street, J. (1997), *Politics and Popular Culture*, Cambridge: Polity Press.

Street, J. (2004), 'Celebrity politicians: popular culture and political representation', *British Journal of Politics and International Relations* 6 (4): 435–52.

Temple, M. (2005), 'Carry on campaigning: the case for "dumbing down" in the fight against local electoral apathy', *Local Government Studies* 31 (4): 415–31.

Wintour, P. (2005), 'Postcode data could decide next election', www.spinwatch.org.

Wintour, P. and White, M. (2005), 'Private poll reveals Labour fears: neck and neck in key marginals', *Guardian*, 27 April.

Worcester, R. (2005), 'The day after the election', *The Observer*, 8 May.

Wring, D. (1996), 'Political marketing and party development in Britain: a "secret" history', *European Journal of Marketing* 30 (10–11): 100–11.

Wring, D. (1997), 'Reconciling marketing with political science: theories of political marketing', *Journal of Marketing Management* 13: 651–63.

Wring, D. (2001), 'Selling socialism', *European Journal of Marketing* 35 (9–10): 1038–47.

Wring, D. (2005), *The Politics of Marketing the Labour Party*, Basingstoke: Palgrave.

Web site

www.mori.com

Part II

Communication

Communication is central to election campaigning: it is the means by which parties seek to provide information, reassure, persuade and mobilise different voter segments. Indeed, some elections are better known for an innovation in communication than the actual result, so demonstrating the potential power of the focus of this section. For example, Gladstone's Midlothian campaign in 1880, the use of television at the 1959 election, and the Conservative Party's use of advertising in 1979, especially the 'Labour isn't working' poster. Equally we observe that communication cannot, in isolation, win an election: hence in 1987 many argued that Labour won the campaign while making few gains. Despite this, parties believe that by communicating their vision, policies and personalities they can influence the final result. Communication thus presents positive messages about the product a party has to offer, as well as undermining the case of their main opponents.

During an election campaign parties can communicate either directly or indirectly to their activists, supporters and floating voters. Direct communication implies some degree of personal interaction between the party and the receiver of its message. Typically, direct communication has involved public meetings, doorstep canvassing, and leaflets. Indirect communication uses a third party to pass on, and hopefully amplify, a party's message. Whilst such a third party can include opinion formers such as journalists, celebrities or community workers, it is the print and broadcast media which are the usual channel. Direct communication enables a party to get all its messages across unhindered, but the effect of the message may be less dramatic if the receiver thinks 'Well, you would say that, wouldn't you?' Although, a party has to surmount the hurdle of persuading the third party to transmit its message, once they do so it adds a degree of credibility direct communication may lack. In reality parties use both direct and indirect communication channels, though one may be prioritised as their main form of communication.

Since the 1950s there has been a steady decline in the importance and use by political party headquarters of direct communication channels. With the growing dominance of mass communication since the early 1960s, especially television, parties have turned their attention to this. Probably the single largest campaign expense, for those that can afford it, has since the 1980s been print advertising. In 2005, for probably the first time, the Liberal Democrats received a large and timely donation which allowed them to compete with Labour and the Conservatives on advertising spend and therefore reach of audience. However, with the dramatic growth of the availability of broadcast and print media, advertising has, to some extent, lost some of the 'bangs for its buck'. Increased media fragmentation has simply made it more difficult to reach the same number of voters as an advertisement could in the early 1980s. As a result, the three main parties in particular have turned to media relations as an effective and cheaper means of getting their messages across to the electorate. However, the market orientation of the communication industry has also encouraged the parties to use information technology to reach voters directly through targeted direct mail and the Internet. Thus, in the pursuit of competitive advantage, political parties now exploit the potential of a wide range of communications media.

The three chapters in Part II look at how parties have used different communication channels – advertising, media relations and the Internet – to market their product, and to enter into a dialogue with the electorate. In Chapter 5 Dermody and Hanmer-Lloyd suggest that Labour's and the Conservatives' advertising was essentially negative in tone, which in turn had an effect on public trust. So clearly communication via advertising did affect the electorate, but perhaps not in the way parties wanted. In Chapter 6 Gaber points out that there were at least six different media agendas, and that of the public and the parties was not necessarily the same. Therefore, through their advertising and media relations campaigns, the parties were communicating to, or at, and not with, the electorate. In Chapter 7 Jackson suggests that for the major parties the main audience of the Internet was activists. In addition, he suggests, owing to limited access to the media via either advertisements or media relations, smaller parties in part turned to the Internet as a means of getting their message across to the electorate. However, despite attempts to reach the target segments, in 2005 party communication appeared to be too divorced from both party product and the electorate.

5

A marketing analysis of the 2005 General Election advertising campaigns

Janine Dermody and Stuart Hanmer-Lloyd

In this chapter, we set out to achieve two primary objectives. First, to review, in detail, the national 2005 election advertising communication of the three main parties in the UK – the Conservatives, Labour and the Liberal Democrats. Second, in analysing their advertising strategies, we consider the question pertinent to this book – was the 2005 election campaign marketing-oriented? Let us begin, however, by exploring the backdrop against which the election was held, or, in marketing parlance, the market place.

The 2005 electoral market place

Each election has its own set of distinctive circumstances, which contribute to the style and tone of each of the contesting parties' election campaign. In 2005 the British economy was strong (using traditional measures: unemployment statistics, inflation and interest rates), although there was some concern over the perceived increasing control from Brussels. The dominance of the three major parties – the Conservatives, Labour and the Liberal Democrats – remained intact. For the first time the Liberal Democrats were being perceived as a credible opposition, while the Conservative Party, although plagued by leadership changes, appeared to be returning from the political wilderness. Labour, sensitive to public attitudes on the war, and so recognising that this was going to be their toughest election since they came to power in 1997 – was going for a record: a third term in office.

However, the political landscape of the 2005 General Election was markedly changed from the internal issues characterising the 1997 and 2001 elections (Butler and Kavanagh 1997, 2001; Crewe *et al.* 1999; Denver 1997; Dermody and Scullion 2000, 2001). Gone were the halcyon days of New Labour's 1997 election landslide and, in 2001, public confidence that Labour would get public services 'right'. The 2005 election contest took place in the shadow of 9/11 and the 'war on terror', which culminated in the Iraq conflict and consequently the charges, later found unproven by the Hutton inquiry, made against the Prime Minister, Tony Blair, that he had lied to Parliament and to the people about weapons of mass destruction (Waugh 2004). The critical issue facing all three parties in this election was that of trust – or rather the lack of it. Given the Iraq war, could Labour be trusted to govern for a third term? Had the Conservative Party redeemed itself sufficiently following the sleaze dominating its latter years in office between 1992 and 1997 (Jowell and Curtice 1997: chapter 5) – could they be trusted to provide good governance in the future? Could the Liberal Democrats – a party that had never been in government – be trusted to govern the country? It is not surprising, therefore, that the issue of low trust dominated the 2004 Conservative, Labour and Liberal Democrat party conferences: 'the public is deeply disaffected with the entire political class. Trust – the lack of it and how to rebuild it – was the underlying theme of the entire party conference season' (Rawnsley 2004: 29). Commenting specifically on Tony Blair and the attitudes of the electorate, Lord Saatchi – speaking at the 2004 Conservative conference – argued:

> the electorate is like a 'girl' who has had her heart broken by Tony Blair. Having once succumbed to his charms, now she feels betrayed. . . . [she] has become mistrustful of any politician who comes bearing 'boxes of chocolates and bouquets of flowers'. So wounding has been her experience . . . that she has become suspicious and cynical about the promises of them all. (Cited in Rawnsley 2004: 2)

These distrusting attitudes of the electorate were also evident in the 2001 General Election (Bromley and Curtice 2002: chapter 7; Dermody and Scullion 2005; Mattinson 2000; Putnam 2000; Russell *et al.* 2002; Spogard and James 2000). These caused some concern over turnout, which proved to be justified, with the 59.4% turnout. What is remarkable is that during the intervening years, between the two elections, the public's low political trust received cursory attention from politicians and the government – with the exception of the 2004 advertising campaign from the Electoral Commission encouraging the public to vote. Thus it is not surprising that low trust dominated the 2005 electoral landscape too, principally through the issue of the legitimacy of the Labour government taking Britain to war with Iraq, but also its perceived broken promises on higher education through the introduction of 'tuition fees' and its perceived attack on 'rural living' after the ban on hunting.

Hence a problem identified in the 2001 election was compounded in the 2005 election. Low trust can result in a number of actions, includ-

ing engendering sufficient anger in the electorate that they are motivated to vote; thus turnout increases, or increasing apathy; thus turnout
remains static or declines. The 61.3% turnout at the 2005 election – an
increase of 1.9% compared with 2001 – highlights the consequences of
low trust on political participation. Of the 9.5 million people who voted,
22% voted for Labour – symbolising the lowest mandate of any governing party in Britain ever and 'a fairly profound statement of disillusion
and indeed disfranchisement' (Liddle 2005: 24). While the Conservatives perceived themselves to be on the 'road to recovery', they received
a million fewer votes in 2005 than they did in their devastating 1997
election defeat. Thus, of the 5 million estranged voters, 700,000 voted
for the Liberal Democrats and many abstained. However, most notably,
given the nature of this turnout, coupled with the high number of marginal seats:

> the most spectacular result of the election last week came in the perfor-
> mance of the so-called mavericks, the misfits, the curmudgeonly one-issue
> independents, the nutters, the people who the mainstream politicians and
> commentators are accustomed to telling us are no-accounts and who are,
> often, quite beyond the pale. (Liddle 2005: 24)

We do not find this surprising. As we have argued elsewhere, a perceived
lack of empowerment, coupled with low trust and high distrust, can
result in more self-focused individuals who either do not vote or who
reject the mainstream in favour of single-issue parties that serve their
individual needs or allay their fears (Dermody and Hanmer-Lloyd 2003,
2004).

Regrettably we are unable to present a detailed account of the political trust and distrust scholarship here (see Dermody and Hanmer-Lloyd
2003, 2004). However, given its importance in this election, it should
be noted that political trust involves an evaluative orientation that can
be directed at the political system (regime-based trust) or at politicians
(incumbent-based trust) (Craig *et al.* 1990; Miller 1974; Schiffman *et
al.* 2002). While the public tend to support the political system, their
trust in politicians and leaders (incumbent trust) is waning, typically
because politicians are deemed to be failing to meet the public's expectations (Citrin and Green 1986; Hetherington 1998; Miller 1983). For
example, the electorates' reduced tolerance of Labour's efforts to redress
the inherent problems in the public services.

In turn this dissatisfaction fuels their distrust of politicians, creating a
cycle of dissatisfaction and distrust (Hetherington 1998). Additionally
the further an individual's attitudinal position is from the government
the less trustful they are (Miller and Borelli 1991). This helps to explain

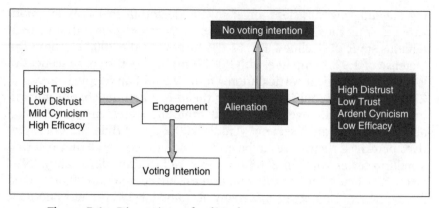

Figure 5.1 Dimensions of political engagement and alienation
Source: J. Dermody and S. Hanmer-Lloyd (forthcoming), 'Safeguarding the future of democracy: (re)building young people's trust in parliamentary politics', *Journal of Political Marketing*

why the attitudes of a significant proportion of the public over the legality of the war in Iraq so undermined their trust in Tony Blair. Further, individuals can hold simultaneously trusting and distrusting political relationships (Cacioppo and Bernston 1994; Dermody and Hanmer-Lloyd 2003, 2004; Lewicki *et al.* 1998; Luhmann 1979; Mancini 1993). This helps to explain why voters trust the integrity of the Liberal Democrats yet distrust their ability to govern – hence they do not vote for them.

In order to restore incumbent-based trust, politicians need to persuade the electorate to believe – through their successful delivery of policies – that they do serve them, and will satisfy their needs. Furthermore, the electorate need to believe that they are sufficiently empowered to influence the decisions of government (Berman 1997; Bok 1997). In conclusion, without trust, cynicism grows, which impacts on efficacy and alienation and in turn can cause the electorate not to vote, thereby undermining the democratic process (Figure 5.1), as witnessed by Labour's 22% mandate.

Thus, from a trust-building perspective, it is somewhat surprising that a significant proportion of the election advertising was negative. Negative political ads, particularly image attack ads, 'impute inferiority, denigrate or destroy the competitions image' (James and Hensel 1991: 55); they are malicious, vicious and violate 'fair play'. Consequently, while there are some shorter-term electoral benefits in employing an attack advertising strategy (Dermody and Scullion 2003), a considerable amount of research indicates its use is strongly related

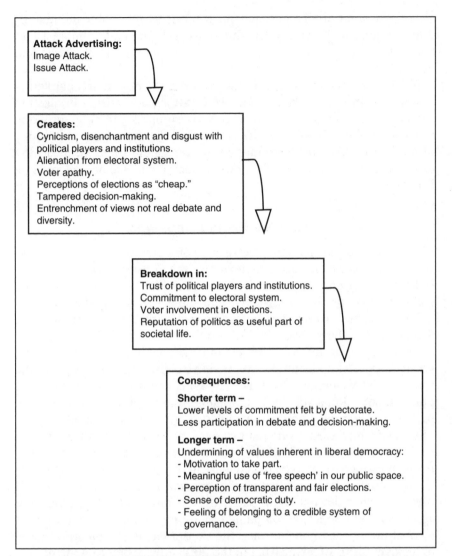

Figure 5.2 The societal consequences of political attack advertising
Source: J. Dermody and R. Scullion (2003), 'Exploring the consequences of negative political advertising for liberal democracy', *Journal of Political Marketing* 2 (1): 94

to individuals' cynical political attitudes, voter alienation and the ignominy of political argument, thereby resulting in increased cynicism and reduced turnout (Figure 5.1) – a democratic deficit (Ansolabehere and Iyengar 1995; Ansolabehere *et al.* 1994, 1999; Cappella and Jamieson 1997; Diamond and Bates 1992; Germond and Witcover

1996; Johnson-Cartee and Copeland 1989, 1991a, b; Kahn and Kenney 1999; Procter and Schenck-Hamlin 1996; Salmore and Salmore 1989; Schenck-Hamlin *et al.* 2000). These consequences are illustrated in Figure 5.2.

A paradox thus emerges when we consider the notion of a marketing orientation in this election – the use of attack advertising in election campaigns has the potential to prevent consumption, thereby shrinking the market place. Clearly this does not reflect the underlying philosophy of marketing. In order to examine this issue more fully, we must first examine the Conservative, Liberal Democrat and Labour advertising campaigns.

The advertising campaigns

With respect to the election advertising, compared with 2001, ad spend was higher for the LibDems, but lower for the Conservatives and Labour (who both concentrated more on direct marketing), and the advertising still remained unregulated. However, while the advertising was not quite as visible in this election, compared with 2001 (Dermody and Scullion 2001), political communication *per se* was expected to continue to play an important role (Butler and Kavanagh 1997; Gould 1998; Wring 2000). The Electoral Commission's consultation exercise on the future of party election broadcasts (PEBs) concluded that while there is much dissent, PEBs still have a valuable role to play in election campaigning (Electoral Commission 2003; Scullion and Dermody 2005). The media mix used to disseminate the advertising messages varied slightly compared with 2001 in that there was a little more press advertising; bolstered perhaps by the increase in the Liberal Democrats' advertising budget. The Conservative, Labour and Liberal Democrat use of their Web sites did not significantly differ from 2001 – featuring their advertising straplines, accompanied by online ads and election poster competitions. The online ads and the Conservative cinema ad were the only novel forms of advertising in the 2005 advertising campaigns.

As already identified, the backdrop against which the political parties were planning their advertising campaigns was one of a lack of trust in both politicians and parties. The Labour Party, and in particular Tony Blair, were especially vulnerable in relation to the trust issue. However, it is also true to say, as illustrated by Lord Saatchi earlier in this chapter, this did not automatically confer trust on the main opposition party. Indeed, the Conservatives themselves 'enjoyed' the mistrust of the electorate too, partially because of their latter years in government in the 1990s, partially because they 'approved' the war with Iraq, and partially because a lot of the electorate do not trust any political party. Even the Liberal Democrats suffered from lower trust – not so much in terms of their integrity, but whether they possessed the skills to govern the country. As will be seen, trust, or rather the lack of it, was at the core of much of the election advertising – delivered largely via issue and image attack styles.

Our accounts of the Conservative, Liberal Democrat and Labour advertising campaigns are based on secondary sources, e.g. media reports, opinion polls, as well as in-depth interviews with senior members of the agency account teams and content analysis of the print and PEB advertising. For each we focus on the aims and tone of the campaign, providing a rich description of their print and PEB advertising, and in so doing enabling us to more fully consider the question of the presence of a marketing orientation in this election campaign.

The Conservatives

The agency Immediate Sales (owned by M. & C. Saatchi) had been working with the Conservative Party for around twelve months before the election took place, and through Lord Saatchi had potentially an excellent insight into the way in which the party operated. They were instructed by Lynton Crosby, who had been appointed campaign director by Michael Howard. They worked with Crosby to identify and agree their advertising plans for the election battle in May 2005. Crosby, accompanied by his dog-whistling (highly negative) tactics, required the agency to focus on the five key policy issues on which the Conservatives would fight the election: taxes (lower, value for money), immigration, crime (more police), education (school discipline) and the NHS (cleaner hospitals); while the trustworthiness of Tony Blair, particularly over 'weapons of mass destruction', was to be used to attack the Prime Minister directly and the Labour Party generally. At one level this might be viewed as a marketing orientation. However, as our analysis later in this chapter indicates, this assumes that these five key issues reflected the needs and aspirations of their loyal and potential 'customers'.

The main remit for the advertising agency was to help the Conservatives to win the 2005 General Election. Low trust had important implications for how the agency translated this goal into its advertising campaign. Research conducted going into the election confirmed that while there was considerable distrust of Tony Blair, this distrust was contaminating the whole election process. This created a demanding challenge for Immediate Sales, who needed to successfully transmute the party's five policy statements into attack ads that would further decrease trust in Labour – and in particular the character of Tony Blair –

without compromising the electability of the Conservative Party. The complexity of the agency's task was further compounded by the legacy of the former Conservative government, coupled with the electorate's wider distrust of politician's promises. Thus while the core objective was to win the election, the advertising also needed to clearly communicate key Conservative policies, create empathy between the Conservatives and the public and suppress the Labour vote by decreasing trust in Labour and Tony Blair. While the core objective was the same, the trust issue distinguished their 2005 from their 2001 advertising.

Given these complexities, an initial frontal attack suggesting 'We can do better' was not appropriate. Immediate Sales recognised that it needed to get the public listening to the Conservative Party again, to understand that the Conservatives were on 'their' side and were, as then party chairman Theresa May told the 2004 party conference, no longer the 'nasty' party that the electorate rejected so overwhelmingly in 1997. As a result, the agency considered the relative merits of a rational and/or emotional appeal to the electorate, and concluded that a more emotional appeal would be more successful in engaging voters. This mirrored the 'emotional strategy' adopted by Yellow M in their advertising campaign for the Conservatives in 2001 (see Dermody and Scullion 2001). The thrust of the appeal was research-based and played mainly on the view that Tony Blair, and by association Labour, had misled the British public about weapons of mass destruction in Iraq and had not delivered on his promises: things had not got better since Labour took office in 1997. Interestingly, previous research by O'Cass (2002: 72) concludes: 'When voters are less emotional, they tend to believe the incumbents and positive messages delivered through advertising; when they are emotional, they tend to believe negative messages more.' Whether the agency or Crosby were aware of, or believed in, such research is unknown; certainly there is a belief in the persuasive power of negative advertising, but their overall campaign could be perceived as following this research conclusion. Thus stage one of the process became one of raising the emotional temperature of the election by creating an emotional link between the potential voter and the Conservatives, portrayed through 'Are you thinking what we're thinking?' which appeared in all the print advertising and featured heavily in their PEBs. This enabled them to begin to address the objective of encouraging the public to listen to the Conservatives, and then to persuade them to vote Conservative because they empathised with the electorate's frustration with Tony Blair and the Labour Party. It was certainly not to present the 'solution' to vote Conservative, but rather to emotionally link the party with voters through empathy.

Indeed, it was evident that the advertising was not 'solutions driven' (Conservatives will do better) but instead driven by a more negative message, attacking Labour in order to suggest that they were not governing properly and had broken their election promises, i.e. they were failing and they were untrustworthy. The 'notepad' empathy messages created by Immediate Sales targeted the policy issues identified by the party as being critical to their election campaign – taxes, the NHS, immigration, crime, Iraq, school discipline (Figure 5.3), all wrapped around 'Are you thinking what we're thinking?' For example:

> My taxes keep going up, but what have we got to show for it? Are you thinking what we're thinking?
> I mean, how hard is it to keep a hospital clean? Are you thinking what we're thinking?
> Its not racist to impose limits on immigration. Are you thinking what we're thinking?

These print ads were designed to provoke the electorate: to make them realise it was time for change by challenging them to question 'If things are so great, why is this going wrong?' The tactic was similar to that used by New Labour in 1997 against the Conservatives. This cross-fertilisation of tactics perhaps indicates that the parties were no more marketing-oriented in communicating their electoral platforms in this election than they were in the 1997 and 2001 elections.

What is interesting about the print advertising created by Immediate Sales is that the majority of it is issue-attack – their two attacks on Tony Blair are rather mild (Figure 5.4). In one they write, 'Imagine another five years of him' (featuring a smiling Tony Blair) and in the other: 'Iraq. Stealth taxes. Immigration. It's now or never to tell him what you think. Take a stand on the issues that matter.' Interestingly, this ad features a different strapline – a direct reference to one of the Conservative PEBs, entitled 'Take a stand'.

As 5 May approached, it became even more critical to ensure that loyal and marginal Conservative voters actually turned out to vote Conservative, whilst suppressing the Labour vote. Thus the tone of the advertising became much more aggressive, with a personal attack on Tony Blair: 'If he's prepared to lie to take us to war, he's prepared to lie to win the election. If you value the truth, vote for it' (Figure 5.5). This 'truth' strapline is a play on Labour's parallel message telling the electorate, 'If you value it, vote for it.' Additionally this ad echoes the Conservatives 'demon eyes' poster ad of 1997. This particular ad was created by Conservative Central Office to the instructions of Lynton Crosby and was designed to receive considerable media

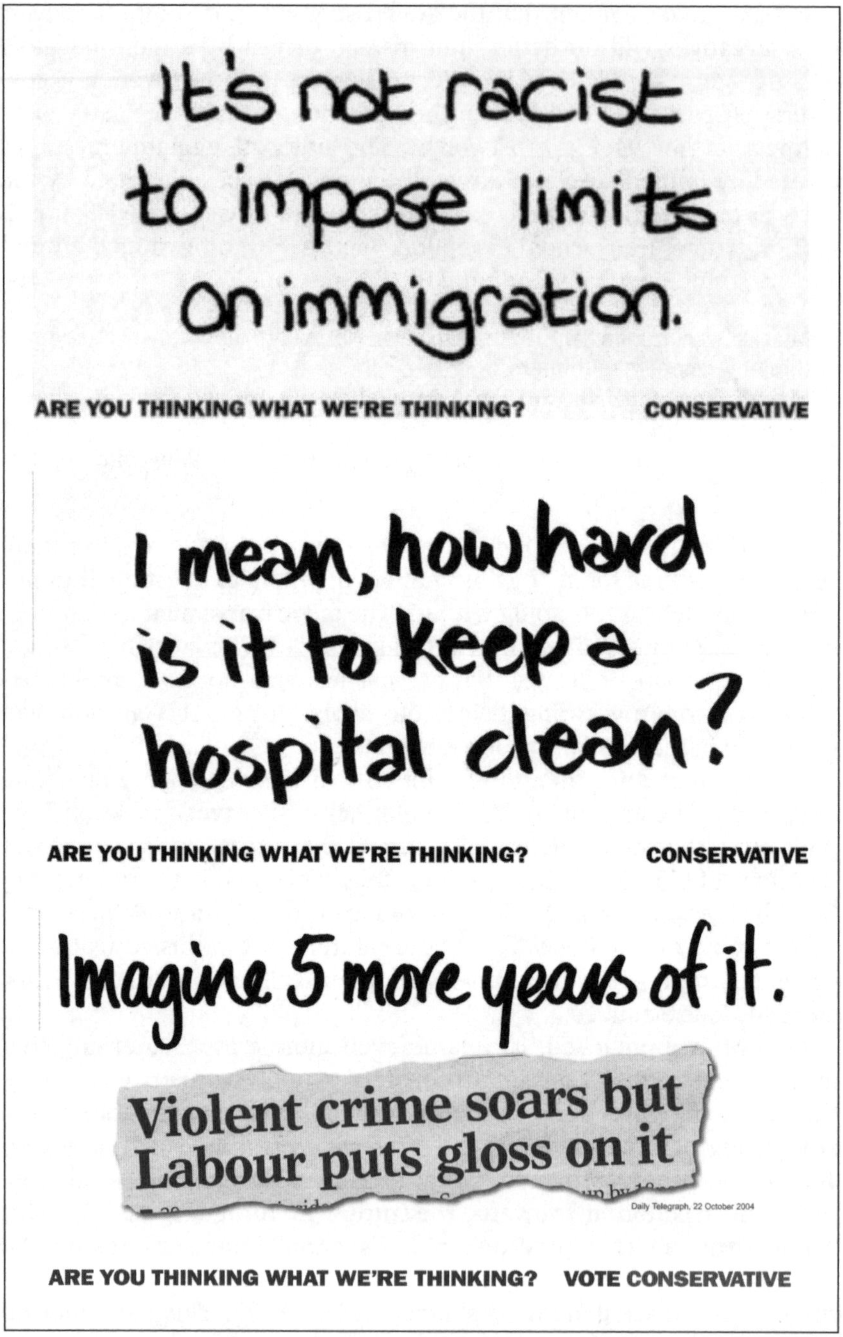

Figure 5.3 Conservative 'questions' posters

Figure 5.4   Conservative 'him' posters

attention – which of course, by calling Tony Blair a liar, it did. To journalists' questions about the ad Michael Howard responded, 'I'm a very
direct person. I say it as it is. Character is an issue at this election. It is
about trust' (cited in Watt and White 2005).

   In addition to the print advertising the party commissioned a novel
piece of election advertising in the form of an eighty-second cinema ad
designed to be shown throughout the election campaign. This ad was
created from edits of material Immediate Sales put together for the 2004
Conservative Party conference. This personal attack on the Prime
Minister starts with footage of Tony Blair standing outside Downing
Street saying, 'Enough of talking, enough of talking, enough of talking,
it is time now to do,' set against a red background. During this 'Are you
thinking what we're thinking?' flashes up on screen. The ad goes on to

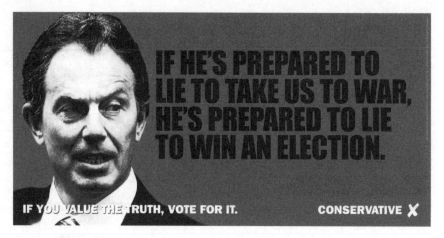

Figure 5.5   Conservative 'lies' poster

show a litany of Mr Blair's broken election promises on education, crime, the NHS and immigration, and his 'lies' about weapons of mass destruction. The ad concludes with 'Imagine another five years of him' followed by 'Are you thinking what we're thinking?' It then flashes back to Tony Blair, saying, 'Enough of talking, it is time now to do,' with 'Vote conservative' flashing up on the screen and Tony Blair saying thank you. What increases the potency of this ad is the background song lyrics – 'Take that look off your face, I can see through your smile . . .', a clear reference to a 'smirking' Tony Blair, an image that was used in other Conservative ads and which echoed Michael Howard launching the Conservative election manifesto, in which he claimed Mr Blair was already smirking at the likelihood of victory. This demonstrates a cohesive and integrated communication strategy, and thus, potentially, a more strategic approach to marketing communication.

With respect to their PEBs, while Immediate Sales was not involved in their production, it was involved in the early briefings for them. Hence there was synergy between the cinema, print and PEB advertising via the key policy themes chosen to attack Labour and Tony Blair. This integration is particularly strong in the second and third PEBs, 'Values' and 'Take a stand'. The 'Values' broadcast features Michael Howard being praised as a man of duty who believes absolutely in honesty and accountability. He talks about his achievements as former Home Secretary and identifies the failings of the Labour government – principally the sixty-six tax increases. He tells the viewer his mother-in-law died in hospital from an MRSA infection and asks, 'How difficult is it to keep a hospital clean?' He tells the viewer he respected his teachers and asks, 'What's wrong with a little bit of discipline in the classroom?' He tells the viewer his grandmother was a victim of the Holocaust and that no one can accuse him of being a racist and states, 'It's not racism, it's common sense to impose limits on immigration.' In this PEB Howard tells the viewer some of the actions his government would take – putting more police on the streets, cutting taxes and imposing tougher sentences on criminals. Overall the viewer is told, 'For a government you can trust to take action on the things that matter – vote Conservative.'

In 'Take a stand', the final PEB of their election campaign, they again list the failings of the Labour government but this time they focus on Tony Blair: the failings are *his* broken promises. Additionally they attack the Liberal Democrats on their plans to abolish mandatory life sentences for murder, to give criminals the vote and to set no limit on immigration; and they give a very disparaging comment on the Labour–Liberal Democrat relationship. Overall this PEB is very negative in tone – using a sneering male voiceover. Their first PEB, 'Choices', was linked with their five key policies; however, the majority of it was dedicated to why people should choose the Conservative Party. For example, 'Because I want lower tax and value for money,' 'I want cleaner hospitals,' 'So I won't be scared when I go out at night.' Howard concludes, 'I'll speak out for Britain's forgotten majority. The people who work hard, play by the rules and take responsibility for themselves and their families.' He then fades and is replaced by their central question:

Are you thinking what we're thinking?
More police
Lower taxes
School discipline
Controlled immigration
Vote Conservative

Inherent within this PEB are the values of Howard the man, and Howard as leader of the Conservative Party. Yet explaining the persona of this relatively new leader to the electorate (as the LibDems did with Kennedy) was, surprisingly, not an objective of the campaign. The failings of the Labour government are implied here too, although they are not as explicit compared with the other two, later, PEBs, suggesting an increasing belief that negativity would pay dividends as the campaign progressed.

The Liberal Democrats

The print advertising campaign for the Liberal Democrats was again conducted by BANC, arising out of the relationship between the chief executive of BANC, the leader of the party, Charles Kennedy, and senior members of the party, a relationship that started in the latter days of the 2001 election campaign. Their ensuing discussions confirmed the need for Kennedy, as party leader, to remain at the heart of the campaign, as he was in 2001 (Dermody and Scullion 2001), and for their entire campaign, including the advertising, to be unremittingly positive, presenting the party as honest and trustworthy. These were underpinned by three core LibDem values: freedom, fairness and trust (through honesty). Thus the advertising campaign aimed to present Kennedy as a trustworthy leader of a viable and principled party. These aims and values resulted in BANC creating the 'single organising principle' of the Liberal Democrats as 'the real alternative', which appeared in every single piece of advertising and other forms of unmediated communication, including Charles Kennedy's speeches. In this respect this was a very integrated communications campaign that echoed the 2001 advertising campaign and consequently created message consistency from the Liberal Democrats to their stakeholders.

While the Liberal Democrats did attack Conservative and Labour policies and their stance on the war with Iraq, their advertising campaign, alongside their wider election campaign, was largely positive. This positive tone was represented by both 'the real alternative' and by the addition of 'We oppose/We propose', which featured in the majority of the print advertising. By opposing and proposing the advertising attempted to present a trustworthy leader and party, thereby meeting the aims of the campaign. It gave an optimistic view of the world, not a negative one, and it gave hope – unlike the Conservative advertising campaign. In so doing it attempted to embrace the public's distrust of politicians and political parties. This is particularly evident in the ad 'Ten good reasons to vote Liberal Democrat', where they tell the 'truth' about their policies, tax and public services, and restate their position on Iraq. The endorsement ad too – 'More and more people are voting for the real alternative. How about you?' – is an equally powerful ad execution of why the Liberal Democrats and Charles Kennedy can be trusted.

This ad features endorsements from twelve broadcasters, artists, musicians, scientists, journalists and businesspeople. For example, Andy Kershaw (broadcaster) states, 'I'm voting LibDem because they are the only party of any honesty, integrity and, most importantly, of any humanity.' Germaine Greer (writer and broadcaster) states, 'The Tories work on the worst in people. Labour treat everyone with contempt. I'm voting LibDem because they believe in the best in people.' Their second PEB – 'Would you buy a used car from this government?' – concentrated on why Labour could not be trusted: the Iraq war and their broken promises on public services, and equally why the Conservatives were untrustworthy: again the Iraq war and their eighteen-year record in government 1979–97. Endorsements from public figures and professionals in public services were used to illustrate the sincerity and veracity of the Liberal Democrats. For example, Air Marshal Tim Garden states, 'The Liberal Democrats were against the war in Iraq. They were the only party with the courage to oppose this government and they have been proved right.' Echoes of the Conservative advertising campaign are visible in the conclusion to this PEB, where Charles Kennedy asks, 'Do you really want five more years of this discredited Labour government?'

Placing Charles Kennedy at the core of the campaign resonated with the advertising strategy of 2001, where Kennedy as 'a young visionary' was introduced to the world. In 2005 there was still a need to launch him as a serious statesman who had matured as a person, a politician and a leader and as someone who rejects 'the rules of engagement' of mainstream politics. Furthermore, BANC recognised that the majority of people 'buy' leaders, not parties, therefore, strategically, it was sensible for the party's main asset, Charles Kennedy, to feature in all their mass communication. While the agency also recognised the importance of the leader in their 2001 campaign, the nature of the 2005 electoral market place perhaps made the character of Kennedy (particularly contrasted with Blair and Howard) even more critical to voters' decision making in this election. This is perhaps why, in all their print advertising, with the exception of the map ad (first shown in 2001), the same black-and-white photograph is used, of a serious Kennedy, the statesman appearing to converse with or be listening to his audience. Thus Kennedy embodies the party and its policies and consequently he was central to all their campaigning. This was visualised in a variety of ways in their print and PEB advertising. Their print ad of their stance on Iraq provides a good illustration (Figure 5.6), the ad with the emotive rhetoric 'We oppose: Bush and Blair on Iraq. We propose: never again.'

Their third PEB, 'A political journey', tells the story of Kennedy's twenty-three years in politics and the evolution of the man himself – from young visionary to father, to leader – whilst wrapped around this are their educational policies and their anti-war stance on Iraq. Their fourth and final PEB, 'There is a wolf', tells the story of Iraq and weapons of mass destruction (WMD), where the wolf is used as a metaphor. Having presented the 'myth of weapons of mass destruction' the PEB once again focuses on Kennedy and his and the party's values. In this PEB Kennedy states, 'If we couldn't trust Labour over Iraq how can we trust them now over health or education or crime or anything else? And what trust can we have in a Conservative Party which simply went along with the government on Iraq?' There are echoes of the Conservative 'liar' print ad here.

Figure 5.6   Liberal Democrat poster 'Iraq'

BANC perceived the 2005 advertising campaign to be a tougher challenge than in 2001 – it was still values-driven but also needed to present
what Kennedy had accomplished since 2001 and, overall, to present him
as a man the electorate could trust and who was authentically different
from Labour and the Conservatives. Kennedy's endeavours were not
particularly well represented in the print advertising, which tended to
revolve around values. However, the first PEB provided a litany of his,
and thus the Liberal Democrats', accomplishments as part of the government in Scotland, whilst also presenting why they are a trustworthy
party: principally through their policies on university fees and health
care for the elderly.

These ads appeared to be more confident than the 2001 print ads,
taking a stand on a number of core issues: in the print ads opposing and
proposing and using the semiotics of capital letters to express commitment to them (see Figure 5.6). In their PEBs they are standing up to the
Labour and Conservative Parties – indeed, they are quite critical of them,
their policies and their character. There was a very strong sense that in
this election they were a credible alternative for a very disenfranchised
electorate. The 700,000 votes that they won are testimony to this.

Labour

While both the Liberal Democrats and particularly the Conservatives
were a much stronger opposition in this election, what was particularly

evident was that New Labour was very vulnerable. Tony Blair recognised that public trust in him was low as a result of Iraq, Thus for the first time since being elected in 1997 'brand Blair' was no longer an asset to the Labour Party. He did not appear on the front cover of the Labour manifesto, and their advertising featured Howard more often than Blair, a feature in common with the Conservative advertising, which featured Blair more frequently than Howard! Thus for Labour the marketing of their leader was not really an option.

As in 2001, TBWA was responsible for Labour's print advertising. Overall the objectives of the 2005 advertising campaign echoed those of the 2001 advertising campaign. In 2001, in helping Labour win a second term in office, it was asked to 'create a sense of connection between the public and politics', 'communicate the achievements and future plans of Labour' and 'remind people how bad things were under a Tory government' (Dermody and Scullion 2001). In 2005 the goal was to win a third term in office. Thus the task of the advertising was to 'communicate the economic stability achieved by Labour', 'to communicate their achievements and future plans for public services' and 'to motivate the Labour vote – particularly wavering Labour voters and swing voters'. The title of Labours' manifesto, *Forward not Back*, indicated how they needed the public to understand that the election campaign was a clear choice between Labour's achievements and future promises and the past Conservative record and 'suspicious' promises. Commenting, Tony Blair asked voters to consider whether they trusted Labour or the Conservatives to run the country, particularly based on Labour's economic record and the Conservatives' policies, which, he claimed, would seriously threaten jobs, mortgages and living standards.

Labour's election strategists, headed by Alan Milburn, clearly recognised that their economic performance was their most powerful weapon against declining public trust and Conservative attacks on their 'failings' on public services and Iraq. Interestingly, an ICM poll found that while the public were not particularly impressed by Labour and Tony Blair, their expectations of Michael Howard and the Conservatives were significantly lower: thus they preferred a Labour government led by Blair to a Conservative one led by Howard (news.bbc.co.uk). How, then, was this portrayed in their advertising?

Labour's advertising has been described by a variety of commentators as themeless. However, we believe that their print ads, with their mix of straplines, clearly reflects their advertising objectives and their overall strategy of 'forward not back'. Thus their first collection of poster ads concentrated on their economic achievements and on the Conservative economic record in government (Figure 5.7). Stating, for example,

Figure 5.7   Labour posters 'Britain is working

'Lowest unemployment for twenty-nine years. Britain is working. Don't let the Tories take us back to 3 million unemployed,' creatively designed to hark back to the 1970s. 'Lowest mortgage rates for forty years. Britain is working. Don't let the Tories take us back to 15% interest rates' – designed to reflect the hippy era of the 1960s.

This emphasis on the economy continued with more stark reminders of the Conservative period in government, with personal attacks on Margaret Thatcher, John Major and their successor Michael Howard on recession, unemployment and repossession. For example, 'I was only seven but I'll never forget repossession. Remember the Tories' 15% mortgage rates. Let's take Britain forward with economic stability.' This ad featured the emotive image of a little girl sitting against a packing chest

Figure 5.8   Labour posters 'Forward not back'

in an emptied room (Figure 5.8). The threat to the economy from the Conservatives also featured in TBWA's rather garish 'warning' ads and 'Britain is working. Don't let the Tories wreck it again', a re-engineering of the infamous 1979 Conservative poster ad created by Saatchi, 'Britain isn't working'. Such similarities, once again, give the impression that this election was no more marketing-oriented than previous elections.

   Their 'If you value it, vote for it' posters presented the harsh choice open to the electorate: a Labour government or a Conservative government. These ads, in addition to reminding the electorate of Labour's economic record and public service agenda, and the Conservatives' historical and potential future cuts in public service spending, were also designed to motivate Labour voters to actually

Figure 5.9　Labour's 'hidden agenda'

turn out and vote. Thus the posters state, 'If you value it, vote for it. Continued investment in schools or Tory education cuts,' 'If you value it, vote for it. A free and fair NHS or Tory charges for hospital operations.' This remit extended to their ads: 'Vote Labour. Or wake up with Michael Howard' – featuring a sleeping Michael Howard dreaming of charges for hospital operations and cuts in schools and hospitals (the hidden Tory agenda). Additionally the ads aimed to appeal to Labour voters who intended to vote Liberal Democrat to 'punish' Tony Blair over Iraq, thereby essentially electing Michael Howard and the Tory hidden agenda to government. These ads possibly illustrate a crude attempt to segment and target Labour's traditional voters. Commenting, Tony Blair remarked:

Figure 5.10   Labour 'economic stability' posters

the danger of wasting your vote on the Liberal Democrats is real . . . it is a back-door way to a Tory government. But beyond this very practical reason, I ask people to stand with us and help us to do what is right and good – to build a fairer society, to ensure every child has the best start in life, and to provide debt relief to tackle injustice in the developing world. (Tony Blair, 2005, www.politics.co.uk)

These threats to public services were also echoed in their warning ads: 'Warning: the Tories will bring in charges for hospital operations. Britain forward not back', 'Warning: the Tories will cut £35 bn from public services. Britain forward not back' (Figure 5.8).

In the final days of the election campaign their print advertising concentrated wholly on economic stability – Labour's creation of 2 million new jobs versus the Tories' 3 million unemployed (Figure 5.10); Labour's lowest-ever mortgage rates versus the Tories' 15% interest rates; and, interestingly, the talents of Blair and Brown versus Howard and Letwin.

Not surprisingly, the themes portrayed in their print advertising were also apparent in their PEBs. In their second PEB, 'Remember?' – with the strapline 'Forward not back' – we witnessed emotive images of economic recession, unemployment, 'Black Wednesday', repossession, cuts in police numbers, the rise of Michael Howard as Home Secretary and the hidden agenda of cuts it was suggested he would make in public services if elected, all set to the music of 'Memories' sung by Barbara Streisand. This legacy of the previous Conservative government was echoed in their fifth (and final) PEB, 'One in ten', aired on 3 May in an attempt to persuade more Labour voters to vote and to vote Labour, not LibDem. It opened by stating, 'If one in ten Labour voters don't vote, the

Conservatives get in.' Once again 'normal' people are talking about what life was like under a Tory government and the inevitable cuts in public services if they get in again. It concludes by telling the viewer that the good things that Labour have achieved will be at risk: 'If you value it, vote for Labour on May 5th.'

There were some policy messages, however. Their third PEB focused specifically on the NHS: 'The NHS expresses fundamental Labour values.' This PEB focused on Labour's health plans and achievements and scare stories about not being able to pay for hospital treatment, again repeating the Conservative NHS legacy: underfunding and privatisation. It concluded with 'Keep the NHS free'. Their fourth PEB, 'Happy families', focused on the achievements Labour had made in helping to improve the standard of living among families, contrasting this with Conservative proposed cuts. Thus: 'Choice 1 – tax credit for families or your prosperity at risk. Choice 2 – investment in education or Tory cuts. Choice 3 – NHS investment or Tory cuts. Choice 4 – 'stability or Tory higher mortgage rates' – featuring a collapsing Lego tower reminiscent of their towering inferno ad from 2001! The risk to family life if the electorate did not vote for Labour was heavily emphasised. Once again the PEB concluded with 'If you value it, vote for it'.

It was Labour's first PEB, however, featuring Blair and Brown, that generated the most media interest – partially because of the supposed volatility of their relationship, because of its filmic qualities (with its ridiculed soft focusing and creative inconsistencies), and because it was their only PEB featuring Tony Blair. Here Blair and Brown discuss the values of Labour and how they both personify those values, hence their investment in public life whilst simultaneously modernising it. This PEB very much focuses on the progress made by Labour since 1997, wrapped around their social justice agenda. Indeed, it is only here we begin to see the ideology of Labour and not just their election promises – a missed opportunity perhaps to begin to address some of the electorate's low trust. Perhaps the objective to win left little room for the promotion of ideology; while we contend that ideology and a market orientation can work in unison, clearly there is equally a necessary 'battle of wills' between them.

Conclusion: the advertising campaign's character

The overall character of the parties' advertising campaigns
Overall, the Conservatives' advertising was very negative in tone – adopting a strategy of image and issue-attack advertising similar to their 1997 and 2001 advertising campaigns. This is not surprising, given

Crosby's campaign focus and his highly controversial 'dog whistle' tactics. His critics maintain the vision of the campaign was too narrow and it failed to focus on the issues most important to the electorate, taxation and health, instead paying too much attention to asylum and immigration (Pierce and Webster 2005). His 'liar' ad too was criticised for portraying Michael Howard and the Conservative Party as unstatesmanlike (Pierce and Webster 2005). Lord Saatchi described the Conservative campaign as a 'tragedy of failed communication . . . it lacked idealism and was detached from the hopes and dreams of voters . . . Mrs Thatcher and Mr Blair became important epoch-makers because they understood that dreams are important' (cited in Kite 2005). Thus while the advertising mix was highly integrated, and highly focused, and even though it aimed to trigger an affective rather than a cognitive response, it would appear that once again, as we have argued elsewhere, the advertising failed to harness the hopes of the electorate.

The Conservatives, arguably, concentrated too much on the failings and untrustworthiness of Labour and Tony Blair and not enough on promoting Conservative policies and aspirations for the future, therefore failing to meet Berman's 'rules' for trust building. Accordingly, did they satisfy their advertising objectives? It is certainly debatable whether they created empathy between the Conservatives and the electorate. Clearly, they did not win the election, but, given Labour's reduced mandate, they may well have helped to suppress the Labour vote by generating distrust through their issue and image-attack advertising.

The goals of the Liberal Democrat campaign were well met by the print and PEB advertising. There was a continuation of the story they started to tell in 2001, thereby creating message consistency for their audience. Their unifying principle of 'the real alternative' facilitated integration across all their unmediated communication, creating further message consistency, and for a disillusioned electorate it provided the hope of a credible, trustworthy alternative. As in 2001, hope again featured strongly in the Lib Dem campaign. Reflecting on Berman's trust-building strategies, we see clear evidence of them addressing the electorate's needs and satisfaction; however, we do not see evidence of trust in the Liberal Democrats as an effective government – a continued major obstacle in instilling public confidence in them.

Like the Conservatives', Labour's campaign was essentially negative in tone, with the majority of their ads being issue-attack, supplemented by a few image-attack ads. A negative advertising strategy is not surprising, given the vulnerability of the party and the decline of 'brand Blair'. However, unlike the Conservatives, Labour very much concentrated on their one area of strength and achievement, economic stability, which permeated their advertising campaign in various guises, e.g. the ability to fund investment in schools and the NHS, underpinned by 'forward not back'. Additionally, even where they were instilling fear into the electorate, with respect to the consequences of electing a Tory government, they still presented their achievements and their aspirations for the future. Thus, like the Liberal Democrats' campaign, they offered the electorate shades of hope. Furthermore, like the Liberal Democrat and Conservative ad campaigns, their print and PEB advertising was well integrated, even though their ads had a more eclectic creative mix.

Labour therefore satisfied a number of Berman's incumbent trust-building strategies – the successful delivery of policy and serving and satisfying public needs – and in doing so their advertising objectives, economic stability, achievements and future plans, were reasonably well met. What, though, of their third objective: to mobilise the Labour vote? With their small mandate it is clear the public sent a very strong message to Tony Blair, yet even so Labour managed to motivate enough of their voters to win the election. Furthermore, while the Conservatives and Liberal Democrats made much of the Iraq war and weapons of mass destruction, research by MORI (Worcester 2005) indicated that Iraq was low down on the electorate's list of priorities, with health care being ranked first. Consequently Labour's advertising campaign was very salient in addressing the needs of their voters – it was very astute and not at all the themeless campaign depicted by its critics.

Reflecting on the role of trust in this election, even though some of the advertising satisfied Berman's trust-building strategies, it is clear that the Conservatives were less interested in building trust in themselves, concentrating instead on creating distrust in Labour, and Tony Blair specifically, through the use of attack advertising. Labour also used attack advertising to attempt to create and reinforce distrust of the Conservatives; however, they were also attempting to restore some trust in themselves, through claims of successful policy delivery. The Liberal Democrats, while they adopted a more positive campaign, aiming to build trust and credibility in themselves, still attempted to create distrust of Labour and the Conservatives.

Figure 5.11 reflects the advertising strategies adopted by the three main parties in terms of their attempts to benefit from positioning their opponents in the Distrust–Policy non-delivery quadrant. At the same time Labour attempted to position themselves in the Trust–Policy delivery quadrant, through emphasis on their successful economic policy. The Liberal Democrats also went for the Trust–Policy delivery quadrant by emphasising their achievements in the Scottish Parliament, linked

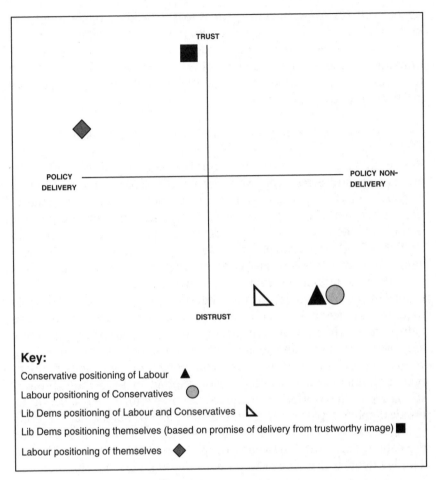

Figure 5.11 Positioning map

with their already trusted position in the eyes of the electorate. The Conservatives did not really focus on identifying a clear positioning strategy for themselves. Thus the decision on who to vote for involved, *inter alia*, deciphering the competing advertising messages in order to ascertain which party and leader were most likely to be telling the truth about themselves and the opposition. Consequently, in choosing who to vote for, was it more a case of 'Who do you distrust least?' than of 'Who do you trust the most to govern the country?'

Overall, these campaigns demonstrate some of the shorter-term benefits of attack advertising – helping parties to increase their market share and thus to win elections, and/or strengthen their position as a viable opposition. However, having spent weeks attacking, denigrating and undermining their competitors' reputations, what impact does this have on a largely suspicious, cynical and distrusting electorate? Consequently, longer-term, as illustrated in Figure 5.2, how likely are the electorate to rediscover trust in politicians and thus re-engage in the political process?

Was there a marketing orientation in the parties' electoral campaigning?

Where, then, does this leave the central question of this book? Did the advertising strategies employed during the 2005 General Election suggest a marketing-oriented stance in parties' electoral communication? Most markets operate within a competitive framework, and the political 'market place' where parties compete for voters seems very similar. Advertising strategies are used by organisations to help them compete more effectively, and certainly the political parties used their advertising to attempt to gain competitive advantage. Market research is carried out by organisations to underpin their strategies, and again there is evidence that the political parties carried out research and this helped shape their advertising strategies. In most market places there are loyal customers, and again with political parties there are loyal voters (customers). Further, many commercial organisations segment their customer base and often target different messages and product strengths to those differing segments. Some examples may exist in the political market place, for example the Liberal Democrats targeting younger voters through their 'no fees' stance for university study, and the Labour Party targeting young couples who have children with their 'family credit' policy. However, perhaps this is taking the argument too far. Is it more the case that the parties have a set of values that automatically generate certain policies? In such situations the notion of a marketing orientation starts to become a little more blurred.

There are other features of the political environment that challenge the claim by some that a marketing orientation is now being applied in politics. In reflecting on this it is worth reminding ourselves of some of the factors that militate against the 'marketing' view. For example, most organisations competing in the market place have the overall intention to expand the market whilst seeking an increasing share for their product, service or brand. Not so for the political parties: they do not share such market growth ambitions, focusing instead on increasing their market share on election day with little consideration of the health of the electoral market *per se*. Indeed, with membership of political parties declining significantly in the UK, there seems to be little effort, by parties, to market themselves to the electorate outside election periods. And of course, particularly for Labour and the Conservatives, the perceived lack of difference between them raises the risk of motivating the electorate only for them to join the ranks of the opposition!

Reflecting on the 2005 election, it is clear that the political parties recognised that the electorate viewed them as generally untrustworthy. This is not totally unusual, as many have argued that consumers see aspects of banking in the same way. However, the banks do not reinforce the belief by pursuing attacking advertising strategies that support their public's distrusting position. As we have discussed above, the Labour, Conservative and Liberal Democrat advertising campaigns deliberately set out to do so. Their use of attack advertising deliberately focused on the negative aspects of their competitors rather than 'selling' the benefits of their own positions, policies and potential MPs. Most notable were the Conservative ad calling Tony Blair a liar and the Labour ads portraying Michael Howard's 'hidden agenda'. Thus, while their advertising campaigns led to a degree of consistency – a positive feature in presentational terms – their appropriateness in a market place already permeated with distrusting 'customers' has to be questioned. Indeed, with the evidence suggesting that attack campaigns are more likely to depress participation than encourage it, questions arise surrounding the role of advertising within the electoral battle and the paradox that emerges when considering the issue of a marketing orientation by political parties in election battles.

It is also worth considering the issue of the 'voter-consumer' within the market place. There appears to be some acceptance, and thus encouragement, from parties that voters have adopted the 'mantle of consumer' rather than citizen. Thus they will not be looking for ideology but instead policies that best suit their needs and wants: the realm of the selfish voter (Dermody and Hanmer-Lloyd 2004). In responding to this, parties might be construed as adopting a marketing orientation. However, this assumes a rather narrow and superficial remit for marketing where the temptation to over-promise and consequently the risk of under-delivery is very real for a party chasing 'voter-consumers' solely to win the election without consideration of the wider consequences of these promises that might emerge, once they are governing the country. Ammunition indeed for electoral advertising, and thus the disengagement cycle is perpetuated: not particularly marketing-oriented! Further, in considering the choices that these 'voter-consumers' might make, they are faced with a number of decisions – vote for 'their' party, not vote, or vote tactically, in marketing terms buy the brand, do not buy the brand or . . . It is perhaps this third choice that raises interesting issues in terms of the marketing metaphor. A voter can 'buy a product' they do not want in order to influence the outcome they require: their party elected nationally. It is not easy to identify parallel situations in other market places.

Thus is it possible to say that political parties adopt a marketing orientation in their election campaigning? They certainly use the tools and concepts of marketing – including research, segmentation, targeting, positioning and promotion. They also compete fiercely for voters to support them so they get elected. However, at the same time they pursue strategies that will shrink the market place and create an increasingly cynical and distrusting customer-voter base; not very marketing-oriented! Their product offerings (policies) are shaped by a mixture of ideology (production orientation) and customer research (marketing orientation), so resulting in confused objectives – get elected but do not pursue ideology – and strategies of attack advertising causing a decreasing and disenchanted customer base. The media drive us down the path of celebrity, which crosses over to politics, thus the election becomes a contest of personalities as ideology and trust continue to evaporate. Is this a marketing orientation? The answer is probably increasingly yes, but in 2005 it was more the tools of marketing than the philosophy of marketing – all utilised to build electoral distrust. As we have argued elsewhere, marketing, and thus a marketing orientation, in its true sense, is about offering people hope for the future (Dermody and Scullion 2001). With the exception of aspects of the Liberal Democrat campaign, there was little evidence of this in the 2005 election campaign. The way in which promotional marketing tools and concepts are being used in election campaigns, with the emphasis on creating distrust and suspicion of the competing political parties, does not bode well for the future of democracy in Britain.

References

Ansolabehere, S. D. and Iyengar, S. (1995), *Going Negative: How Political Advertisements Shrink and Polarize the Electorate*, New York: Free Press.

Ansolabehere, S. D., Iyengar, S., Simon, A. and Valentino, N. (1994), 'Does attack advertising demobilize the electorate?' *American Political Science Review* 88 (December): 829–38.

Ansolabehere, S. D., Iyenger, S. and Smith, A. (1999), 'Replicating experiments using aggregate and survey data: the case of negative advertising and turnout', *American Political Science Review* 93 (4): 901–9.

Bellah, R. N., Madsen, R., Sullivan, W. M., Swidler, A. and Tipton, S. M. (1991), *The Good Society*, New York: Vintage Press.

Berman, E. M. (1997), 'Dealing with Cynical Citizens', *Public Administration Review* 57 (2): 105–12.

Bok, D. (1997), 'Measuring the performance of government', in J. S. Nye, Jr, P. D. Zelikow and D. C. King (eds), *Why People don't Trust the Government*, Cambridge MA: Harvard University Press.

Bromley, C. and Curtice, J., (2002), 'Where have all the voters gone?' in A. Park, J. Curtice, K. Thomson, L. Jarvis and C. Bromley (eds), *British Social Attitudes: The Nineteeth Report*, National Centre for Social Research, London: Sage.

Butler, D. and Kavanagh, D. (1997), *The British General Election of 1997*, Basingstoke: Macmillan.

Butler, D. and Kavanagh, D. (2001), *The British General Election of 2001*, Basingstoke: Palgrave Macmillan.

Cacioppo, J. T. and Bernston, G. G. (1994), 'Relationship between attitudes and evaluative space: a critical review, with emphasis on the separability of positive and negative substrates', *Psychological Bulletin* 115 (3): 401–23.

Cappella, J. N. and Jamieson, K. H. (1997), *Spiral of Cynicism: The Press and the Public Good*, New York: Oxford University Press.

Citrin, J. and Green, D. P. (1986), 'Presidential leadership and the resurgence of trust in government', *British Journal of Political Science*, 16 (October): 431–53.

Craig, S. C., Niemi, R. G. and Silver, G. E. (1990), 'Political efficacy and trust: a report on the NES pilot study items', *Political Behaviour* 12 (3): 289–314.

Crewe, I., Gosschalk, B. and Bartle, J., eds (1999), *Political Communications: Why Labour Won the 1997 General Election*, London: Frank Cass.

Denver, D. (1997), *Elections and Voting Behaviour in Britain*, Englewood Cliffs NJ: Prentice Hall.

Dermody, J. and Hanmer-Lloyd, S. (2003), 'Segmenting Young People's Voting Behaviour through Trusting–Distrusting Relationships', Proceedings of the Academy of Marketing Political Marketing Conference, University of Middlesex Business School, 18–20 September.

Dermody, J. and Hanmer-Lloyd, S. (2004), 'Segmenting youth voting behaviour through trusting–distrusting relationships: a conceptual approach', *International Journal of Nonprofit and Voluntary Sector Marketing*, 9 (3): 202–17.

Dermody, J. and Scullion, R. (2000), 'Perceptions of negative political advertising: meaningful or menacing? An empirical study of the 1997 British General Election campaign', *International Journal of Advertising* 35 (1): 201–25.

Dermody, J. and Scullion, R. (2001), 'An exploration of the advertising ambitions and strategies of the 2001 British General Election', *Journal of Marketing Management* 17: 969–87.

Dermody, J. and Scullion, R. (2003), 'Exploring the consequences of negative political advertising for liberal democracy', *Journal of Political Marketing* 2 (1): 77–100.

Dermody, J. and Scullion, R. (2005), 'Young people's attitudes towards British political advertising: nurturing or impeding voter engagement?' *Journal of Nonprofit and Public Sector Marketing*, special edition on political marketing 14(1/2): 129–50.

Diamond, E. and Bates, S. (1992), *The Spot: The Rise of Political Advertising on Television*, 3rd edn, Cambridge MA: MIT Press.

Electoral Commission (2003), *Party Political Broadcasts: Report and Recommendations*. London: Electoral Commission

Germond, J. W. and Witcover, J. (1996), 'Why Americans don't go to the polls', *National Journal* 28 (47): 2562–4.

Gould, P. (1998), *The Unfinished Revolution*, London: Little Brown.

Hetherington, M. J. (1998) 'The political relevance of trust', *American Political Science Review* 92 (4): 791–808.

James, K. and Hensel, P. (1991), 'Negative advertising: the malicious strain of comparative advertising', *Journal of Advertising* 20 (2): 53–70.

Johnson-Cartee, K. S. and Copeland, G. A. (1989), 'Southern voters' reaction to negative political ads in 1986', *Journalism Quarterly* 66 (4): 888–93.

Johnson-Cartee, K. S. and Copeland, G. A. (1991a), 'Candidate-sponsored Negative Political Advertising Effects Reconsidered', paper presented to the Association for Education in Journalism and Mass Communication convention, Boston MA.

Johnson-Cartee, K. S. and Copeland, G. A. (1991b), *Negative Political Advertising: Coming of Age*, Hillsdale NJ: Erlbaum.

Jowell, R. and Curtice, J. (1997), 'Trust in the political system', in R. Jowell, J. Curtice, A. Park, L. Brook and K. Thomson (eds), *The End of Conservative Values? British Social Attitudes: The Fourteenth Report*, Aldershot: Ashgate.

Kahn, K. F. and Kenney, P. J. (1999), 'Do campaigns mobilize or suppress turnout? Clarifying the relationship between negativity and participation', *American Political Science Review* 93 (4): 877–89.

Kite, M. (2005), 'Tory party chairman: we lost because they didn't offer hope', *Telegraph* online, 8 May 2005, www.telegraph.co.uk/news, accessed 10 June 2005.

Lewicki, R. J., McAllister, D. J. and Bies, R. J. (1998), 'Trust and distrust: new relationships and realities', *Academy of Management Review* 23 (3): 438–58.

Liddle, R. (2005), 'Victory for the fringe', *The Spectator*, 14 May, p. 24.

Luhmann, N. (1979), *Trust and Power*, Chichester: Wiley.

Mancini, P. (1993), 'Between trust and suspicion: how political journalists solve the dilemma', *European Journal of Communication* 8 (1): 33–51.

Mattinson, D. (2000), 'People power in politics', *Journal of Market Research Society* 41 (1).

Miller, A. H. (1974), 'Political issues and trust in government, 1964–1970', *American Political Science Review* 68: 951–72.

Miller, A. H. (1983), 'Is confidence rebounding?' *Public Opinion* 6 (June–July): 16–20.

Miller, A. H. and Borelli, S. (1991), 'Confidence in the government during the 1980s', *American Politics Quarterly* 19 (April): 147–73.

O'Cass, A. (2002), 'Political advertising believability and information source value during elections', *Journal of Advertising* 31 (1): 63–74.

Pierce, A. and Webster, P. (2005). 'Moderniser quits as donor berates Tory campaign', *Times* online, 9 May, www.timesonline.co.uk, accessed 10 June 2005.

Procter, D. E. and Schenck-Hamlin, W. J. (1996), 'Form and variations in negative political advertising', *Communication Research Reports* 13: 1–10.

Putnam, R. B. (2000), *Bowling Alone: The Collapse and Revival of American Community*, New York: Simon & Schuster.

Rawnsley, A. (2004), 'The Big Idea is now small ideas', *The Observer*, 10 October, p. 29.

Russell, A., Fieldhouse, E., Purdam, K. and Kalra, V. (2002), *Voter Engagement and Young People*, London: Electoral Commission. Online at www.electoral-commission.org.uk, accessed 4 July 2005.

Salmore, B. G. and Salmore, S. A. (1989), *Candidates, Parties and Campaigns: Electoral Politics in America*, Washington DC: *Congressional Quarterly* Press.

Schenck-Hamlin, W. J., Procter, D. E. and Rumsey, D. J. (2000), 'The influence of negative advertising frames on political cynicism and politician accountability', *Human Communication Research* 26 (1): 53–75.

Schiffman, L. G., Sherman, E. and Kirpalani, N. (2002), 'Trusting souls: a segmentation of the voting public', *Psychology and Marketing* 19 (12): 993–1007.

Scullion, R. and Dermody, J. (2005). 'The value of party election broadcasts for electoral engagement: a content analysis of the 2001 British General Election campaign', *International Journal of Advertising*, 24 (3): 345–72.

Spogard, R. and James, M. (2000), 'Governance and Democracy: the People's View', a global opinion poll, address to the United Nations conference, www.gallup-international.com/survey/18htm, accessed 7 July 2005.

Watt, N. and White, M. (2005), 'Tories focus on Blair lies claim', *Guardian*, 27 April, http://politics.politics.guardian.co.uk/election, accessed 27 April 2005.

Waugh, P. (2004), 'After Hutton, the verdict: 51% say Blair should go', *Independent*, 7 February (lead story).

Worcester, R. M. (2005), 'Women's Support gave Blair the Edge', 8 May. Online at www.mori.com, accessed 11 May 2005.

Wring, D. (2000), 'Machiavellian communication: the role of spin doctors and image makers in the early and late twentieth-century British politics', in P. Harris, A. Lock and P. Rees (eds), *Machiavelli, Marketing and Management*, London: Routledge.

6

The autistic campaign: the parties, the media and the voters

Ivor Gaber

This was one of the oddest campaigns I've ever covered. – Peter Riddell, Political Editor, *The Times* (Riddell 2005)
This is the most dislocated, perhaps even distracted, general election campaign I can remember. – Adam Boulton, Political Editor, Sky News (Boulton 2005)

It is not the argument of this chapter that the media campaigns fought by the parties in the four weeks leading up to polling day played a critical role in deciding the outcome of the General Election; in fact it is unclear if they ever do. However, it is undoubtedly the case that the media exposure that the minor parties (and the Liberal Democrats in particular) receive during a campaign does result in these parties increasing their visibility and hence their standing both in opinion polls and, presumably, at the ballot box. This overall lack of measurable impact of the parties' election media campaigns is probably the result of three causes. First, because the media are just one part, and arguably a decreasingly important part, in the parties' overall campaign armouries, which now involve the full gamut of marketing and communications techniques. Second, because the impact of an intense media campaign (no matter how well conceived and implemented) is marginal, compared with the impact of the media's political coverage in the periods between elections. And finally, because the evidence of a direct relationship between media consumption patterns and people's voting behaviour still remains, despite the best efforts of generations of researchers, tenuous at best.

This all therefore begs the 'So what?' question. What is the point of studying the parties' media campaigns if they apparently have so little impact? From the parties' perspective one answer is that even if they are 99% certain that campaigns have no discernible effect on the election outcome, to renounce campaigning is not a gamble that any of them feel they can afford to take. A senior party staff member, speaking at the post-election briefing at the Guildhall, suggested that, 'taken together, the campaigns made little or no impact on the result, which was much as the opinion polls had predicted before the four weeks of intense campaigning began'. But what if one party had not campaigned? It is not dissimilar to the probably apocryphal advertising executive who said, 'I know that 90% of the money my clients spend on advertising is wasted – I just don't know how to identify the 10% that works.'

But elections are valuable moments for media researchers, for they provide conditions in which, as near as possible, the success or failure of the parties' attempts to influence the media's, and subsequently the voters', perceptions of what are the important issues can be assessed. Much of the debate surrounding election campaigns revolves around discussions about the 'setting of the news agenda'. The usual debate, inside both newsrooms and academia, focuses on whether it is the politicians' or the media agenda that is predominating, leading to further discussions as to whose agenda should predominate. On the basis of this research it is possible to identify no fewer than six distinct news agendas swirling around during the 2005 election campaign.

First, there are the three separate agendas pursued by the main parties, and this research demonstrates quite how different they are. Then there are the media agendas. Conclusions about this are based on the detailed textual analysis of election coverage carried out by researchers at Loughborough University for the Electoral Commission. This research indicates that there are essentially two distinct media agendas in play. There is the broadly similar one pursued by the broadcasters, the 'qualities' (*The Times, Guardian, Independent, Daily Telegraph* and *Financial Times* and their Sunday equivalents*)* and the mid-market papers (the *Daily Mail* and the *Daily Express*). In contrast there is a very different agenda pursued by the 'red-tops': the *Sun*, the *Daily Mirror* and *Daily Star*, which can be characterised almost as a 'no interest' agenda (Deacon *et al.* 2005). The final, sixth, news agenda is that of the electorate, as revealed by opinion pollsters, who, throughout the campaign, ask voters which issues they believe to be the most important in determining how they will vote. Thus what one calls the 'election agenda' is in fact six separate agendas all competing for attention and all, to some extent, influencing each other.

Judgements about parties' campaigns are inevitably influenced by how the media have reported the campaign, but this throws only limited light on how the parties themselves campaigned through the media. This is because the media 'mediate' – they select, rewrite and, sometimes, distort party media pronouncements. Hence what one can ascertain about the parties' media intentions, from the way their campaigns are

reported, is limited. Interviews and insider accounts can be equally problematic. Interviews conducted prior to the campaign suffer from the fact
that whilst interviewees might fully intend to undertake the strategy and
tactics they have outlined to the researcher, as Harold Macmillan, in
response to the question during a 1957 television interview 'What keeps
you awake at night?' said: 'Events, dear boy, events,' frequently intervene
to throw such plans off course. Participant accounts and interviews,
written or conducted after elections, are hampered by the natural tendency of respondents to rewrite and refight the campaign in the light of
subsequent events. An arguably more effective way of judging a party's
media strategy is not by what participants say they will do, or indeed say
they are doing, or meant to do, but by the hard evidence of what they
actually did do (Norris *et al.* 1999; Brandenburg 2005).

At least since the 1980s, media management, the deliberate management of public image and information (Cottle 2003), has become a
normal component of party election campaigns. A number of broader
socio-political factors have been suggested as the driving force behind
this development: the permanent campaign (Ornstein and Mann 2000);
postmodernist campaigning (Norris 2000); the growth of professional
public relations advisers (Plasser 2002). This suggests that political
parties are being swept along on a tide, whereas in fact party media
management is a quite deliberate strategy. Parties want to deliver their
message and improve the image of the overall party and individual
politicians (Street 2001). For example, in the 1980s, the Conservative
Party very successfully raised the profile of Mrs Thatcher, and in the
1990s New Labour managed the media to change its overall image from
a negative to a positive one. Although an art, rather than a precise
science, media management offers parties the potential for strengthening their message through the third-party endorsement of the journalist. The logic of this argument is that if a reader sees an advert, their
response is likely to be 'You would say that, wouldn't you?' whereas if
the journalist reinforces a party message a reader may be more likely to
respond positively. Moreover, in a period of rising voter dealignment and
declining partisanship, parties believe – and it is this suspicion rather
than reality which is important – that media management influences
voting behaviour. As a result, the media campaign is a central part of the
three main parties' election communication strategy.

Throughout the year the main political parties use their Web sites as
repositories for all their press releases and media initiatives. It is in the
'Press', 'News' or 'Media' sections of their Web sites that a record can
be found of all the national press notices they have issued. During an
election campaign such sites become important sources for identifying

the parties' media priorities, particularly given that the releases are presented in headline format only with journalists having to click on the headlines in order to see the detailed release. Thus how party press offices choose to headline releases, and thus attract the attention of 'time poor' journalists, is a matter of some significance, arguably representing 'snapshots' from the 'front line' of the battle for the election news agenda.[1]

That is not to say that the parties reject other means of communicating with the media, e-mails, phone calls, text messaging, etc., but the significance of the parties' online media activity is that it represents their own proactive output. Many of their other contacts are reactive: dealing with specific enquiries or trying to steer a particular correspondent in one direction or another. The online newsroom encapsulates the parties' considered media priorities. This output consists of formal press releases, often put out to coincide with a press conference, extracts from speeches they wish to publicise, statements issued either in reaction to a breaking news story or to rebut something from another party, messages drawing reporters' attention to articles in the press that reflect key party themes and announcements about upcoming party election broadcasts poster launches, etc.; this latter category was deemed 'operational' and ignored for the purposes of this analysis unless the release highlighted the content of the broadcast or poster.

Press releases from the national press offices aimed at the national media, not those from regional or local branches of the parties, were analysed covering the four weeks of the official campaign, i.e. 6 April until polling day on 5 May. It could be argued that the election campaign had in fact been under way for a good deal longer – indeed, in the age of the 'permanent campaign' it is becoming increasingly problematic to decide when one campaign has ended and the next has begun. Certainly from the beginning of 2005 it was plain that an election campaign, albeit undeclared, was well under way. In March it increased in intensity as the Conservatives launched a series of so-called 'hit and run' attacks on the government (including highlighting the case of Margaret Dixon, a sixty-nine-year-old whose NHS operation had been postponed seven times) but the Prime Minister did not formally launch the election campaign until two weeks later, on 5 April, hence this analysis begins with the press coverage on 6 April.

The media campaign

Perhaps the most striking aspect of the 2005 media campaign was the extent to which coverage, particularly across the tabloids, mid-markets and broadcasters, was down compared with the previous election. Researchers at Loughborough University have been analysing media coverage of elections since 1997. At the start of the campaign the *Guardian* reported their initial findings thus:

> Between April 4 and April 11, during which time the parties launched their manifestos and sought to grab the initiative, the election was afforded less than half the amount of front page space in the red tops than was the case in 2001. Among the mid-market tabloids – the *Daily Mail* and the *Express* – the lack of interest was even more pronounced, with less than a quarter as much front page space devoted to politics. Broadcasters, who have vowed to do better than 2001 to capture the public's imagination, devoted around 10% less airtime to the election during their main evening bulletins. (*Guardian*, 18 April 2005)

And, as the *Guardian* again reported, the situation had not improved by the time the campaign drew to a close:

> Over the past four weeks more than three-quarters of tabloid front pages have featured stories other than the election. Among the red tops, the number of non-election front pages rises to 87% . . . The *Sun* and the *Daily Mirror* each devoted more than 10 times as many column inches to the Beckhams' marriage than to the leaking of Lord Goldsmith's legal advice on the legality of war in Iraq. (*Guardian*, 2 May 2005)

If media coverage is one factor behind the decline in interest in, and engagement with, formal politics[2] then one has to look not just at the quantity of media coverage of politics, but at the tone as well. In this respect the omens, at the start of the 2005 campaign, were not good. Only on one day throughout the campaign did the popular end of the press (the *Daily Mail, Daily Express, Daily Mirror, Sun* and *Daily Star)* all lead their front pages on the election – and that was not on polling day but on the day following the official opening of the campaign. And their coverage, even on that day, would have done little to encourage the disengaged to take a more positive interest in the election. The *Daily Mail's* page 1 headline, reflecting a strong Conservative theme designed to cast doubt on the validity of the new arrangements for postal voting, was: 'Can we trust the result?' (*Daily Mail*, 6 April 2005). The *Daily Star*, a paper not famed for its political coverage, headlined the election news 'May 5: a good time to take a holiday, folks' (*Daily Star*, 6 April 2005) and *The Sun*, unsurprisingly, ran with a picture of three topless women under the headline 'They're OFF. Page 3 girls keep you abreast of election swings: see centre pages', which, apart from featuring more topless women, told its readers, '*The Sun* is No. 1 for politits' (*Sun*, 6 April 2005). The broadcasters made greater efforts to cover the election but not with any greater success, in terms of audience. The two main terrestrial bulletins – the BBC *News at 10* and the *News on ITV* at 10.30 – lost on average 200,000 viewers throughout the campaign. (*Broadcast* 2005)

This diminution in media coverage does not represent a new phenomenon as such but more the continuation of a trend clearly discernible in preceding elections. Apart from growing public disenchantment with the formal political process, evidenced by turnout declines and a plethora of poll findings, it is arguable that the trend has also been hastened by the political parties themselves, motivated both by distrust of the national press in particular and by the development of new methods of campaigning. Thus the importance of the national media as the central election battleground appears to be in decline. One explanation for the 'autistic' campaign was that the parties had decided to concentrate their resources on the 'ground', in targeted campaigns in specific seats, using the whole range of marketing and communication techniques, rather than relying on the big guns of the national media to boom out their messages – or not, as the case may be. The technique was summed up by the Conservatives' chief election strategist, Lynton Crosby, who had successfully masterminded campaigns for the Australian Premier John Howard:

> Many media commentators do not see much of the real campaign these days. It does not take place on the TV, on the radio or even in newspapers. It is the local activity on the ground that really counts – letters to voters, postcards, newsletters, telephone canvassing, door-knocking . . . (Miller 2005)

Labour's leading election strategist, Phillip Gould, speaking in January 2005, came to a similar view:

> Four years ago the national campaign mattered, now it's the ground campaign that deals with individual voters that is central. That's because the electorate are now cynical about national messages, they don't believe them. But they do believe messages from local sources especially their local MP. (Gould 2005)

This 'bifurcated' campaign came to be described as the 'ground war' and the 'air war' (Walkington 2005; Wood 2005). Journalists in London were concerned that they were increasingly out of touch, that something was stirring in the political undergrowth, and that come 7 May they would all be left with the proverbial egg on their faces. Peter Riddell of *The Times* observed, 'We knew that a different campaign was taking place in the country than the one we were observing'

(Riddell 2005), and Andy Bell, Political Editor of *Channel Five News*, wrote:

> I was based in Westminster throughout the campaign and by the last 10 days that became uncomfortable. It was like sitting in a command bunker far removed from the battle while ever-more interesting rumours filtered back from the front line. (Bell 2005)

The parties' campaign

But it was not just the media's sense of 'being out of touch' that made this a very different campaign. The parties adopted a different approach, too. Modern British general election campaigns have tended to follow a well worn pattern. During campaigns the day used to begin with a series of early-morning press conferences at fixed times in central London, usually fronted by the party leader. He (or she) would then board a much decorated party 'battle bus' to undertake a regional tour, returning to London in the evening for major media interviews or simply to rest and recuperate. In 2005 the Liberal Democrats stuck closest to this model, with a daily press conference usually fronted by the party leader, Charles Kennedy. But, for the most part, Kennedy did not then proceed to the usual 'regional tour' which used to give reporters an opportunity of 'sniffing the air' in a particular part of the country. The Liberal Democrats did have a battle bus but it was more often than not used simply to transport Kennedy to an airport or heliport whence he would be transported to, say, Birmingham for a mid-morning meeting, followed by a lunchtime event in Bristol and an afternoon gathering in Exeter and thence back to London. The Conservatives undertook similar 'hit and run' tours, dispensing with a London-based battle bus, and did not always feature party leader Michael Howard at their press conference. Labour had no battle bus and no fixed time for their press conferences, which were not always fronted by Tony Blair.

But there were other factors that gave this campaign a particularly odd flavour. There was the fact that, somewhat bizarrely, neither of the two major parties appeared keen to want to promote its own leader and yet conversely appeared very keen to 'promote' the leader of the other party. Labour's press releases during the election period headlined Tony Blair nineteen times but Michael Howard was headlined twenty-five times and Charles Kennedy three times (Blair's deputy, John Prescott, was headlined just four times). And it was the same story with the Conservatives. They headlined Michael Howard twenty-eight times during the campaign but Tony Blair thirty-two times; Charles Kennedy received one mention, which was one more than the Conservatives' deputy leader at the time, Michael Ancram. Only the Liberal Democrats seemed to feel they had a leader worth headlining; Charles Kennedy received thirty headlines from the Liberal Democrats, Tony Blair thirteen and Michael Howard seven.

Another odd aspect of the parties' media campaigns was their 'negativity'. Not in the normal sense of the word but in what might be described as 'tactical negativity': all parties, for differing reasons, sought to play down their own electoral chances. This 'tactical negativity' was linked with the notion of 'permission politics' – a variation of 'permission marketing', a phenomenon which has been seen in recent election campaigns but was, in the 2005 campaign, used in a very particular manner.

Seth Godin, one of the pioneers of the concept, describes permission marketing as offering:

> the consumer an opportunity to volunteer to be marketed to. By only talking to volunteers, Permission Marketing guarantees that consumers pay more attention to the marketing message. It allows marketers to calmly and succinctly tell their story, without fear of being interrupted by competitors or Interruption Marketers. (Godin 1999: 44)

From this has developed what could be described as the 'traditional' notion of 'permission politics': parties used direct mail, telephone and e-mails to seek voters' 'permission' to send them further information about particular topics. For example, if someone expressed a concern about, say, the government's policy on education, it was seen as a cue, or 'permission', to send them further material about the topic. However, 'permission politics' came to be used in a different way in the 2005 media campaign', and this was bound up with what was earlier described as the 'tactical negativity' that characterised the election.

The most obvious, and consistent, way that the Conservatives used this new form of 'permission politics' was in their promotional strapline 'Are you thinking what we're thinking?' It was the party's attempt to break out of the 'spiral of silence' (Noelle-Neumann 1974), the notion that certain views were considered outside the parameters of the 'normal' political consensus. It can be argued that through the 1980s the effects of spiral were seen to hamper Labour's efforts to achieve electoral success; since 'Black Wednesday' in 1992 the spiral has been one of the key explanations for the Conservatives' electoral failures. Hence the 'Are you thinking what we're thinking?' can be seen as the Conservatives' attempting to give voters 'permission' to hold views that they might have been thinking were 'unacceptable'. Unfortunately, because the slogan was carried at the bottom of posters, it lent itself to parody and attack – most commonly seen was the simple word 'No!' at the end of the sentence; another variation was 'Are you thinking that we're stinking?' and a third was 'Labour are doing what we're thinking'.

The Conservatives, in pursuit of 'tactical negativity', sought to use the media to downplay their own chances of winning the election. This was because they were keen to 'give permission' to voters who wanted to 'send Blair a message' that they were unhappy with his policies but who might be alarmed by the prospect of a Conservative government. This was evident in a string of headlines on Conservative press releases, including:

'Take that look off your face,' Mr Blair told. (13 April 2005)
It's now or never to tell Mr Blair what you think. (29 April 2005)
Wipe the smile off Mr Blair's face on May 5th. (29 April 2005)

Equally there was also none too subtle acceptance of the fact that, come 6 May, Labour would still be in power, evidenced by headlines such as:

Labour's secret pensions 'tax' agenda: Blair will make people pay for pensions crisis his government created. (2 April 2005)
Which taxes will Mr Blair raise? The heavy costs of a Labour third term. (13 April 2005)

Labour also played the 'permission politics' game by indulging in 'tactical negativity'. Labour's big fear was that their supporters would stay at home or, worse, vote Liberal Democrat, Nationalist or Green as a way of punishing Tony Blair, primarily for the war in Iraq but also as a reflection of the general disillusionment that all the polls showed was infecting Labour's core vote. Hence Labour sought to 'give permission' to their voters to vote Labour without having to approve of the government's involvement in Iraq or, even, without supporting Tony Blair. Throughout the campaign, and well before, Blair went out of his way to assure Labour voters that they could disagree with his policies whilst still supporting a Labour government, and that if they sought to 'send him a message' by not voting Labour the result could be to let the Conservatives in 'by the back door'. This message was reflected in press release headlines such as:

[1970] Year the anti-war vote cost Labour its third term. (1 May 2005)
Tories trying to sneak into No. 10 through the back door. (3 May 2005)

Labour also sought to give their supporters 'permission' to vote Labour by publicising arguments from less than obvious supporters of Tony Blair, in particular using the *Guardian*, regarded by many in New Labour as the spiritual home of disillusioned middle-class Labour voters. The late Robin Cook, who resigned over the Iraq war, wrote an article in the *Guardian* explaining why he was still campaigning for the return of a Labour government, despite the fact that he was a candidate, and therefore *not* campaigning for the return of a Labour government would have been odd in the extreme. Nonetheless Labour still thought it worth publicising the article with a press release headlined 'Why I am on the campaign trail for Labour by Robin Cook' (8 April 2005). Equally, Lord Attenborough, an uncontroversial figure who was seen to have credibility with recalcitrant Labour supporters, also used the *Guardian* to voice his support. This too was picked up by the party and press-released: '"Labour has achieved so much," Lord Attenborough writes in the *Guardian*. "Whatever we do, we must not take the return of our government for granted"' (8 April 2005).

Liberal Democrats were also in the 'permission' game. They were anxious to give disillusioned Labour supporters 'permission' to vote Liberal Democrat without risking Michael Howard slipping into Downing Street by default. The Liberal Democrats were particularly angered when Labour tried to blow this strategy apart by claiming that their 'research' demonstrated that if one in ten Labour voters didn't vote, or switched parties, the victory could go to the Conservatives. Alan Milburn – one of Labour's key campaigners – kicked off this offensive at a Labour press conference on 25 April, warning:

> Our message to every Labour supporter is simple and direct. If you vote Tory you get Michael Howard. If you vote Liberal Democrat you are in danger of getting Michael Howard. And if you don't vote at all you are in danger of getting Michael Howard. (Milburn 2005)

The Liberal Democrats reacted angrily. The following day, in an attempt to reassert 'permission' for Labour voters to vote Liberal Democrat, they led their morning press conference with Brian Sedgemore, who until the dissolution had been a left-wing backbench Labour MP whom the Liberal Democrats believed had credibility with disillusioned Labour voters. Charles Kennedy told the press conference on 26 April:

> Brian Sedgemore's message for other people who are considering voting Labour but who are unhappy with the Party's policies on Iraq, tuition fees and civil liberties. At this election, the only party which has taken principled stands on these issues is the Liberal Democrats. They should follow their beliefs and vote Liberal Democrat – certain in the knowledge that however the vote goes, Michael Howard's Conservatives cannot win this election. (Kennedy 2005)

Labour hit back the next day when the *Guardian* led on 'Private poll reveals Labour fears' (*Guardian*, 27 April 2005). In a story that bore all the hallmarks of a stage-managed 'leak' the *Guardian* gave Alan Milburn space to repeat his warnings about the 'dangers' of Labour supporters voting Liberal Democrat in order to 'punish' Tony Blair. But the Liberal Democrats appeared to have won this little spat when, on 30 April, the Liberal Democrat-supporting *Independent* ran a piece from its respected psephologist John Curtice which analysed the substance of Labour claims and reported in a front-page headline, 'Vote for Lib Dems will *not* let in Tories' (Curtice 2005).

In appealing to disillusioned Labour voters the Liberal Democrats highlighted issues such as Iraq, tuition fees and civil liberties. By choosing these subjects they were clearly pitching their appeal to traditional Labour supporters and also highlighting individuals and groups who were now supporting the Liberal Democrats, who were likely to evoke a positive response. Apart from the defection of Brian Sedgemore the party publicised the fact that university lecturers and readers of the *New Statesman* magazine were, according to polls, showing majority support for the Liberal Democrats:

> Higher education polls show momentum is with the Liberal Democrats. (30 April 2005)
> Liberal Democrats as the first choice among students.
> Liberal Democrats ahead amongst *New Statesman* readers. (28 April 2005)

This tactic represented both the use of 'permission politics' and – the other new factor in this election – 'dog whistle' policies, an innovation which Labour 'blamed' on the Conservative's Australian adviser Lynton Crosby. As the *Independent* reported on the eve of the campaign:

> Labour claims that Crosby has imported 'dog-whistle politics' into Britain. Used by the Australian Liberals, the Tories' sister party, it means sending a message which – the way a dog whistle is inaudible to humans – is heard only by the people at which it is aimed. (*Independent*, 26 March 2005)

The concept of the 'dog whistle' policy is nothing new, but the use of the term highlights the fact that the parties were making more use of this technique than ever. Even before the campaign officially opened both Labour and the Conservatives were sending messages to their own supporters. At the start of the campaign, but on Easter Monday, so media attention was less intense, Labour held a press conference on the theme of 'workers' rights'; they put out three linked press releases headlined:

> Workers benefit from paid bank holidays. (28 March 2005)
> Rights at work not safe under the Tories. (28 March 2005)
> 28 days' paid holiday with Labour. (29 March 2005)

The theme of defending employment rights was clearly targeted at Labour's traditional supporters in the trade union movement, who were feeling alienated from the government, but the message was also put out at a time when there was less chance of it being picked up by Conservative-supporting newspapers, which might otherwise have used it to resurrect stories about the trade unions 'dominating' the Labour Party.

Labour brought out their dog whistle again later in the campaign when they sought to reach their reluctant voters with a release headlined 'This is now the values election' (18 April 2005). This marked the launch of the slogan 'If you value it, vote for it', a message which Labour used to try and remind its core vote that they all shared 'Labour values'. In the last week of the campaign the front page of the party's main Web site read:

If you value it, vote for it:
Minimum wage,
Strong stable economy,
Free and fair NHS,
Make Poverty History,
Sure Start and tax credits.

Putting the minimum wage at the top of the list and including 'Make poverty history' and 'Sure Start and tax credits' were indicative of the fact that this appeal was aimed directly at traditional Labour supporters who were thinking of voting Liberal Democrat, rather than the party attempting to win over centre-right voters who might be thinking about voting either Labour or Conservative.

The Conservatives too, under Lynton Crosby's tutelage, were blasting on their own dog whistles throughout the campaign. Clearly Michael Howard's frequent references to the immigration and asylum issue was aimed at a specific audience that felt strongly about the issue, but other, less obvious uses of the technique were also made. The slogan 'Are you thinking what we're thinking?' was not only a form of 'permission politics' but was also a 'dog whistle', saying to would-be Tories, 'It's OK to be a Tory, there are lots of us around.' Another 'dog whistle' was blown by Conservative leader Michael Howard when he told *Cosmopolitan* magazine, just before the formal campaign began, that he favoured reducing the time limit for abortions (*Cosmopolitan* 2005). Despite the fact that he also said that he did not believe that abortion should become an election issue the whistle had clearly been blown. Not only did anti-abortion voters get the message, but it was also a signal for various public figures to join in the debate, not least Cardinal Cormac Murphy-O'Connor, the head of the Roman Catholic Church in England and Wales, who made it clear that he was closer to the Conservatives' policy on abortion than to that of Labour or the Liberal Democrats.

An example of a possible 'dog whistle' that clearly went wrong came when Michael Howard was forced to sack his frontbench colleague Howard Flight and prevent him from standing as a Conservative candidate. In a private speech Mr Flight suggested that the true extent of the Conservatives' public spending cutbacks was being concealed until after polling day. Mr Flight had apparently blown the dog whistle a little too loudly. The Conservative leader acted quickly, sacking Mr Flight. He was no doubt mindful of the 2001 election, when another senior Conservative, Oliver Letwin, appeared to make a similar suggestion. Letwin was forced to go to ground and Labour made great political capital out of his 'disappearance', even going to the lengths of staging a televised stunt involving a Sherlock Holmes look-alike, complete with bloodhound, scouring the streets of Westminster 'looking' for Mr Letwin. This time round Michael Howard wanted no repetition: Mr Flight had blown the wrong whistle at the wrong time and had to go.

The Liberal Democrats' dog whistle was particularly targeted at former Labour voters who were contemplating deserting Mr Blair. Examples of this can be found, as previously mentioned, with reference to Liberal Democrats giving Labour supporters 'permission' to vote Liberal Democrat. In particular they sought to send Labour supporters three separate but related messages. One was that they could 'send Mr Blair a message' about the Iraq war by voting Liberal Democrat, since they were the only major party who opposed the war. Second, that their policies, as on Iraq, tuition fees and civil liberties, were more 'left' than Labour's. And third, that it was safe to do so – the Conservatives could not win, and Labour's attempts to convince their recalcitrant supporters otherwise was scaremongering. Their press release headlined:

> Blair crying wolf when he says voting Liberal Democrat will let Howard win. (30 April 2005)

This, issued just a few days before polling, was a good example of such attempts to reach Labour voters.

All three parties laid great emphasis on their efforts to woo the regional, as opposed to the national, media, but to what effect? Labour's Chief Press and Broadcasting Officer, Adrian McMenamin has admitted that whilst the press offices took the regional media seriously they had a problem convincing politicians that they really mattered. For whilst any amount of research might demonstrate how the public are far more trusting of the regional media than of its national counterparts, politicians, particular senior ones (of all parties), are creatures of Westminster. They make the right noises about the importance of the regional media but instinctively believe that the political editors of the national media remain the big beasts in the jungle. Their 'disdain' for the regional media, despite the lip service they paid to it, did not go unnoticed. The journalists' trade paper *Press Gazette* carried a headline, 'Regionals attack politicians for stage-managed campaigning' (*Press Gazette*, 29 April 2005), covering a report of a survey of regional editors who complained that, although much had been made of parties' regional media strategies, their opportunities to really question leaders on tour had been severely limited. Labour's deputy leader, John Prescott, spectacularly enunciated this disdain when he told a reporter from a Welsh newspaper who had asked about a Labour row in one local constituency:

> Why are you asking me about this? I don't care, it's a Welsh situation. I'm a national politician. . . ..You're an amateur, mate . . . Bugger off. Get on your bus, you amateur. (*Guardian*, 21 April 2005)

One final aspect of the media campaign worth commenting on was Labour's so-called 'masochism' strategy. Speaking before the election, Labour's Phillip Gould outlined it thus:

> We have to engage with the public in a way that might involve the PM in getting shouted at. So in order to control the election we have to give up control and allow people into our campaign in a way that has never happened before. We are looking at ways of enabling the public to have direct and continuous contact with the PM throughout the campaign. We intend to campaign in a revolutionary way. This campaign will be different to any other. (Gould 2005)

It was a high-risk strategy. Television producers, faced with editing the Prime Minister meeting members of the public, were unlikely to focus on the fifty-nine minutes which showed the PM in charge of his brief, as opposed to the one minute in which he might be seen to be on the back foot, and this is precisely what happened. In a number of encounters Blair found himself wrongfooted on the National Health Service. In Leeds he met a group of shoppers and ended up being berated by a disillusioned Labour voter, which resulted in a sea of negative headlines the following day. This was hardly the 'result' that Labour's media team had intended: for example, the *Daily Telegraph* (21 April 2005) ran the headline 'Jessica, 20, tells Blair how she lost faith in him'. This was perhaps not just masochism, but an instance of Blair shooting himself in the foot.

The media campaigns tabulated

This analysis of the parties' media output focused on all national press releases issued by the Labour, Conservative and Liberal Democrat parties during the period of the official campaign – 6 April 2005 to 5 May 2005. The releases were analysed by headlines, but only those subject areas receiving more than one press release were included in the tabulation. Thus, for example, on Sunday 24 April all three parties put out press releases about development, as part of the Make Poverty History campaign, but this was a one-off – none of the parties returned to the topic in the four weeks of the campaign. Hence 'Development' does not appear in this tabulation. Equally, some press releases fell into two categories – for example, a Conservative release headed 'GP targets: Tony Blair is out of touch' (29 April 2005) would be classified as being both about the NHS and attacking Labour. However, it should be noted that the vast majority of news release headlines covered only one subject. Thus Labour's total of subjects tabulated here is 126, but based on 106 releases; the Conservatives' 111 was based on eighty-six releases and the Liberal Democrats' 113 topics were covered by 107 releases.

Labour

Labour ran a fiercely disciplined campaign. In a memo 'leaked' at the start of the last week of the campaign Alastair Campbell, their director of campaigning, was quoted as saying, 'The strategy – root everything in the economy, focus on values/dividing lines in public services – is on track and working' (*Sunday Times*, 24 April 2005). This can be tracked to the fact that the economy was Labour's leading policy area, in terms of the number of press releases they issued on the topic; it was followed by the 'values/dividing line' issues of health and education. Ironically the closure of the Rover MG plant – which some commentators saw as 'bad news' for Labour – meant that the news agenda remained focused on the economy, which, as per the Campbell memo, Labour saw as an area of strength. The next most favoured topics, in terms of press releases, were Labour responding to two key areas of Tory attack – immigration/asylum and crime (including terrorist crime) – and the last two topics (housing and women/families) can be seen as 'dog whistle' issues which Labour used to signal to their own supporters that they were still, 'at heart', Labour.

However, perhaps the most striking aspect of Labour's news agenda is the extent to which it was dominated, not by their favoured policy areas as such, but by tactical messages (Table 6.1). These consisted of messages attacking the Conservatives or the Liberal Democrats, which accounted for 33% of all Labour's news output (broken down as 27% devoted to attacking the Tories and 6% to attacking the Liberal Democrats) or positive messages urging people to vote Labour or defensive ones, mainly consisting of warning of the 'dangers' of not voting or

Table 6.1 Labour news initiatives, 4 April–5 May 2005 ($n = 126$)

	Week					
Topic	1	2	3	4	Total	%
Attacking Con. or LD	14/0	7/3	7/5	6/0	42	33.0
Lab.Pos./Def.	2	4	6	7	19	15.1
Economy	12	1	2	4	19	15.1
Health	1	9	5	0	15	11.9
Education	1	0	4	4	9	7.1
Immigration/Asylum	1	0	4	4	9	7.1
Crime	2	0	2	5	9	7.1
Housing	0	0	0	2	2	2.0
Women	1	1	0	0	2	1.6

voting for another party. These accounted for 15% of all messages. Thus almost half (48%) Labour's entire media output was what might be termed 'tactical', the majority of it negative.

Conservatives

The Conservatives followed a similar pattern (Table 6.2). They devoted 41% of their news output to attacking the other parties (split 39% attacking Labour and 2% attacking the Liberal Democrats) and 9% promoting or defending themselves or urging people to vote Conservative. Thus their total for non-policy messages was identical to Labour's at 48%. The policy areas they gave most prominence to, each accounting for just under 10% of their output, were two topics that had served the Conservatives well in the 1980s but, in recent times, appeared to have been less effective. These were crime (including terrorism) and taxation (which was mainly focused on national levels of tax but also included attacks on opponents' plans to reform Council Tax). These two 'traditional' Tory areas were followed by a topic not usually considered natural Tory territory – health. Perhaps this was because the Conservatives' internal polling was telling them that it was a subject of great concern to the electorate and about which Labour was seen as potentially vulnerable (MORI 2005), particularly given Howard's ability to personalise the story owing to his mother-in-law's death from the MRSA virus.

There were many accusations by Labour that the Tories in general, and Michael Howard in particular, were giving undue attention to the highly sensitive subject of immigration and asylum. This analysis only partially bears out the accusation. The Conservatives put out six

Table 6.2 Conservative news initiatives ($n = 111$)

Topic	Week				TOTAL	%
	1	2	3	4		
Attacking Lab./LD	8/0	15/2	10/0	6/0	41	36.9
Crime	2	3	5	1	11	9.9
Tax	2	5	4	0	11	9.9
Con. Pos./Def.	0	2	1	7	10	9.0
Health	1	5	0	2	8	7.2
Economy	3	1	2	1	7	6.3
Immugration/Asylum	0	4	1	1	6	5.4
Education	0	3	1	1	5	4.5
Pensions/Social Security	2	3	0	0	5	4.5
Voting irregularities	1	0	1	3	5	4.5
Iraq	0	0	1	1	2	1.8

separate press releases in the period under review – more than Labour or the Liberal Democrats – but they also devoted more press releases to tax, health and crime. Certainly Michael Howard was making speeches on the topic throughout the campaign but these were not being reflected in the party's official media output. Speaking after the election the Conservatives' director of campaigning, David Canzini, confirmed that the party centrally had tried to ensure that it was not seen to be narrowly campaigning on this single issue but that the issue's promotion was driven by the media (Canzini 2005).

Liberal Democrats

The most notable aspect of the Liberal Democrats' media initiatives was the wider range of topics they covered (Table 6.3). The party issued two or more press releases during the campaign covering ten subjects, the Conservatives covered nine and Labour seven. If we include those topics which received only one news release then the Liberal Democrats covered eighteen subject areas (not including tactical messages) whilst Labour covered fifteen and the Conservatives thirteen. Also striking was the Liberal Democrats' emphasis on promoting a positive rather than a negative agenda. Only 28% of their output was devoted to attacking the other parties (19% aimed against Labour and 13% against the Conservatives) with 7% devoted to urging people to vote Liberal Democrat or defending themselves from attack. In other words, more than two-thirds of their output (72%) was devoted to positive messages about their polices; this compares with 52% for both Labour and the

Table 6.3 Liberal Democrat news initiatives ($n = 113$)

Topic	Week				Total	%
	1	*2*	*3*	*4*	*Total*	*%*
Attacking Lab./Con.	3/5	1/6	6/0	9/2	32	28.0
Economy	5	4	2	2	13	11.5
Iraq	1	–	4	7	12	10.6
Health	5	1	1	4	11	9.7
Education	3	1	3	1	8	7.1
LD Pos./Def..	1	2	1	4	8	7.1
Pensions/Social Security	0	5	1	2	8	7.1
Tax	2	2	3	0	7	6.2
Environment/Energy	1	1	3	0	5	4.4
Crime	0	2	0	2	4	3.5
Ethnic issues	1	1	0	1	3	2.7
Voting irregularities	1	1	0	0	2	1.8

Conservatives. The Liberal Democrat output on Iraq is seen to be skewed towards the end of the campaign as the leak of the Attorney General's advice to the government about the Iraq war came to dominate both the Liberal Democrat and the media news agenda. Conversely, it is noticeable how the Liberal Democrats totally ignored the issue of immigration and asylum.

Overall we can see that throughout the campaign the three parties were running separate news agendas, which only occasionally came together (Table 6.4). There was some consensus, if that is the right word, that the economy/tax was the key issue. At least it was for the parties (if not for the media or the public) and that health was also a key issue (and here the public, but not the media, seemed to agree). But for the other topics the parties had their own agendas and sought, more or less, to stick to them.

The media

Turning to the media, Loughborough University's detailed textual analysis of the range of topics covered during the campaign reveals that there were two, more or less distinct, agendas running through the campaign (Deacon 2005) (Table 6.5). Television, the broadsheets and the mid-market papers followed a broadly similar agenda – with Iraq, 'voting irregularities' and asylum scoring highly. In contrast, the red-tops hardly followed any recognisable agenda at all (with no fewer than nine topics falling in the 4–7% range of coverage). However, in order to make some

Table 6.4 Party news agendas

Ranking	Labour	Conservative	Lib Dem
1	Economy	Tax =	Economy
2	Health	Crime=	Iraq
3	Education=	Health	Health
4	Immigration/ asylum=	Economy	Education =
5	Crime=	Immigration/ asylum	Pensions/Social Security=
6	Housing	Education =	Tax
7	Women/ families	Pens/social. security. =	Environment/ Energy
8	–	Voting irregularities.=	Crime
9	–	Iraq	Voting irregularities
10	–	–	Ethnic issues

Note:

Equals signs denote that these issues had equal prominence with those contiguous.

Table 6.5 Media news agendas

Agenda	Television	Broadsheets	Mid-market	Red-tops	%
Election process	41	49	28	45	44
Iraq	10	8	10	4	8
Voting Irregularities	7	7	16	6	8
Asylum, etc.	9	6	9	6	7
Crime	4	2	5	5	7
Taxation	4	5	7	4	5
Economy	2	4	3	5	4
Health	4	3	7	7	4
Education	3	3	4	5	3
Pensions/Social security	2	2	4	4	2
Local government	4	1	1	–	2
Environment	2	2	1	1	1
Europe	1	2	–	1	1
Miscellaneous. (less than 1%)					7

generalisations possible the Loughborough researchers have averaged out a media news agenda and these figures will be used in the analysis that follows.

In common with the parties, the single biggest subject of the media's election coverage was what the Loughborough researchers describe as the 'election process'. This equates with the parties' attack, defence and promotion messages – characterised in this analysis as 'tactical messages'. It is significant that this subject receives an average of 44% of the coverage across all media, compared with an average of 43% for the parties' tactical messages. But the *policy* area receiving most media coverage during the campaign was one that featured nowhere on Labour's priority list, was ninth on the Tory list but second on the Liberal Democrats': Iraq. The subject that attracted second most interest (although here the running was very much made by the mid-market tabloids) was that of 'voting irregularities' (which arose after recent cases of electoral fraud). Asylum and immigration came next on the media's agenda, followed by crime, the economy, health, education, pensions and social security, and 'local government' (which was how the Loughborough researchers classified stories about Council Tax rises). So although, in overall terms, the subject areas that the parties wanted to talk about did attract some media attention, what is striking is just how different the priorities of the two 'sides' were.

All three parties made health one of their top three priorities, but for the media it stood in seventh place. For the media the top three topics, after 'election issues', were Iraq, 'voting irregularities' and asylum; none of the parties put any of these issues in their top three. But, as this figure, reproduced from Loughborough's interim report, makes clear, it was not until late in the campaign that Iraq, and concerns about voting, moved up the media's agenda, whilst the immigration/asylum issue fell away (Deacon 2005) (Figure 6.1)

So which party was most successful in terms of seeing its agenda items reflected in the media's election coverage? If we cross-tabulate the media's agenda (excluding 'election issues') with the parties' own priority lists we find the opposition in a stronger position than the government: see Table 6.6. Looking at this list, it is clear that Labour was the furthest off the media's agenda, with just four of the media's top ten in its priority list; by contrast both the Conservatives and Liberal Democrats shared nine out of the ten of the media's priorities. So if the battle for election agendas represents a battle to gain (or perhaps follow) media coverage then both the Conservatives and the Liberal Democrats were more successful. However, if we ask a different question – how close were the parties to the voters' agenda? – a different

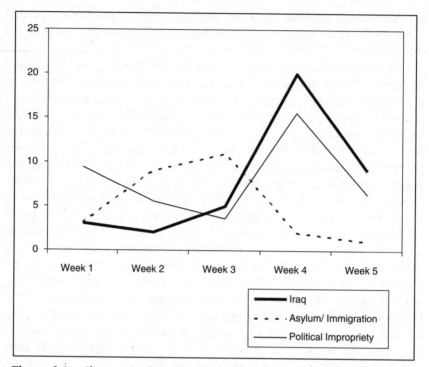

Figure 6.1   Changes in the national media campaign, 4 April–6 May 2005

pattern emerges. A YouGov poll[3] conducted on election day (involving 3,461 respondents) asked, 'Which two or three of the following issues will be most important to you in deciding which party to support?' Table 6.7 compares the 'public agenda' with that pursued by the parties and the media.

It can be seen from the data that, of the public's top five issues, the media had just two in their own top five but, strikingly, Labour had all five in its top five, the Conservatives had four of the five and the Liberal Democrats three of the five. Thus, in terms of agendas, the analysis reveals that Labour was the most effective at pursuing an agenda that matched the concerns of the voters, possibly indicating a stronger market orientation, and the media were the least successful in terms of reflecting these concerns. However, for parties, lining up policy priorities with the priorities of the public is only half the battle, for if the agenda is *not* being covered by the media then a party's campaign will almost certainly fail to achieve an impact, or at least will need to use other methods of 'message delivery' such as direct mail, leaflets etc., to get its messages across to the voters.

Table 6.6 Party and media news agendas

	Public	Media	Lab.	Con.	Lib Dem
Health	1	7	2	3	3
Asylum	2	2	4	5=	–
Economy	3	6	1	4	1
Crime	4	5	5	1=	8
Education	5	8	3=	8=	4=
Tax	6	4	–	1=	7
Pensions/Social Security	7	9	6	7	4=
Iraq	8	1	–	10	2
Families	9	–	7	–	–
Europe	10	–	–	–	–

Table 6.7 The differing news agendas

	Public	Media	Lab.	Con.	Lib Dem
Health	1	7	2	3	3
Asylum	2	2	4	5=	–
Economy	3	6	1	4	1
Crime	4	5	5	1=	8
Education	5	8	3=	8=	4=
Tax	6	4	–	1=	7
Pensions/Social Security	7	9	6	7	4=
Iraq	8	1	–	10	2
Families	9	–	7	–	–
Europe	10	–	–	–	–

Labour *were* successful on both these fronts. Not only did they coincide their agenda with that of the public they also succeeded in winning the lion's share of media attention, despite the fact that there was a discordance between their and the media's priorities. But this was probably not so much because of the perceived effectiveness of the party's campaign – indeed, one senior staff member privately expressed strong doubts – as a graphic demonstration of the importance of 'incumbency'. Factiva, a commercial media monitoring organisation, tracked the election coverage and found that Labour's 'share of voice' was dominant. At the start of the campaign Labour was receiving 61% of all coverage, falling only to 55% in the last week; this compares with the Conservatives, who ended with 29% against 28% in the opening week, and the Liberal Democrats, whose coverage grew from 12% to 17% (*Guardian*, 6 May 2005).

Conclusion

Bearing in mind the necessary limitations of using only the parties' news Web sites to analyse their media campaigns, it is, nonetheless, still possible to tease out certain conclusions. First, that general talk about an 'election news agenda' is misleading. What this research reveals is that there are arguably five or six news agendas in competition throughout the campaign. These are the agendas of the three main parties – the 'red-tops'' agenda, the rest of the media's and the public's – and that these different agendas both interact with each other but also, in some ways, act in isolation: for example, the media's attention to Iraq and 'voting irregularities' did not spark any proactive reaction from Labour's media machine.

Second, the claims of the parties that they campaign on 'policy' are thrown into doubt by this evidence. All three parties devoted more media output to the election battle itself than to any specific area of policy. In the case of the Labour and Conservative parties, virtually half their media initiatives were tactical or strategic, rather than policy, messages. And, of these, the majority constituted attacks on the other parties rather than positive messages about themselves.

Third, Labour's desire to make the economy a central issue, and the Conservatives' belief that 'tax' was a strong area for them, resulted in all three parties highlighting this issue. However, the media did not follow suit – tax and the economy were in fifth and sixth place in the media's priority lists and would have been even lower had the closure of the Rover MG plant not kept the issue in the news during the first weeks of the campaign.

Finally, that whilst the Conservatives and Liberal Democrats succeeded in mirroring nine of the media's ten top policy areas (or perhaps the media mirrored their agendas), Labour featured only four of the media's top ten in their list of policy priorities. But when it came to matching the parties' agendas with that of the public, the situation was reversed, with Labour and the public sharing the same five priority areas, the Conservatives sharing four, the Liberal Democrats three and the media just two. Thus Labour's media campaign can be seen to have been the most disciplined and the one which most closely followed the concerns of the electorate. Whether any of this actually affected the election results is another issue and one that cannot be investigated here. What this study does is to throw some light on how the parties develop and shape their news agendas during a campaign and the extent to which this is reflected in the media and by the voters.

Notes

1 The Liberal Democrats and Conservatives maintain archives of their press releases; Labour's goes back only a month. However, this does not mean that the Conservative and Liberal Democrat archives represent a 'time frozen' account of the parties' media campaigns. Culling takes place, and what currently appears in the archive for the period 6 April–5 May represents less than the full day-by-day output. For the purposes of this analysis the parties' Web sites were monitored continuously throughout the campaign, with the last 'reading' for all the sites taken on 7 May 2005.
2 See the special issue of *Journal of Public Affairs* 4, 4 (November 2004) based on papers delivered at the conference 'Can vote, Won't vote: is the Media to blame for Political Disengagement?' held at Goldsmiths' College, University of London, 2003.
3 YouGov, for Sky News, questioned 3,461 adults aged eighteen-plus throughout Britain online on 5 May 2005. The results have been weighted to the profile of all adults. This question is preferred to the one used by the British Election Study, 'As far as you're concerned what is the most important issue facing the country at the present time?' which consistently ranked 'immigration' higher than was found by YouGov. Given the election result, and the emphasis put on immigration by the Conservative leader (if not his party), it is suggestive that the YouGov poll is a more useful measure of the public's election priorities.

References

Bell, A. (2005), 'The election: a dog's breakfast', *British Journalism Review* 16 (2): 7–11.

Boulton, A. (2005), 'They said this time would be different', *Press Gazette*, 29 April.

Brandenburg, H. (2005), 'Party Strategy and Media Bias: A Quantitative Analysis of the 2005 UK Election Campaign', paper presented to EPOP, University of Essex, September.

Broadcast, 28 April 2005.

Canzini, D. (2005), 'The Conservative Party Campaign', paper presented to EPOP, University of Essex, September.

Cottle, S. (2003), 'News, public relations and power: mapping the field', in S. Cottle, *News, Public Relations and Power*, London: Sage.

Curtice, J. (2005), 'Vote for Lib Dems will not let in Tories', *Independent*, 30 April.

Deacon, D., Wring, D., Golding, P., Billig, M. and Downey, J. (2005), *Media Coverage of the 2005 UK General Election: Interim Report to the Electoral Commission*, Communication Research Centre, University of Loughborough.

Godin, S. (1999), *Permission Marketing*, New York: Simon & Schuster.

Gould, P. (2005), addressing Russian mayors, House of Lords, 28 January.

Kennedy, C. (2005), speaking at the Liberal Democrat press conference, 26 April.

Milburn, A. (2005), speaking at the Labour Party press conference, 25 April.

Miller, D. (2005), 'Election Spin mostly Underground', 2 May, online at www.spinwatch.org

Noelle-Neumann, E. (1974), *The Spiral of Silence*, Chicago: University of Chicago Press.

Norris, P. (2000), *A Virtuous Circle: Political Communication in Post-industralised Societies*, Cambridge: Cambridge University Press.

Norris, P., Curtice, J., Sanders, D., Scammell, M. and Semetko, H. (1999), *On Message: Communicating the Campaign*, London: Sage.

Ornstein, N. and Mann, T., eds (2000), *The Permanent Campaign and its Future*, Washington DC: American Enterprise Institute/Brookings Institution.

Plasser, F. (2002), *Global Political Campaigning*, Westport CT: Praeger.

Riddell, P. (2005), speaking at a post-election briefing, Guildhall, 23 June, organised by the Corporation of the City of London.

Street, J. (2001), *Mass Media, Politics and Democracy*, Basingstoke: Palgrave.

Walkington, S. (2005), speaking at a post-election briefing, Guildhall, 23 June, organised by the Corporation of the City of London.

Wood, N. (2005), speaking at a post-election briefing, Guildhall, 23 June, organised by the Corporation of the City of London.

Acknowledgements

I am grateful to the Loughborough team, and particularly David Deacon, for allowing me access to some of their final, albeit preliminary, data. The research will be published by the Electoral Commission later in 2005 but was made available in preliminary form as *Media Coverage of the 2005 UK General Election Interim: Report to the Electoral Commission, 20 May 2005* (Loughborough: Communication Research Centre, University of Loughborough), analysts: David Deacon, Dominic Wring, Peter Golding, Michael Billig and John Downey.

7

Banking online: the use of the Internet by political parties to build relationships with voters

Nigel A. Jackson

As a simple tool for political marketing, the Internet is unlikely to have a significant influence on British politics, although it will continue to be a resource for parties to make unmediated appeals to target voters. (Coleman 2001a: 12)

Voting can be likened to depositing money in a bank savings account. The citizen is investing their vote with a political party in the hope that it will lead to longer-term benefits for both themselves and society as a whole. The party hopes to build sufficient equity that it can achieve its political goals. The cornerstone of this relationship is trust. As soon as the voter believes that the party has lost their 'money', they will withdraw support. The relationship between a voter and a political party, therefore, is akin to that of a bank and a customer. As a service industry a bank is not very interested in one-off deposits, rather it wants lifetime customers. A political party will happily accept a one-off vote at an election, perhaps as a tactical or protest vote, but it is only with the stability that long-term associations bring that it can hope to fundamentally change society. A relationship marketing strategy offers parties a potentially effective means of mobilising support.

As a political campaigning tool, the Internet has been on a steady, but not very dramatic, upward curve. In the UK political parties were first recorded as providing Web sites from the mid-1990s. The advantage to parties is that the Internet enables them to market their product to voters both directly and indirectly at the same time. This chapter will first outline the importance of the Internet to political parties during election campaigns. Then by looking at how political parties used the Internet during the 2005 General Election campaign we will use a model to test whether online relationship marketing had a role to play. Ultimately, we hope to assess whether the Internet, and e-campaigning, have now truly come of age.

The Internet and elections

Following the use of the Internet in the 1996 US presidential election, some commentators felt that the 1997 General Election would be the first UK election where the Internet played a role. Technically they were correct, but at this stage it was little more than an experiment by interested volunteers rather than the party hierarchy, and the online campaign was judged not to have had a significant effect on party behaviour (Ward and Gibson 1998a). The parties' use of the Internet in 2001 was considered an advance over 1997 in terms of the quality of party Web sites and their use of e-mail (Coleman 2001a). Coleman also suggested that parties were seeking a role for the Internet; therefore the use of e-mail by four of the parties (McCarthy and Saxton 2001; Coleman and Hall 2001) must be seen as a part of an experiment. The 2001 General Election offered a useful 'road test' for how parties might use the Internet in subsequent elections.

The main use of the Internet in 1997 and 2001 was as an electronic brochure that disseminated information (Ward and Gibson 1998a; Gibson *et al*. 2003a). However, the potential for resource generation is growing. There is evidence that in the more candidate-centred US the Internet has been a powerful new tool for generating funds and securing volunteers. In the more party-centred UK resource generation plays a lesser, but a still tangible and growing, role. In 1997 there was very little attempt to use the Internet to secure volunteers and new members (Ward and Gibson 1998b; Gibson *et al*. 2003a). By 2001 the party Web sites were beginning to deliver new members and volunteers (Gibson *et al*. 2003a; McCarthy and Saxton 2001), especially for the Liberal Democrats, Green Party and Socialist Alliance. However, at no time was the Internet considered an effective tool for raising money in the UK.

The parties have largely ignored the interactive possibilities of the Internet (Ward and Gibson 1998a; Auty and Nicholas 1998; Coleman 2001b). A survey of party officials in 2001 found that the ability to gather feedback from members and the wider public was the least important function of a Web site (Gibson *et al*. 2003a). Looking at the use of e-newsletters, Jackson (2004) explains this reticence to enter into a dialogue was due, in part, to the fact that interactivity necessitates additional resources to handle feedback. The political parties, therefore, generally view the Internet as a top-down, one-way communication tool that informs supporters and the undecided voter.

Most research has focused on the use of the Web by political parties during an election campaign (Bimber 1998; Painter and Wardle 2001; Gibson *et al*. 2001b), but the evidence suggests that e-mail is growing in popularity. In 1997 e-mail, and the use of e-mail lists by parties, are barely recorded (Ward and Gibson 1998b) but by 2000 five of the eleven London mayoral candidates had e-mail lists that visitors to their Web site could sign up to (Auty and Cowen 2000). In the run-up to the 2001 general election four parties provided e-newsletters, and during the election campaign some of the parties, most notably Labour, experimented with e-mail lists (Coleman 2001a). However, for the Labour Party e-mail was considered secondary to their Web site, which was the key to their online strategy (McCarthy and Saxton 2001). In the run-up to the 2005 campaign Jackson (2004) has pointed out that e-newsletters are more likely to have been used by parties to reach and mobilise their own supporters than to persuade floating voters. With the growing importance of e-mail, e-mail lists and e-newsletters, the focus of Internet use has shifted from just election use, but also between elections to build up relationships.

Relationship marketing

Marketing is based on an exchange, be it a product or service, and there are two main strategies open to political marketers: transactional or relationship marketing. Transactional marketing dominated commercial marketing in the post-1945 period. As its name implies transactional marketing focuses on the sale, which is the ultimate goal of any interaction with the customer. It uses the traditional 'four Ps' marketing mix to communicate with customers, so the emphasis is on untargeted mass communication (O'Malley *et al.* 1999). The key to a transactional strategy is to constantly attract new customers (Wang *et al.* 2000; Lindgreen *et al.* 2004). Critics have suggested that this strategy was applicable until the 1970s but since then has lost its relevance (Brady and Davis 1993). Others suggest that transactional marketing still has a place, but that is increasingly limited to manufacturing and consumer markets (Lindgreen *et al.* 2004). If this strategy is applied to the political arena we would expect parties to view the voter as a one-off customer to be won or lost for each election campaign, starting all over again at the next campaign. The focus would be primarily on floating voters, who have to be won over, and they would communicate primarily through mass communication channels. Indeed, traditionally UK political parties were judged to be using a transactional approach (Mauser 1983; Niffenegger 1989; O'Shaughnessy 1990; Lees-Marshment 2001; Wring 2001).

Coined by Berry (1983), and closely associated with the Nordic school (Gronroos 1994; Gummesson 2002), 'relationship marketing' stresses the importance to long-term profitability of the relationship between companies and clients. Underpinning it is the observation by Reichheld and Sasser (1990), that it can cost five times more to attract a new customer than it does to retain an existing one. The cornerstone of relationship marketing, therefore, is the emphasis on customer loyalty. Rather than relying on the four Ps to retain customers the relationship marketing school suggests that personal relationships are as, or even more, important (McKenna 1986; Kandampully and Duddy 1999). Close relationships are based on trust, so that the customer believes the message they are receiving (Gronroos 1994; Veloutson *et al.* 2002). Ultimately trust of the producer should lead to commitment by the customer.

We can identify four key elements that need to be present for a relationship marketing approach to be successful. First, the collection and analysis of data from customers (Wang *et al.* 2000; O'Connor and Galvin 2001). Second, based on such data, key target audiences needed to be identified so that a conversation can begin. Third, building trust and commitment is essentially a communication process (Duncan and Moriarty 1998), so the message to each individual customer needs to be appropriate. Fourth, one-way communication will not enhance a relationship, therefore feedback from the customer needs to be encouraged (Yau *et al.* 2000; Geissler 2001; Arnott and Bridgewater 2002). To help build trust the customer must be empowered to be able to respond to any message conveyed to them (Papadopoulou *et al.* 2001).

A number of commentators suggest that relationship marketing is more achievable via the Internet than via traditional communication channels (Krol 1999; Wang *et al.* 2000). Both companies and customers have more access to information which helps them to make the appropriate decisions for mutual benefit. Moreover, the interactive nature of the Internet further facilitates the sharing of that information through enhanced feedback mechanisms (Geissler 2001). What is new is some of the methods and tactics marketers need to use in their communication techniques, most important of which is that the design and navigability of a Web site need to be simple and easy to follow. Therefore, the structure of an online presence is as important as the sharing of information through its interactivity.

Although transactional marketing has been traditionally associated with politics, more recently a number of studies have suggested that a relationship marketing approach is more appropriate. Bannon (2003) simply suggests that this is the case because relationship marketing is more appropriate for all organisations, and political parties are organisations. More specifically, political parties are viewed by Jackson (2004) as part of the service industry which is the most widely associated with relationship marketing. Dean and Croft (2001) argue that the transactional approach is unsuitable because parties do not concentrate on the 'sale' of securing a vote at each election. Relationship marketing provides mutual political benefits, interested citizens (both current and the next generation of voters) can find out whether they like political parties, their personalities and policies, and in return the party gets to educate the electorate about itself. This suggests that winning elections is as much a result of nurturing relationships, as it is of other campaign strategies and tactics.

Although a relationship management strategy cannot be limited to a single medium, a number of researchers have suggested that the Internet has indeed been used as part of a relationship management approach. Looking only at Web sites, Martin and Geiger (1999) concluded that political parties were using them as part of a relationship marketing approach. Bowers-Brown (2003) came to a similar conclusion during the 2001 election. Concentrating on e-mail, Jackson (2004) refined this to suggest that parties with a publicly available e-newsletter were deploying a relationship marketing strategy for internal audiences such as members and activists; but only Labour during the 2001 Parliament appeared to be conducting a relationship marketing strategy towards floating voters.

Relationship marketing is part of a wider permanent campaign between elections when parties seek to dominate the political agenda, therefore the 2005 General Election lasting only four weeks can be considered only a snapshot. However, within this tight time frame we will focus on which political parties are using an online relationship marketing strategy, and with what effect.

Methodology

The research conducted so far in the UK has focused on one element of the Internet, either the Web (Geiger 1999; Dean and Croft 2001; Bowers-Brown 2003) or e-mail (Jackson 2004). This chapter considers the use by parties of both their Web sites and e-mail in order to get a more balanced perspective on their use of the Internet. Whether it has considered relationship marketing or not, with the exception of Ward and Gibson (1998a), most research has focused on the major parties' use of the Internet. By looking at the combined use of the Internet by all parties that contested the 2005 General Election we can gain a more complete impression of its role.

This chapter seeks to add significantly to the knowledge of the use of the Internet by UK political parties by addressing two questions:

1 How important to party election campaigns is the Internet?
2 Did parties use a relationship marketing strategy online during the 2005 General Election campaign?

To answer these questions we used three separate research measures. First, an analysis of party Web sites, which were accessed once during the campaign between the second and third weeks of a four-week campaign. As we were seeking to find out how important the Web was to the parties this analysis did not look at the content, rather we focused on how many parties provided a Web site, how soon their Web sites offered content tailored to the election and whether the Web site was used to 'Get Out The Vote' (GOTV) in the final days of the campaign. Second, an analysis of all publicly available party e-newsletters.[1] Again, as the intention was to use indicators which might suggest the importance or otherwise of the e-newsletter we did not assess the content. Such indicators were: how many issued a publicly available e-newsletter,[2] how soon once the election was called their e-newsletter was available, the frequency of e-newsletters, whether they were used to Get Out The Vote. Third, interviews with the e-campaigners of parties which had a Web site and/or provided a publicly available e-newsletter.

In order to avoid the peculiar nature of the election in Northern Ireland, research data were collected only on parties contesting the 628 seats in England, Scotland and Wales. For the purposes of this research the parties were divided into four categories. 'Major' were the three largest parliamentary parties, Labour, Conservative and Liberal Democrat. All three major parties were interviewed. 'Minor' were those other parliamentary parties which represented seats in Great Britain such as the Scottish National Party (SNP), Plaid Cymru and Respect; one minor party was interviewed. 'Fringe' were those parties which, although without parliamentary representation, had representation at other levels of government and usually had a structure which in nature, if not size, was similar to that of the parliamentary parties. Examples of fringe parties included the Green Party, Scottish Socialist Party and British National Party (BNP); two fringe parties were interviewed. Lastly, 'Hopefuls' were the remaining parties which could probably aspire at best to save their deposit, such as Legalise Cannabis Alliance, Community Action Party and Mebyon Kernow; two hopefuls were interviewed. The non-parliamentary parties have been divided into two because the fringe parties had national organisations, could expect some national media coverage and had expectations of challenging seriously in some seats. The hopefuls, however, were much smaller parties with far less ambitious, short-term objectives, usually limited to contesting only one or a few seats.

To determine whether a party's Internet presence indicated a relationship marketing approach the following framework was used:

1 *Structure:* the importance of the design and navigation on the impact of a Web site or e-newsletter.
2 *Value* provides something of value to the receiver – it contains information not easily available elsewhere.
3 *Targeted.* Communication is tailored to the requirements of the visitor/receiver.
4 *Recruitment.* The Internet presence is used to build closer links with voters.
5 *Feedback.* The Web site or e-newsletter seeks to identify and understand the needs and views of the visitor/receiver, so communication is two-way, not just one-way.

Table 7.1 outlines the content analysis coding which was used for the party Web site and/or e-newsletter which was assessed to meet this framework. Within the structure a site search engine or site map helps the visitor navigate themselves around a Web site in the way that suits them. Enmeshing is the use of hyperlinks within the site, which also helps the visitor navigate (Ollier 1998). The Internet requires text to be short and to the point (Morris 2000), and brevity was measured by whether the text on a Web page exceeded the size of a computer screen or an e-newsletter exceeded three pages. A privacy statement gives guarantees on how any information collected may be used. Value is a difficult concept to assess, but it is taken to mean the provision of information which may be of interest to the visitor or subscriber. A Web site or e-newsletter that would be of interest to a member of the general public would probably provide a wide range of general information about the party. Something of value only to members and activists would cover only specific party-based activity and news. Value has been measured by how it would apply to a non-party member visiting a party Web site or subscribing to its e-newsletter. To be effective, communication must be targeted, and this requires capturing appropriate data from visitors/subscribers. Recruitment signifies the use of the Internet to attempt to develop a longer-term relationship through ever closer commitment by the voter. In effect recruitment acts as a loyalty ladder

Table 7.1 The measurement of Internet relationship marketing

Structure	
Own search engine/site map	Yes/No
Enmeshing	Yes/No
Brevity	Yes/No
Privacy statement	Yes/No
Value	
Of relevance to non-members	Yes/No
Targeted	
Capture e-mail addresses	Yes/No
Gather information from visitors	Yes/No
Tailored to the needs of the visitor	Yes/No
Recruitment	
Join party	Yes/No
Volunteer	Yes/No
Donate	Yes/No
Feedback	
E-mail contact	Yes/No
Surveys	Yes/No
Opinion polls	Yes/No
Guest book	Yes/No
E-newsletter	Yes/No
Competition, games and quizzes	Yes/No
Live discussions	Yes/No

(Christopher *et al.* 1991) so that customers, the voters, are encouraged to ascend rungs of the ladder. During an election campaign we identify three particular 'rungs' that are important for a party: joining the party, volunteering to help the party during the election and donating money so that the party can fight the election campaign. Lastly, a party which has identified the specific needs of the receiver is likely to be more effective in delivering its recruiting message. Generating two-way communication not only gives the party valuable information but makes visitors to the Web site, or subscribers to an e-newsletter, believe that their opinion is valued. Seven different forms of generating feedback were identified.

One note of caution is that a relationship marketing strategy is a long-term one (Jackson 2004), and an election campaign of four weeks provides only a snapshot. However, this framework can be used to see whether the parties seek, and have in place, the basis of a relationship marketing approach.

Online relationship marketing

The importance of a Web site

When the election campaign started in April 2005 the Electoral Commission recorded 301 registered political parties; however, only 107 different party labels were identified as contesting seats in Great Britain at the 2005 General Election.[3] That only twenty-four (22.4%) of parties contesting the election had a Web site which recognised an election was taking place might suggest that the Web is not considered an important communication tool. However, closer analysis suggests that, among those parties with a realistic expectation of either winning or coming second or third in some parliamentary seats, the Web is a normal part of their armoury. All the three major, four minor and seven fringe parties provided an election Web site, whereas only 9% of the ninety-three parties classed as hopefuls did. While our overall percentage is skewed by the large number of hopeful parties for whom the Web was largely irrelevant, this could suggest that a Web site is now a mainstream communication channel for all parties hoping to win a parliamentary seat.

That a party provides a Web site in itself does not explain the importance of its role. Two possible indicators of the salience to the overall campaign are how soon a party's Web site reflected that the election campaign had been called, and whether it was used on election day to help Get Out The Vote. Both uses suggest that resources were allocated in advance because the party strategists believed that doing so might have a beneficial effect. Within three days of 5 April 2005, the day the election was called, the home page of ten (42%) of the parties with a Web site acknowledged that the campaign had started and brought to the visitor's attention their distinct approach. All three major parties were quick off the starting block, only two of the minor parties, four of the fringe candidates and surprisingly one of the hopefuls.

Getting Out The Vote includes both encouraging constituents to vote and offering a means of getting them to the polling booth. Unsurprisingly no party used its headquarter Web site to offer lifts to the polling station. Only five of those parties with a Web site used it to remind people to vote. Size of party does not appear to be a relevant factor in whether parties use their Web site to Get Out The Vote, as a party from each category sought to remind visitors that it was election day.[4] The Alliance for Green Socialism's and Scottish National Party's Web sites both merely said it was election day, stated when the polls were open and reminded people to vote for them. The Liberal Democrats, United Kingdom Independence Party (UKIP) and Labour additionally suggested reasons for why visitors should vote for them. For example, the Labour Party Web site quoted

Tony Blair and Gordon Brown's mantra 'If people want a Labour government they have to go out and vote for it'.

The importance of e-newsletters

Overall, publicly available e-newsletters are less commonly used as a campaign tool than Web sites, with only the three major parties and one fringe party (the Green Party) offering an e-newsletter.[5] Additionally, two parties, UKIP and Veritas, collected e-mail addresses but did not send out any e-mails to this list, though UKIP did send a thank-you e-mail the day after election day. Therefore, of all the parties with a Web site, only 17% considered an e-newsletter worthy of allocating the necessary resources. However, it would appear that private, pass-protected, e-mail lists of party members, activists and donors were more popular. For example, of our eight interviewees, six (all four parliamentary parties, one fringe and one hopeful) used such an e-newsletter.

Three factors might indicate how important these parties thought their publicly available e-newsletter was: how quickly once the election was called they sent the first one out; how frequent it was; and whether it was used on election day to GOTV. The Liberal Democrats sent out the most e-mails, seventeen during the campaign, then Labour, with sixteen, the Green Party, fourteen, and the Conservatives, nine. The three main parties each sent out an e-mail on the first day of the campaign, but the Green Party took a week before its first e-newsletter. Most e-newsletters were sent out at fairly regular gaps of between two and four days, though after their initial e-mail the Conservatives waited another week for the second. In the last ten days of the campaign there appear to have been different approaches so the tone of each party's e-newsletter was distinctive. The Labour Party's e-newsletter particularly stressed the importance of raising money and getting volunteers to fight their key marginals. The alternative approach of the Conservatives, the Liberal Democrats and the Green Party was to stress their distinctive policies and attack their opponents. Labour, Conservatives and the Greens sent out an e-mail either on the eve of the election or on election day specifically calling on people to vote for them on 5 May. The Labour Party and the Green Party also sent out a thank-you e-newsletter on 6 May. For these four parties a publicly available e-newsletter appears to have been a regular additional means of getting out their message at all stages of the campaign.

The parties' view of the Internet

During a short election campaign all parties have extra resources to use; therefore, they can attempt to use the Web in different ways than between elections. The role of a Web site appears to have been to support other communication channels. For example, the English Democrats' Web site allows people 'To get a fuller explanation of what we do' (interview, Uncles 2005). UKIP point out that 'The Internet is really a back-up' to traditional communication (interview, Gulleford 2005). For Plaid Cymru, the 'Web site was almost a reference site, in that if people wanted more information about our policies and manifesto they could access them via the Web site' (interview, Trystan 2005). This was equally true of the major parties, with Labour stating, for example, 'Our viewing rate went through the roof on the day the manifesto was launched' (interview, Saxton 2005). Overall, therefore, all parties viewed their Web site as a useful supplementary information tool.

However, two parties suggested that the Web was more than just an information tool. The Green Party assumed that many electors predisposed to vote for them would first find out about them via the Internet. 'Therefore, the Internet is the first impression they have of the Green Party' (interview, Wootton 2005). Third Way also viewed their Web site from a philosophical and not just a campaigning point of view. 'We believe that the Internet allows people to discuss ideas in their own time, without the pressures they might face in a meeting. The Internet provides a safe environment to discuss ideas' (interview, Harrington 2005). The smaller parties, thus, may be more likely to see a relational orientation to the Web.

A Web-based relationship marketing strategy?

The first criterion that is indicative of a relationship marketing approach in a Web site is that it is easy to navigate. Table 7.2 shows that parties have broadly recognised the importance of design. For example, the home page of the Alliance for Green Socialism has both a search engine and headed sections of pages within the site which may be of interest to the casual visitor. The second criterion of relationship marketing is that the communication has value. This was assessed on the subjective basis of whether the site provided information of interest to a non-party member. Not unsurprisingly, all party Web sites did provide value for the visitor, often in the form of downloads of manifestoes, press releases and details of who their candidates were. Parties appear to have recognised, and to be meeting, the requirement from visitors that a Web site is easy to understand and provides relevant information.

Marketing theory suggests that good data collection is a prerequisite of effective relationship building, but only a minority of parties recognised this. Only 46% of parties collected e-mail addresses and even less, 38%, gathered any other data from visitors such as age, policy interests and whether they support the party. We might expect there to be a link between the collection of good data and the use of those data for targeting, yet despite the limited number of parties collecting data they all target messages. This can be explained by the fact that their Web sites are all very comprehensive in nature, trying to reach all possible interests.

In terms of using recruitment to encourage visitors up the loyalty ladder, the parties have generally seized the resource-generating possibilities of their Web site. Some parties created additional lower rungs in the loyalty ladder, with a pop-up page with a pledge that visitors could sign up to before they actually entered the Web site. For example, the Liberal Democrats had a pledge on opposing the Gulf war, and the SNP invited visitors to register their support of the party.

The election Web sites were clearly considered a means of attracting new members, with all twenty-four parties' Web sites attempting to encourage new membership. Indeed, eleven of the party Web sites provide an online membership form for visitors to join straight away. Fifteen parties asked visitors to donate money and six sought volunteers, for example Veritas asked people whether they would help leafleting or even set up a branch. However, on the whole Web sites do not appear to be a major tool for volunteers. This might be because, as a public document, a party's opponents could work out where its targets were, or just simply that the party does not view the Web site as good at securing volunteers.

Table 7.2 suggests that parties are generally poor at using their Web sites to deliberately create a dialogue with visitors. However, parties do expect to receive feedback in the form of e-mails, often in response to their published policies, for example Third Way engaged in e-mail conversations with some visitors to their Web site (interview, Harrington 2005). The impact of such feedback could influence the message parties send. For example, following e-mail responses early in the campaign the Conservatives adjusted their message on pensions and tax revaluation policy (interview, Westlake 2005). Such responses did not necessitate a change in party policy, but did help them set the tone which visitors felt was appropriate.

Table 7.3 shows that the major parties fully meet the design and layout needs of a 'good' site, with the other parties much less likely to meet the structure criteria. The minor and fringe parties lie in between the two extremes, mostly but not fully meeting the requirements. This may be explained by the availability of resources. All the major parties have a team of several people working at party headquarters on their e-campaigning, whereas the other parties had far fewer numbers working on their Web site. For example, Third Way had four volunteers who managed their Web

Table 7.2 The use of party Web sites as part of a relationship management strategy

	No.	%
Structure		
Own search engine/site map	12	50
Enmeshing	17	71
Brevita	14	58
Privacy statement	8	33
Value		
Of relevance to non-members	24	100
Targeted		
Capture e-mail addresses	11	46
Gather information from visitors	9	38
Tailored to the needs of the visitor	24	100
Recruitment		
Join party	22	92
Volunteer	11	46
Donate	17	71
Feedback		
E-mail contact	24	100
Surveys	3	12.5
Opinion polls	2	8
Guest book	1	4
E-newsletter	8	33[a]
Competition, games and quizzes	1	4
Live discussions	2	8

Note:
[a] Only four of the eight actually delivered an e-newsletter.

site (interview, Harrington 2005), whereas the Conservatives employed at least six people in managing their e-communications.

There were clear differences in targeting between the three major parties and the rest. First, most of the smaller parties merely had only one Web site (though Plaid Cymru had a 'Members' Page' and the Green Party a 'Members' Web site'). For example, the Conservative Party had at least six separate Web sites, each aimed at a different audience in terms of age, geography and policy interest; similarly Labour had at least four, while the Liberal Democrats had nine distinct sites. Second, the smaller parties nearly all aimed their Web site at the general public, whereas the major parties focused more on existing supporters than on floating voters. This approach was summed up by Andrew Saxton for

Table 7.3 The Use of party Web sites to build relationships by party classification

	Major		Minor		Fringe		Hopeful	
	No.	%	No.	%	No.	%	No.	%
Structure								
Own search engine/site map	3	100	2	50	3	60	5	42
Enmeshing	3	100	3	75	4	80	6	50
Brevity	3	100	4	100	3	60	4	30
Privacy statement	3	100						
Value								
Of relevance to non-members	3	100	4	100	5	100	12	100
Targeted								
Capture e-mail addresses	3	100	2	50	4	80	2	17
Gather information from visitors	3	100	1	25	4	80	1	8
Tailored to the needs of the visitor	3	100	4	100	5	100	12	100
Recruitment								
Join party	3	100	3	75	5	100	11	92
Volunteer	3	100	2	50	3	60	3	25
Donate	3	100	3	75	5	100	6	50
Feedback								
E-mail Contact	3	100	4	100	5	100	12	100
Surveys							3	24
Opinion Polls					1	20	1	8
Guest Book					1	20		
E-newsletter	3	100	1	25	3	60	1	8
Competition, games and quizzes							1	8
Live discussions					1	25	18	8

the Labour Party: 'Common sense suggests that the average voter, if they use the Internet, might look at the BBC or a newspaper Web site, but they are less likely to look at party Web sites. Really it is our supporters who come to our Web site.' With a more sophisticated approach to tailoring their messages, the three largest parties were more likely to use a relationship marketing strategy.

Quite clearly the main reason for the difference of approach between the parties is one of resources, with the smaller parties unable to maximise their use of the Web. For example, 'If we had the resources we would have sought to collect information on Web site visitors' (interview, Trystan 2005). However, one of the smaller parties, the Green Party, did focus on a narrow range of people, namely what they referred to as potential Green voters. These were, they believed, predisposed to find out about the Green Party through the Internet rather than other media. Therefore the one smaller party which appeared to try to target its Web site also believed that the Web was a particularly salient communications tool for building relationships with its target audience.

Gaining membership was an important long-term benefit of Web sites: once a person has joined, the party hopes to build on the relationship. For the smaller parties elections are one of the few occasions when voters may initiate contact with them. As a result, gaining new members appears to have been one of the key benefits of their Web sites. For example, the English Democrats believed that the number who joined during the election campaign was twice the normal monthly total (interview, Uncles 2005). The larger parties have greater opportunities for contacting voters between elections, therefore their election Web sites are perhaps proportionately less important for them in gaining members than for the smaller parties. However, the larger parties did certainly gain significant numbers of new members, for example the Liberal Democrats found that 'Forty percent of new members who joined during the election did so via the Web site. This was an increase in both numbers and percentage over 2001' (interview, Pack 2005). Getting people on to the first rung of the loyalty ladder, membership, was a universal long-term benefit of a party's Web site. Securing more members during a campaign may offer limited immediate benefits, but may significantly raise fund raising and volunteering for the party over several elections.

However, these figures needed to be tempered by three factors. First, as the Liberal Democrats point out, much of this new membership was in areas where support was generally weak, and so would not necessarily affect the immediate result, so any benefit was long-term. Second, as Sheridan Westlake explained, at times when the Conservative Party is in the news, donations and membership increase, because the amount of traffic visiting the site increases. Elections are no different from any other news story in terms of their effect on membership. Third, although some parties, such as UKIP, suggested that their Web site was an effective fund-raising tool, this does not appear to have been the universal view. The main tangible benefit of a Web site is primarily in encouraging new members, rather than securing funds or new volunteers. A Web site is a good mechanism for encouraging visitors on to the first rung of the loyalty ladder.

Whilst overall the results of using a Web site to develop a dialogue are disappointing, Table 7.3 does suggest that there are different approaches between the parties on feedback. Whilst all parties encourage e-mail contact, it is primarily the larger parties who use e-newsletters. (The fringe and hopeful parties who offered one did not actually deliver an e-newsletter.) The parliamentary parties do not use other interactive features (though the Liberal Democrats did have a Internet campaigning page where visitors could download a number of features). Rather, if more interactive tools were used it was by the smaller parties. Those parties who offered a survey appeared to be using them as market research, for example, Your Party had a New Policy survey the results of which they intended to use during the election campaign to say what people could do about issues of interest to them. Third Way's visitor survey form, Feedback, gave them an interesting insight into how people viewed the party on the political spectrum (interview, Harrington 2005). The only party with a guest book, Veritas, appeared to be using it as another means of gaining market research by asking for names and addresses and what visitors thought the top election issue was. Two parties provided one-question opinion polls. Your Party asked, for example whether 'MPs should have annual appraisals?' UKIP explained that such opinion polls are designed to give both the party and the visitor benefits, 'This feature [Have Your Say – Vote no] was done to draw people to the site, to interest people and make the site lively. It gave people the chance to have their say' (interview, Gulleford 2005). The only party with a competition, the English Democrats, used their Devolution Quiz to help make their political points (interview, Uncles 2005). The nature of the live discussions for the BNP and English Democrats is very similar in that they were an opportunity for visitors to put their views and get a debate going on an issue of their choice. Generating dialogue through their Web site, as a means of initiating a relationship, appears to be particularly important for smaller parties. This is perhaps because of the limited number of other media opportunities for developing contact and getting their views across.

Table 7.3 indicates that there are clear differences between the parties, with the size and resources available to each party having an impact on the likelihood of a party conducting a relationship marketing strategy. Overall, the three largest parties are, with the exception of feedback, the most likely to use a Web site to meet the relationship marketing criteria. Conversely, the hopefuls are, on the whole, the least likely category to follow a relationship marketing approach. This would suggest that those parties with adequate resources are more likely to attempt to build a relational approach.

An e-mail-based relationship marketing strategy?

Table 7.4 suggests a mixed picture of whether parties with an e-newsletter were following a relationship marketing strategy. All the parties recognised the importance of the design and layout of their e-newsletter. Indeed, these scores are generally higher than their Web site scores. There are, however, slight differences between the parties. The Liberal Democrats appear to have given the greatest attention to the structure of their e-newsletter. The Green Party e-newsletter appears to be mostly press releases and so does not appear to enmesh or have a privacy statement.

All of the parties ignore the importance of collecting data. Jackson (2004) suggested that in the eighteen months prior to the election parties could have made more use of targeting of key audiences, with only the Labour Party focusing on the collection of personal data to build up a profile. Whilst the parties mostly use broad-based content, so that a broad range of individuals can pick up the information they require, most do not actually capture information about their subscribers during the election. That the Liberal Democrats seek to capture e-mail addresses is explained by the fact that each e-newsletter contains a link where subscribers can sign up to more e-mail lists.

Most parties still managed to tailor their e-newsletter by providing links to a wide range of stories. Therefore, subscribers could find out more information on a story if they wanted. However, two of the Green party's e-newsletters could have been of interest only to party members, as they were clearly seeking members who could represent the party on television programmes.

Only Labour and the Conservatives sought to use the e-newsletter for resource generation. That the Liberal Democrats and the Greens did not use their e-newsletter for this purpose can be explained by the fact that their limited resources meant that their e-newsletters were essentially press releases. With more resources, Labour and the Conservatives could write their e-newsletters specifically for the purpose, and so could include appeals for help.

The publicly available e-newsletters generated some additional help for Labour and the Conservatives. The Labour Party, in particular, using advice from its US consultants, sent out four humorous e-mails from the writer John O' Farrell appealing for funds. These appear to have been a

Table 7.4 The use of party e-newsletters as part of a relationship marketing strategy

	Labour		Cons.		Lib Dem		Green	
	No.	*%*	*No.*	*%*	*No.*	*%*	*No.*	*%*
Structure								
Own search engine/site map[a]	12	75	7	78	17	100	0	
Enmeshing	14	87	9	100	17	100	14	100
Brevity	16	100	9	100	17	100	0	
Privacy statement								
Value								
Of relevance to non-members	16	100	9	100	17	100	12	85
Targeted								
Capture e-mail addresses	1	6	0	17	100	0		
Gather information from visitors	0	1	11	0	0			
Tailored to the needs of the subscriber	16	100	9	100	17	100[b]	12	85[b]
Recruitment								
Join party	0		1	11	0		0	
Volunteer	7	44	3	33	0		0	
Donate	7	44	4	44	0		0	
Feedback								
E-mail contact	1	6	3	33	0		0	
Surveys	0		0		0		0	
Opinion polls	0		0		0		0	
Guest book	0		0		0		0	
E-newsletter	0		0		0		0	
Competition, games and quizzes	0		1	11	0		0	
Live discussions	0		0		0		0	

Notes:

[a] This measurement does not apply to an e-newsletter.

[b] Whilst the subject matter might appeal to a range of subscribers the written style is primarily in the form of press releases with an initial audience of journalists.

success. For example, on 7 April O' Farrell sent out the first such appeal to the publicly available e-mail list. The next day an e-newsletter was sent out claiming £50,000 had already been raised. A series of more traditional appeals for help were made by Alan Milburn, Tony Blair and Matt Carter, the party's General Secretary. The assessment of their value throughout the campaign was that 'The results suggest that these fundraising e-newsletters were worth their weight in gold' (interview, Saxton 2005). However, this success must be balanced by the fact that at least two of the parties with a publicly available e-newsletter did not attempt to use them for raising funds.

During an election campaign the parties do not seem to want to encourage feedback from subscribers. Tony Blair's first e-mail asked subscribers to contact him by e-mail, presumably so that Labour could build up a database of those willing to volunteer for the party early in the campaign. The Conservatives occasionally encouraged subscribers to ask a question on specialist policy areas. They also invited subscribers to play their online game to 'Wipe Tony's smile off his face'. However, on the whole the e-newsletter was not used during the campaign as an interactive tool, rather the purpose appears to have been to get out key messages and appeals for help to support the campaign in the target seats. Publicly available e-newsletters are not used to develop a dialogue with voters.

It was in fact the internal pass-protected e-mail lists which had greatest impact on building relationships. This was not just because more parties had such an e-mail list but, more important, because of their qualitative effect. Such e-newsletters, targeted at only members, activists and donors, and benefiting from greater security, appear to have been used by all six parties to encourage volunteers to campaign in their key seats. Such e-mails helped the parties mobilise their core support during the election.

All six respondents reported that their e-mail list helped generate funds. For example, Third Way generated 20% of their total donations using this medium (interview, Harrington 2005). The e-mails were also useful in directing volunteers to help in their key seats. For example, the internal list of members was the major part of Plaid Cymru's online election presence.

> We used the e-mail list to organise volunteers during the campaign. For example, we e-mailed members to ask them to telephone-canvass from their home. This worked well and we had up to a hundred people each day doing this. This was something we had not been able to do before. Indeed, we even had colleagues from Australia telephone-canvassing for us. (Interview, Trystan 2005)

To put this in context, Plaid Cymru had a budget for its whole campaign of £50,000, therefore the e-mail list was a significant and cheap mobilising tool. E-mail lists and e-newsletters are a relationship-nurturing and maintaining device aimed at the already committed.

The value of such pass-protected e-mail lists, as opposed to the publicly available e-newsletters, appears to be that the party knows exactly who it is speaking to, and that they are fully committed. Mark Pack, for the Liberal Democrats, pointed out how important these e-mail lists were:

> The Internet is like the telephone system in that it is part of the communicating process. The biggest impact of the Internet is internal communication, and in terms of internal communication it is absolutely crucial. It is easier to survive if the telephone stops but the Internet connection survives than the other way round. (Interview, Pack 2005)

Whereas publicly available e-newsletters are external communication with an uncertain impact, members only e-mail lists are internal communication with a measurable effect.

If a Web site was useful for getting people on to the first rung of the loyalty ladder, membership, e-mail was much better for getting them on to the next two rungs. Publicly available e-newsletters secured some donations, but it was private e-mail lists which were the strongest relationship marketing tool. As part of internal communications such e-mails gave key activists necessary information about the campaign, but also mobilised them to help with practical activities in key seats. This is probably because, as members, they have a higher propensity to desire a relationship with the party.

Conclusion

After much hyping of the role of the Internet during the 2004 US presidential campaign, the 2005 General Election was the third time that people voted for the UK government where the Internet played a role. Since 1997 there has been steady progress in the use of the Internet but it has not revolutionised the way in which parties fight elections. In 1997 and 2001 the focus was essentially on the use of party Web sites. However, in 2005 the parties appeared to pay more attention to the potential of mobilising supporters through e-mail. After the 2005 election we may expect parties to focus more effort on using e-mail to mobilise supporters.

Within this historical context of a growing importance, just how central to party election campaigns was the Internet? In terms of the

Web we can identify a clear division between what might be termed the serious parties and the hopeful parties. The serious parties, which included our categories major, minor and fringe, all provided a Web site. The hopefuls, with probably little or no chance of saving their deposits, largely did not have a Web site. Quite clearly the hopefuls did not consider a Web site a means of breaching the gap between themselves and the other parties.

As the hopefuls form the greatest number of parties their inability to provide a Web site skews our overall results. However, when we look specifically at the parties that do provide a Web site, there are a number of patterns. First, size of party influences whether a party has a Web site, with the major parties the most likely, then the minor ones, followed by the fringe. Second, Web sites do not seem to play a central role in key phases in an election campaign. Only 42% of those with a Web site recognised that an election was occurring within three days of it being called. Even fewer, 21%, believed that their Web site might help to Get Out the Vote on election day. Overall the Web can be judged a supplementary communication channel.

Publicly available e-newsletters were far less popular than Web sites, and primarily the preserve of the major parties. They were used as a regular tool throughout the campaign, from day 1 to election day. However, private e-mail lists of members and activists appear to have been more popular, with parties in all four categories using e-mail in this way. Although fewer parties had e-newsletters than Web sites, those that had a private e-mail list appear to have used it to help generate new resources.

There is evidence that the parties have most of the basis of a relationship marketing strategy in place for their Web site, though they are generally weak on targeting and feedback. Most parties recognise the importance of the structure, value and see the membership recruitment opportunities that the Web provides. However, we might argue that the capacity for developing a dialogue which feedback helps create is the most important element in building relationships. Therefore, with the very important exception of feedback, the larger parties are the most likely to use their Web site as part of a relationship marketing approach to members of the public. This leaves us with a paradox. Are the main parties really conducting a relationship management strategy if they are not focusing on the key element of a relationship management approach?

Size and access to resources is the key factor which influences how well parties meet the relationship marketing framework through their Web site. The larger parties are more likely to understand and meet the structures criteria, and more likely to tailor their messages to a wider range of target audiences, because they have a larger number of Web sites. Conversely, it is the smaller parties which are more likely to consider interactive elements such as polls, live discussions and competitions. The aim of such activities is, in part, a marketing function in that they generate some market research data, but the key reason is that they help offset some of the disadvantages of being a small party. Interactive features can attract and help to keep visitors who may know very little about a 'hopeful' party.

The fact that only four parties provided a publicly available e-newsletter reinforces the fact that this is primarily a communication channel for the well resourced, or, as in the Green Party, those very interested in the Internet. E-newsletters are primarily a one-way tool, as the parties do not seek to encourage feedback. Only the Liberal Democrats collected additional data on their subscribers to further target their use. However, those parties with e-newsletters are even more likely than those with only Web sites to recognise the structural aspects. With adequate resources to rewrite and tailor the text of their e-newsletters only the Conservatives and the Labour Party were able to generate more resources in the form of volunteers and donors. Therefore a publicly available e-newsletter is a sign of a more sophisticated e-campaign, which offers another channel for getting out their message – but only two of the parties, Labour and Conservative, may have been using it as part of a relationship marketing strategy.

However, whilst resources may influence the ability of parties to have, and make effective use of, a publicly available e-newsletter such is not the case with member-only e-mail lists. This use of e-mail was much more common among parties of all four categories. Moreover, the benefits accruing from their use are more concrete. They enabled parties to communicate key messages direct to activists and generate significant additional resources. Those parties with a pass-protected e-mail list of party members conducted an internal relationship marketing strategy. The Internet was used in this election primarily to maintain a relationship with a small focused group of loyalists.

During the election campaign the Internet provided parties with three practical benefits. First, Web sites and e-mail helped parties both promote their key messages and wider background information. For example, visitors to a Web site could download detailed information such as a manifesto. In this way a Web site provided an efficiency gain for parties that did not wish to respond to large numbers of individual requests for the same information, and offered visitors ease of use in return. Therefore Web sites were a helpful convenience. Second, Web sites act as the first port of call for many people and can prove a useful recruiting tool for new members. Again this is an issue of convenience for members of the public and an organisational supplementary function for the parties. However, it is possible that members recruited by the Web may be less loyal because of limited personal contact. Third, e-mail, publicly available e-newsletters or private e-mail lists can mobilise supporters into action and generate funds. The effect of the Internet on parties in 2005 was limited, but it is likely that the resource-generating characteristics of e-mail will grow in importance in subsequent elections.

For the smaller parties, especially the fringe and hopefuls, starved of the oxygen of media attention, the Internet can raise their profile. Yet the vast majority of hopeful parties did not have an election online presence. For the parliamentary parties the Internet is merely a supplementary tool, one of many such channels. The conclusion might be, therefore, that the Internet was an irrelevance during the 2005 campaign. Largely this is probably true, except in one aspect, namely that if the Internet did not come of age it was surely developing a distinct purpose. The Internet did generate resources, perhaps not as dramatically as in the US presidential elections, but it is clearly a new seam of support. The Internet did not deliver the floating voter, but by enhancing the relationship between supporters and the party it did attract a body of future activists in the form of new members, it directed volunteers to help in key seats and to participate in activities, and it encouraged donors. Clearly this had some benefit in 2005, but the real test of how successful this relationship management strategy is is how much money and volunteer help it raises in future years. The average saver was not encouraged to bank online, but those who might be considered shareholders in the party develop closer ties online.

Notes

1 The term 'e-newsletter' is used, but it could include phrases such as 'e-mail lists' or 'further updates as we have news of interest to you'.
2 Parties could provide a freely available e-newsletter to all who signed up for it, a password-protected e-newsletter for activists, or both. Jackson (2004) suggests that only the three largest parties which had the resources outwith an election could do both. The analysis will look at the publicly available e-newsletters, but the interviews will address the parties use of pass-protected e-newsletters.
3 This figure was compiled by Richard Kimber, who made a number of minor changes to the raw data he accessed from the Press Association. Richard Kimber's data online at www.psr.keele.ac.uk/area/uk/ge05/candidates.htm, accessed 1 June 2005.

4 The five parties were: Alliance for Green Socialism, Labour Party, Liberal Democrats, Scottish National Party (SNP), United Kingdom Independence Party (UKIP).
5 The SNP did provide a regular publicly available e-newsletter prior to the election, but an e-mail of 6 April 2005 suggested that their approach was to be changed for the election. Rather than delivering updates via e-mail their news would appear on a daily basis on their Web site.

References

Arnott, D. and Bridgewater, S. (2002), 'Internet, interaction and implications for marketing', *Marketing Intelligence and Planning* 20 (2): 86–95.

Auty, C. and Cowen, A. (2000), 'The London mayoral Web sites: cyberdemocracy or cybermediocracy?' *Aslib Proceedings* 52 (8): 277–84.

Auty, C. and Nicholas, D. (1998), 'British political parties and their Web sites', *Aslib Proceedings* 50 (10): 283–96.

Bannon, D. (2003), 'Relationship Marketing and the Political Process', paper presented to the Political Marketing Conference, Middlesex University, September.

Berry, L. (1983), 'Relationship marketing', in L. Berry, G. Shostack and G. Upak (eds), *Perspectives on Services Marketing*, Washington DC: American Marketing Association.

Bimber, B. (1998), 'The Internet and political mobilisation', *Social Science Computer Review* 16 (4): 391–401.

Bowers-Brown, J. (2003), 'A marriage made in cyberspace? Political marketing and UK party Web sites', in R. Gibson, P. Nixon and S. Ward (eds), *Political Parties and the Internet: Net Gain?* London: Routledge.

Brady, J. and Davis, J. (1993), 'Marketing mid-life crisis', *McKinsey Quarterly* 2: 7–28.

Christopher, M., Payne, A. and Ballantyne, D. (1991), *Relationship Marketing*, Oxford: Butterworth-Heinemann.

Coleman, S. (2001a), 'Online campaigning', in P. Norris (ed.), *Britain Votes, 2001*, Oxford: Oxford University Press.

Coleman, S. (2001b), *Elections in the Age of the Internet: Lessons from the United States*, London: Hansard Society.

Coleman, S. and Hall, N. (2001), 'Spinning on the Web: e-campaigning and beyond', in S. Coleman, ed. (2001), *2001: Cyber Space Odyssey – the Internet at the UK Election*, London: Hansard Society.

Corrado, A. and Firestone, C., eds (1997), *Elections in Cyberspace: Toward a New Era in American Politics*, Washington DC: Aspen Institute.

Dean, D. and Croft, R. (2001), 'Friends and relations: long-term approaches to political campaigning', *European Journal of Marketing* 35 (11–12): 1197–216.

Duncan, T. and Moriarty, S. (1998), 'A communication-based marketing model for managing relationships', *Journal of Marketing* 62 (April): 43–51.

Geissler, G. (2001), 'Building customer relationships online: the Web site designer's perspective', *Journal of Consumer Marketing* 18 (6): 488–502.

Gibson, R., Nixon, P. and Ward, S., eds (2003b), *Political Parties and the Internet: Net Gain?* London: Routledge.

Gibson, R., Margolis, M., Resnick, D. and Ward, S. (2003a), 'Election campaigning on the WWW in the US and the UK', *Party Politics* 9 (1): 47–75.

Gronroos, C. (1994), 'From marketing mix to relationship marketing: towards a paradigm shift in marketing', *Management Decision* 34 (3): 5–14.

Gummesson, E. (2002), *Total Relationship Marketing*, Oxford: Butterworth-Heinemann.

Jackson, N. (2004), 'Political parties, their e-newsletters and subscribers: "one night stand" or a "marriage made in heaven"?', paper presented to Elections on the Horizon: Marketing Politics to the Electorate in the USA and UK, British Library, London, 15 March.

Kandampully, J. and Duddy, R. (1999), 'Relationship marketing: a concept beyond the primary relationship', *Marketing Intelligence and Planning* 17 (7): 315–23.

King, A. ed. (2002), *Britain at the Polls in 2001*, New York: Seven Bridge Press.

Krol, C. (1999), 'Web becomes crucial to relationship efforts: Miller/Huber's new clientele formalises its interactive capabilities', *Advertising Age*, 24 May, p. 52.

Lees-Marshment, J. (2001), *Political Marketing and British Political Parties*, Manchester: Manchester University Press.

Lindgreen, A., Palmer, R. and Vanhamme, J. (2004), 'Contemporary marketing practice: theoretical propositions and practical implications', *Marketing Intelligence and Planning* 22 (6): 673–92.

Martin, S. and Geiger, S. (1999), 'Building Relationships? Political Parties and Marketing on the Internet', paper presented to the Academy of Marketing 'Political Marketing' conference, Bournemouth, September.

Mauser, G. (1983), *Political Marketing: An Approach to Campaign Strategy*, New York: Praeger.

McCarthy, K. and Saxton, A. (2001), 'Labour: the e-campaign is born', in A. Painter and B. Wardle (eds), *Viral Politics: Communication in the new Media Era*, London: Politicos.

McKenna, R. (1985), *The Regis Touch*, Reading MA: Addison-Wesley.

Morris, S. (2000) *Wired Words*, London: Pearson.

Niffenegger, P. (1989), 'Strategies for success from the political marketers', *Journal of Consumer Marketing* 6 (1): 45–51.

O'Connor, J. and Galvin, E. (2001), *Marketing in the Digital Age*, Harlow: Financial Times/Prentice Hall.

Ollier, A. (1998), *The Web Factory Guide to Marketing on the Internet*, London: Aurelian Information.

O'Malley, L., Petterson, M. and Evans, M. (1999), *Exploring Direct Marketing*, London: International Thompson Business Press.

O'Shaughnessy, J. (1990), *The Phenomenon of Political Marketing*, London: Macmillan.

Painter, A. and Wardle, B. (2001), *Viral Politics: Communication in the New Era*, London: Politicos.

Papadopoulou P., Andreou A., Kanellis P. and Martakos A. (2001), 'Trust and relationship building in electronic commerce', *Internet Research: Electronic Networking Applications and Policy* 11 (4): 322–32.

Reichheld, F. and Sasser, W. (1990), 'Zero defects: quality comes to service', *Harvard Business Review* 66 (5): 105–11.

Veloutson, C., Saren, M. and Tzokas, N. (2002), 'Relationship marketing: what if …?' *European Journal of Marketing* 36 (4): 433–49.

Wang, F., Head, M. and Archer, N. (2000), 'A relationship-building model for the Web retail marketplace', *Internet Research: Electronic Networking Applications and Policy* 10 (5): 374–84.

Ward, S. and Gibson, R. (1998a), 'UK political parties and the Internet: politics as usual in the new media', *Harvard International Journal of Press/Politics* 3 (3): 14–38.

Ward, S. and Gibson, R. (1998b), 'The first Internet election? UK political parties and campaigning in cyberspace', in I. Crewe, B. Gosschalk and J. Buttle (eds) *Political Communication: Why Labour won the General Election of 1997*, London: Frank Cass.

Wring, D. (2001), 'Labouring the point: Operation Victory and the battle for a second term', *Journal of Marketing Management* 17 (9–10): 913–27.

Yau, O., McFetridge, P., Chow, R., Lee, J., Sin, L. and Tse, A. (2000), 'Is relationship marketing for everyone?' *European Journal of Marketing* 17 (9–10): 1111–27.

Interviews

Stuart Gulleford, United Kingdom Independence Party, 5 July 2005.
Patrick Harrington, Third Way, 29 June 2005.
Mark Pack, Liberal Democrats, 13 June 2005.
Andrew Saxton, Labour Party, 15 June 2005.
Dafydd Trystan, Plaid Cymru, 9 June 2005.
Steve Uncles, English Democrats 16 June 2005.
Sheridan Westlake, Conservative Party, 13 June 2005.
Matthew Wootton, Green Party, 30 June 2005.

Part III

The consumer

Some commentators would argue passionately that this is the 'natural' starting point for any organisation that claims a market orientation. If the customer is king (or queen), the political parties should have placed them at the centre of all product and communication development, and a sense of palpable satisfaction should be gained from the consumer-voter. In effect the parties should accept that the organisation exists in order to serve them, a feature of behaviour that should be recognised internally and externally. Without dwelling on the history of the three main political parties in the UK it is sufficient to say that each developed in response to the needs and wishes of particular groups of people in society; in this way they can, to some extent, claim market-led origins!

Our placing of the political consumer at the end of the book is recognition that most play a largely *responsive role* in General Election periods: they do not call for the election to take place and their involvement is limited to reacting to those elements of the campaign they, often accidentally, encounter. Politicians are deeply involved in the business of politics; in contrast the political consumer may occasionally take an interest. This is not to say they should be considered of less importance than either the political product or the way the political brands attempt to communicate. Indeed, most contemporary considerations of the communication process place great emphasis on the reception aspect of this process. That is to say, they recognise the value in asking what people do with the messages they come across because this makes a significant contribution to what messages are attended to and the meanings derived from them.

It is important to appreciate that those whom the political parties refer to as voters or the electorate are likely to be more comfortable to be considered as consumers. Is it worth noting here that we are suggesting a change in nomenclature. In part because we are analysing behaviour from a marketing perspective, but also in response to what the chapters in Part III reveal. A lot of our time and effort is devoted to consumption, and it is widely recognised that we live in a consumer culture where the market increasingly permeates all arenas, including politics. Chapter 8 starts from this premise in order to look at the implications for electoral choice. Ultimately the consumers' key role in the election was in making a decision over which, if any, political brand to support. Evidence has been growing since at least the 1980s that suggests the political consumer is less committed to a particular party than was the case; this is often referred to as dealignment. Consequently consumers in the political market place are demanding to be convinced – starting from the premise of asking 'Why should I vote?' and 'Why should I vote for you?' Given such circumstances, the nature of the political product and how it is conveyed take on extra importance and therefore we cover them in the previous two parts of the book.

More recent commentary about the political consumer talks about a growing sense of disengagement, even apathy. This and related issues are at the centre of Chapter 10, which focuses on those consumers who seem to be most inclined to mentally switch off from politics. Inevitably such problems generate calls for solutions, and one possible strategy that tries to tackle the political consumer's sense of detachment from politics – the 'us and them' syndrome – is a focus on local campaigning. Chapter 9 offers some positive findings in its study of local campaigning activity in marginal seats. Collectively these chapters confirm that not all political consumers are equal: some are of more relevance to a party than others. Pragmatically this has always been an accepted reality. For those with a democratic deficit agenda it is at the core of the problem.

Given the above issues, it is clearly not just useful but increasingly vital to gain a fuller appreciation of what the General Election means to political consumers and what their views are about various aspects of the campaign. Part III is dedicated to such an enquiry. It ties in with Part I on the product and Part II on communicating it by dint of the logic that you need to actively listen to the consumer's view on both these stages of the process.

8

Investigating electoral choice through a 'consumer as choice-maker' lens

Richard Scullion

Choice has always been a critical theme within politics – in all forms of democratic systems it has legitimising energy. One strand of political science seeks to understand elections by investigating correlations between social variables and the choices made, class and party identification being historically vital in the UK. More recently, choice has been positioned increasingly as a key element of policy, particularly in terms of public service delivery; see for example Edwards (2000). In part, this seems to be a case of politics learning and borrowing from consumer experience. Consumers, hence electors, desire endless choice, and so politicians must respond in kind. Corner and Pels (2003) and Scammell (1995) address, in various forms, the growing convergence between popular culture and politics. Ewan argues that the 'citizen concept is debased whilst consumer replaces it, whose franchise is his purchasing decision' (cited in Gabriel and Lang 1995: 173). Coleman (2005) points to a contemporary culture where citizenship has no fixed meaning, and where we are ever more consumerist in making political choices. Miller's work (1995, 1998) demonstrates a powerful political dimension of the choices consumers make. However, his case studies also illustrate well that often ill considered, even accidental, political consequences are attached to consumer choice. Miller declares that in politics voters, as individuals, have little power, whilst in shopping we have far more. Power here is located in the degree of choice perceived. As his subsequent empirical study demonstrated, the meaning attributed to these two social realms was affected extensively by the perceived choice they offered (Miller, 1998). Evident here is that people seek to attach importance to those parts of their lives where they feel they have some control. Scholarly literature and practitioners' words increasingly point to a blurring of the once distinct concepts of citizen and consumer. If this is so contemporary elections are being held within an increasingly market-oriented society and that must have potentially profound implications. This chapter addresses the issue by seeking insights by investigating the psychic space where consumer choice connects with politics. That is to say, it locates choice in politics indirectly through another life sphere: consumption. It privileges the idea that, for most, the concept is primarily concerned with consumer activity. By conceiving of electors with agency whose self-identity is appreciably shaped by, and through, being participatory consumers, more light may be shone on contemporary political engagement. It is through plural notions of 'consumer as chooser' that this chapter ultimately seeks to locate and consider modern political election campaigns. It perceives consumers as choice-makers in order to look at their actual practices.

The chapter briefly outlines theory from other disciplines that underpin attribution of meaning to choice. First, the philosophical foundation linked it with the idea of free will, which proffers an existentialist-based ontological and epistemological standpoint. Aligned to this is a socio-cultural base with the structure–agency debate at its centre. A third strand of thought posits choice as critical in the shaping of our contemporary sense of self where choice is concerned with our quest to become recognisable individuals. Consistent with these three ideas of choice – an existentialist philosophical position, the emergence of reflexive agents and the dominance of the enterprising self-identity project – emphasis is placed on choice, as it is manifest within the market. Here, choice legitimises the system (capitalism), and is positioned as inherently virtuous. By looking at choice strategies adopted by consumers and at the variety of meanings attributed to consumer choice-making, this section suggests how such a view of the electorate may generate insights on the subject of electoral engagement. The chapter goes on to briefly outline some of the arguments that position choice as troublesome, again offering tentative links with electoral engagement.

The General Election of 2005 offered fertile ground in which to investigate the meaning of electoral choice through a consumer-as-choice-maker lens. The methods used to collect 'material from the field' are then briefly outlined before the chapter offers the reader a synopsis of each participant's experience. It concludes by drawing out themes and offering a number of provisional speculations as to how these insights help us to understand electoral choice held within consumerist cultures.

Choice in philosophy

Kant posits the idea that humans inherently posses a 'faculty of choice', which requires exercise in order for individuals to be complete (Sullivan 1995). Kierkegaard affords special emphasis to choice when he reminds us of the need to recognise the human experience itself as the essence of humanity (Watts 2003). Existentialism tries to reconcile essence and existence as man's nature and actual experiences. Sartre is lucid on the crucial role of choice within existential thinking. 'I chose myself not in my being but in my manner of being' (cited in Roubiezek 1964: 124). Kierkegaard claims all choice is based on subjective truth. What a person becomes is 'his own responsibility, the product of his will', Gardiner (2002: 111). The political sphere offers opportunities to define the self through deciding on the level of attachment given to any political choices made and when opting to support a particular political party. We should further recognise the possible metaphysical benefit that simply having an opportunity to make an electoral choice offers: facing uncertainty through acknowledging endless possibilities creates tension. For Kierkegaard the solution to this angst was to be found in faith – not surprising, given that he wrote in the mid-nineteenth century, when belief in universal certainties prevailed. Coping, in a contemporary context, where individualism and agency are realised through self-enterprising projects, is likely to be found in fragmented locations, and, this chapter argues, especially in consumption.

A society dominated by a teleological viewpoint (Hooker, cited in Messerley 1995), where a belief in an infinite number of options prevails, fits consumer culture well. It places choice within a broad set of calculations leading to a desired outcome, inevitably privileging judgements made on those outcomes – or consequences. In national politics most individuals witness and experience few direct consequences of their actions. Campbell (1987:18) argues that we live within an increasingly individualised ontology where consumerism creates a context full of opportunities for people to select their own series of experiences: 'I feel, therefore I am.' Personal choice then is what determines not just who we are, but *that* we are. The human need for reassurance and a sense of identity are met well by consumption because it provides opportunities to constantly engage in various activities that satisfy affective self-expression. Campbell states, 'The real location of our identity is to be found in our reaction to products' (Campbell 2004: 32). Choice, then, is a necessary consequence of our inescapable human ability to indulge in wishing, dreaming, hoping and longing. Conceivably, the sphere of politics once dominated human thoughts when they turned to such matters. Now, argue Campbell (2004) and Firat and Dholakia (1998), consumerism occupies this central place in fulfilling human desire. Choice as consumer, rather than as citizen, offers potential in abundance: a profusion of choice, and the more of it we have, the more specific and accurate we are in being, knowing and expressing ourselves (Sen *et al.* 2001).

Choice: free agent or determined by structures?

Giddens maintains that we are reflexive, knowing autonomous agents interacting with pre-existing structures, themselves created by other agents. This interaction, which he refers to as structuration, both sustains and adapts the structures. Choice then somewhat paradoxically both assists individuality and, by helping to shape the future, takes on a structural dimension. This is evident in both consumer and political spheres, where choice can reflect a desire to belong and show allegiance – via fashion purchases through to party activism. Equally, by making a choice that supports an existing structure (high-street store or political party) we are contributing to that structure's empowerment. Structures are prevalent during elections, at the same time electors have agency. For example, the meaning of a carefully choreographed media event (mainly structure) can be dramatically altered when interrupted by the 'deviant behaviour' of electors (mainly agency). Equally, politically motivated sectors of the electorate (agents) may be uninspired when faced with what they see as the pointlessness of their action in a so-called 'safe seat' (structure). The interplay between these two features clearly has significant implications for how we perceive electoral choice.

Political parties present such choice on their terms: support our stance or another party stance, *do not* demonstrate your own stance. This supports the idea that structures in the political sphere are, for many, an impediment to agency. Consequently, many are frustrated by the limiting nature of politics and look to engage in other more agency-friendly spheres (see 'Journey into the field: a brief context setting' below). Douglas and Isherwood (1986) identify themes among the cacophony of contemporary consumer choices. They argue preferences, expressed through consumer behaviour, are a manifestation of macro-cultural choices. Ultimately, behind each micro-choice lies the answer to what kind of society we want to live in. Douglas (1996, 2003) argues such cultural choice is characterised by individualism, competition, minimal rules and reciprocity centred on maximising benefits for oneself. These prevailing cultural qualities reinforce our sense of being autonomous choice-makers and downplay life spheres characterised by a more collective civic ethos such as politics.

Self-identity and choice

In recent times we have constructed a self that Rose (1993) describes as the enterprising self, knowingly unique, therefore aware of one's agency, and of the requirement to use it. Where once identity was fixed and given, it has more recently been transposed by a sense of something to be both sought and created: possibly through consumption. A major consequence of this is the emergence of both expectations and responsibilities for choice making. This set of conditions – where choice is essential to our being, where our agency is ever more apparent, and where this agency is manifest in discovery of the self – is most palpable within consumption activity. Markets produce constant stimuli, premeditated to create shape and celebrate choice, inevitably establishing the notion of choice as a vital and privileged activity. Within this liberal economic tradition choice turns customers into kings. For some, the 'moving spirit' of our times is now located not in politics but in consumption (Comaroff and Comaroff 2000: 295). Firat and Dholakia (1998) argue that the only remaining legitimising force, and therefore the structure with the power to ascribe value via exchange, is the market. Electors less readily equate the casting of their vote for a party with an identifiable process of exchange. As a result they find it difficult to judge the worthiness of such decisions. This may relegate politics to mere squabbling over who is the best management team. Yet despite, or perhaps because of, its desirability in consumer spheres, the allure of choice seems to have waned in election contexts, giving rise to apathy and disengagement (Bromley and Curtice 2002; Dermody and Scullion 2005; Harrop 2001). This chapter explores the nature of any relationship that exists between consumerism, endowed as it is with extravagant levels of choice, and consumers' approach to electoral choice.

Consumer choice and the potential application to election contexts
Schwartz (2004) suggests that being seen to have lots of choice, and to be able to make many choices, seemingly independent of mere precedent, is now a signal of being successful. For Gabriel and Lang consumption is communication – 'the idea that objects form a system by which we communicate to others and ourselves' (1995: 47). Choice becomes a signifier of wide-ranging status positions through the exhibition of possessions; this tells others the very fact that you have it, that you take responsibility for using it, and that you articulate your reasons for the choices made. Consumer choice is usually highly visible even if it is not intended to be conspicuous. Political choice remains private, for many reducing its associated connotations. Gordon and Valentine (2000) also argue consumption is an identity-seeking and matching process. They posit the notion of the mutable subject, a state of being between a fixed sense of self. Brands are communication mirrors: a discourse of signifiers. Through active consumption practices we attach a collection of these signs to ourselves, creating a moment of identity, a

temporary stability for our subjectivity. Political brands are perhaps more limited by the relative stability of what they signify, and how the media represent them, and thus we find it harder to predict or recast the meanings they can communicate.

Consumer choice demonstrates an individual's worldly experience, their willingness to make judgements about (and influence) the future, and their readiness to make a decision, with the accompanying high levels of personal responsibility. Hogarth (1987) links choice closely with judgement, seeing it as the expression of preference and prediction. Consumerism's array of styles, tones and shades means our personal taste becomes an easy expression of preference. Many, well versed in being a consumer, and having a basic grasp of the user-friendly 'laws' of demand and supply, are confident in anticipating their future as consumers. Contrast this situation with the political arena, where most of the electorate struggle to articulate clear preferences, and find it perplexing to anticipate. Political choice that remains private, or at best shared fleetingly between a few others, has little ability to demonstrate one's judgement. Nor is it likely to be used as a key criterion by those judging you. As a signifier a satellite dish fixed to your house resonates in a way that marking a cross by the name of the Labour candidate once every four or five years does not.

When we choose, we often act as a result of that choice and so our choices become our privileged memory bank. Hogarth says, 'you can only observe some potential outcomes related to your initial judgement' (1987: 116). Choice shapes the experiences we have and therefore the sources we can draw on when making future decisions. Primary options selected determine the reality we encounter, which in turn influences both future, secondary, options faced and the recourse we can draw on to help make subsequent decisions. We gain much experience through consumer choice before we are faced with electoral choice. It seems logical, then, to suppose this consumerist referent system becomes dominant. The infrequency of politically oriented choice deprives many of relevant experiences to draw on, and this in turn may reduce motivation to engage in such political choice-making when it is presented.

Deciding not to make a choice is often an attempt to gain a sense of control. This plays a pivotal part in striving for equilibrium between the state of boredom and of anxiety that Csikszentmihalyi (1975) refers to as 'flow'. Some spheres of our lives may present us with opportunities to reach this state of flow more readily than others. We may for example find political choice far more likely to be either extremely boring or so complex as to cause angst. We also strive, in part through our choices, to avoid a state of cognitive dissonance where our attitudes and behaviour do not match. In the political sphere both this desire for flow and aversion to dissonance are actualised through making tactical choices. That is, opting for something in opposition to something else, but the choice is driven by a negative affective state.

Schwartz (2004) refers to the 'fallacy of variety', thinking we want it more than we do, and believing we encounter it more than we really do. This condition inevitably heightens the sense of importance attached to choosing and is readily located in consumption. For example, Gabriel and Lang find that many consumers are driven by curiosity manifest in behaviours characterised by exploration. They talk of the 'relaxed exploration' (1995: 69) offered by much present-day consumption activity, allowing people the exhilaration that goes with exploration without the accompanying apprehension. They also refer to the notion of the 'narcissism of small differences', demonstrating how insignificant alternatives are magnified by one's apparent ability to spot and decode the nuances between 'x and y'. Minor variations in the twenty-seven brands of toothpaste offered become relevant because we believe we can identify them. Expertise is thus verified through consumption choices that reflect our capacity to differentiate between very similar objects: in this example, brands. By stark contrast, in politics, there appears to be a lack of perceived variety during elections accompanied by an inability or/and a lack of motivation to identify small differences. Additionally, when we choose a particular brand of toothpaste, that is the one we get. This is plainly not so in politics for the majority of the electorate.

Choice as burden and its potential application to election contexts
The more potentiality attributed to individual choice, the more we may feel the weight of expectation. The enterprising self may help dissociate feelings of unhappiness and discontent from a systemic problem to one located in the autonomous chooser. Failure is more readily attributed to decisions made by individuals. Electoral choice fits poorly with this sense of self. Individuals who have come to accept the price of autonomous choice cannot easily equate it with a collectivist decision-making frame that is a feature of UK election outcomes. On the other hand structures of electoral choice can act to prevent feelings of blame or guilt, as the outcome cannot be determined by one's individual choice.

Schwartz's (2004) central hypothesis is that an explosion of choice has led to less, not more, satisfaction, in part because we are encouraged to adopt maximising over 'satisficing' strategies. The perfect combination is considered likely to be available, given the huge array offered, and so we get mired in our quest for flawlessness. Our satisfaction becomes more transient as ever more possibilities are envisaged. Decision making becomes more complex, opportunity costs and expectations rise, yet, at the same time, doubt emerges about our ability to cope with the intricacy of the situations we face. This propensity to seek the best in our consumer sphere has important implications for the political sphere. In commercial settings we are more likely to experience situations characterised by satisfaction, as any lingering disappointment with a purchase decision can be channelled through the return of the goods, a speedy move on to the next purchase and detailed Internet searches for an improved offering. Adopting a maximiser strategy in politics, one is likely to be prone to either fundamentalism or disappointment. In the murky, messy, compromise-ridden world of politics and election outcomes maximisers rarely find satisfaction.

The notion of the consumer as victim (Gabriel and Lang 1995), clearly reveals the vulnerability felt by many individuals faced with taking on the responsibility of making their own decisions in the dangerous terrain occupied by corporate power and its manipulative, persuasive marketing techniques. Choice for them is framed primarily as how to respond to their status as prey. Given that electoral choice is a relatively rare event, often not well understood compared with consumer choice, it is easy to see how it might be conceived as a burden, especially for those who experience similar angst in their consumer experiences. Such people may readily use this 'injured party' self-identity when engaged in elections, helping to explain why they view politics with scepticism. Putman (2000) argues that reduced political engagement is a result of widely different levels of social capital. Perhaps those who believe they have little consumer choice transfer this sense of powerlessness into politics too.

However, some react to their sense of anxiety in the market by adopting a consumer-activist stance. For them, choice in the form of 'alternative' consumption patterns may deliver the kind of value-based experiences once offered by a more vigorous form of citizenship, and so these are seen as a far more meaningful act than that of voting. They may be prime drivers of the growth in single-issue transient pressure groups and demonstrations. Consumer as rebel adopts a more individualistic challenge to the system (De Certeau 1984). They too may transfer their consumer perspective to the political arena. They set up the 'vote for none of the above parties'; they put great effort into constructing clever, engaging and satirical anti-mainstream political Web sites. For consumer activists' electoral engagement may be all about how to create meaningful choice within a system that, left alone, offers them little.

Methodology

Ontological and epistemological position

The subjects of this study construct their own meanings of choice, and they do so increasingly in a reflexive manner: what Giddens describes as 'a disturbing liberation' (2002: 87) where we constantly *have to* face metaphysical questions. The author as researcher is aware that his 'intrusion' into the subjects' lives is likely to add to this sense of reality being self-constructed as it is taking place. A consequence is that the 'stories' being told will be as much about the teller as about the participants. Furthermore, this means the reader should accept they are often engaging with second-, even third-hand reality. The position adopted means that it was appropriate to focus on individuals in their own settings, attempting to embrace and be sensitive to the participant's range of attachments to their daily lives. Construction of reality itself can lead to both renewed agency and reinforced structures passed on through cultural truths and social norms (Hughes 1990, cited in Brewer 2000). As Douglas points out, thought itself is socially constructed: 'thought style develops as the communicative genre for a social unit to itself, about itself, and so constituting itself' (1996: xii). Flowing from this, an interpretativist epistemology is embraced, the author empathising with Neuman (1994), who views social life as deliberately created out of the determined actions, thoughts and communications of interacting social beings. Thus transparency is a critical virtue in this research process. The fieldwork was located in settings that can be referred to as capturing 'lived experiences' (Hammersley and Atkinson 1995). The position taken is one that recognises humans as meaning-endowing beings; this applies equally to participants and author. Knowledge is thus perspectival (Altheide and Johnson, cited in Brewer 2000), making all that is discovered here relative to the individual's perspective.

Journey into the field: approach to data collection

A form of longitudinal study over a period of one month using self-completed diaries and a two-stage in-depth interview with each of the participants took place. Sample selection was based on eligibility to vote, potential experience of voting in a previous General Election (twenty-three years old or above), not known to the author and willingness to participate in a time-consuming research process. Clearly, the character of the participants' parliamentary constituency may have been influential but this chapter investigates such a link only if the participants themselves made reference to it. The initial discussion sought to establish mutual rapport and allow better contextualisation of the findings. More specifically, the discussions tried to draw out a sense of how the participants think and feel about, and subsequently use choice, in their everyday lives. These interviews took place in late March and early April 2005. Each participant was asked to complete a daily diary for a period of one calendar month leading up to the General Election. Completion of diaries was made easier by offering participants a specific framing question to consider. Some of the participants were given a very generic frame to consider. 'Tell us a little about the decisions you encountered/made today and what thoughts you have on those experiences.' Others were additionally given an election-specific framing question to consider. 'Tell us about any encounters you have involving the General Election. How, if at all, might they impact on your decision about voting?' This allowed the author to judge the impact of 'hothousing' the issue of the election on participants' reflections.

The final phase of the data collection involved talking to the participants directly about issues emerging from their completed diary. These interviews took place in May 2005, at least a week after the General Election. It became apparent that some of the participants had not completed diaries. Second-stage interviews were conducted but subsequently the author decided not to use any of the material from these participants. Consequently, a total of twenty face-to-face interviews and ten self-completed diaries make up the sample case studies.

From these interactions with participants, along with the diary data, the author constructed several narratives and of these a brief synopsis is presented here. Each of the discourses is an ordering attempt, not an order in itself (Brownlie and Saren 2004). The resultant texts are 'knowingly contrived' (Whyte 1981) and multivocal, offering somewhat 'messy text' (Denzin 1997). Where possible the participants have read and acknowledged their narrative.

Journey into the field: a brief context

This chapter does not seek to offer detail on the electoral system operating during the data collection. Nevertheless it is worth noting some potentially valuable contextual issues pertinent to the participants' circumstances:

1 In all four of the constituencies where participants were based the same four parties stood for election: Conservative, Labour, Liberal Democrat and UK Independence.
2 Two of these four constituencies were generally considered safe seats where the incumbent party was expected to retain the seat.

3 Two of the four constituencies were generally considered to be potentially marginal seats. There was an outside chance that the incumbent
would be defeated by a clear second-place challenger.

The participants' experiences

Inevitably, when you ask someone to offer his or her views on a subject,
that subject is likely to take a more central place than it otherwise
would. Prompting some but not other participants allowed a gauging of
the impact of the research instruments used here. It is evident that those
prompted reflected more frequently on the election. However, two of the
prompted participants wrote less about the election than some of those
participants not prompted. Additionally, all but one participant (he was
prompted) wrote more about choice/decisions relating to non-political
spheres of their lives, most often consumer-related. Reviewing all diaries
and post-completion interviews, what might be described as 'elaborate
distortions' occurred in only one instance (see Geoff's story).

Narrative from those not *prompted to write about the election*
Pam is a thirty-seven-year-old full-time housewife and part-time florist.
She did not mention the election at all in her diary. She was too busy
ensuring life for her and her family included lots of 'little treats and lux-
uries'. Lack of reference to the election was carefully rationalised by Pam
– essentially, the topic was dismissed as something outside her normal
life. 'It's not for me and I'm not for it'. A zero-sum effect was patent here:
if she let herself get involved in extra life spheres it would mean less time
and space for activities already recognised as both enjoyable and beneficial. Equilibrium was attained largely through consumption, where
Pam was able to blend pleasure and integrity. Rather than see political
choice as a weapon to sustain this position, through electing a government likely to protect her *status quo*, she viewed the political sphere as
a threat to the balance. Non-engagement in electoral choice-making was
her way of nullifying this risk.

Sue is a divorced fifty-something with no children and a passion for
gardening, who didn't mention the election in her diary either. A calm
fatalism pervades much of what Sue says about her life. 'I look for an
easy life that I can flow through undisturbed'. Sue seems relaxed that
'big choices are for other people' to make. Sue made one 'big' choice
regarding the election itself: to ignore and avoid it whenever possible.
'Once it was called I stopped watching the BBC news.' To her this is an
area of life where she perceives so little influence that she simply cannot
see the point in worrying about it Drifting characterises much of Sue's

approach to life. For her, consumer choice largely involves 'nothing more dramatic than deciding what I fancy to eat over the weekend'. Consequently, her specific interests seem all the more zealously pursued. Her garden is at the centre of nearly all she writes and talks about, so affording her purpose. Purchases are carefully planned; she devotes a lot of time to considering options and in imagining her garden post-purchase. Sue is vulnerable as a result of believing she has little self-determination. She prevents a state of victim developing by focusing on a very narrow life sphere that offers her personal scope. Engaging in political choice would reveal and bring to the fore her lack of agency, thus it is purposely set aside. Significance in this act of choosing is rationalised away.

Mary is a forty-something with four children. She referred to the election once directly and once indirectly. The direct reference was as a result of being 'accosted' on the street by a candidate and asked to consider voting for them. This clearly caused her angst because she subsequently felt obliged to broaden her range of considerations. Like Sue, she largely feels she faces 'real choices' very seldom. To her, choice and making decisions are not the same things. Choice is 'when the path splits and you don't really have a map to help'. Other people and circumstance have already made many choices for her and she now occupies that space. Shopping occupies a lot of her daily activity and she acknowledged that it could be very stimulating at times when it was of the less directive variety. The stimulation seems to come particularly from the conversation created by being in such an environment. Consumption activity matters because it affords her visible signs and elicits sharp memories that Mary found easy to associate with those people and things that mattered to her. Her sense of civic duty means she reluctantly engaged with electoral choice but was hampered by self-doubt about her judgement in this sphere. Yet her effort to connect with it resulted in experience that aided preference formation in the way Hogarth (1987) suggests.

Ray is self-employed, with a large, close family. He refers to the election on three occasions – once very early in response to an encounter on the doorstep with a candidate. The day before the election he mentions discussing with his partner who to vote for, whilst on the day of the election he says his partner reminded him that they needed to go and vote before the polling station closed. Asked about these three episodes he was rather defensive, and it is evident that he was far more confident to talk about decisions he had made where he felt self-assured in making the choices. The election was not referred to much, as it was not a topic of discussion and therefore not top of mind. By inducing 'private thoughts', politics appeared to count less and so it was considered 'not much to do with choice'. Throughout the diary and discussion there was a palpable sense of his being conscious of having to fill time carefully. Anything that could help avoid wasting time was considered positively. Politics drags on, 'It's so repetitive,' with little clear point, 'I struggle to see what it changes,' and so is an unattractive subject to fill his valuable time with. His primary choice was to maximise every minute by always being occupied. He sought to do this by maximising his variety-seeking experiences, largely realised through what can be called 'experiential consumption'. Purpose for Ray is derived from engaging in novel experiences with clear outcomes. Lack of options, inability to personalise the experience and the brevity of the event all meant political choice was unfulfilling to Ray. His act of choosing who to vote for was largely devoid of meaning to him. The sheer diversity of potential experiences, in the manner discussed by Campbell (2004), afforded through consumption, matched his desires far better.

Jo is an early twenty-something who lives alone but has a 'serious' partner. She referred to the election thirteen times, including twice on the day of the election itself. Most comments she made revolved around a premise of 'I know I have to decide who to vote for. They keep telling me, reminding me, worrying me about it all the time.' The most common response to election stimuli was annoyance because it forced her to face up to something she didn't want to face: making a decision. Life to Jo is full of situations where a strong, compelling force is evident. She simply felt she had no choice but to consider all kinds of options. Her indecision resulted in her constantly pondering, asking herself what was best for her, and reflecting on how something that had happened made her feel. Her consumer experiences generate a sense of being overwhelmed. Shopping should be fun but rarely is, and she blames the most visible sign causing her angst – persuasive advertising. Her indecisiveness is fuelled rather than alleviated by receiving new information. To her the election campaign was one long aggressive advertising campaign where her sense of duty to consider the options entailed a backdrop of growing confusion. Cultural pressure to be autonomous brings mental strife to all her life spheres, resulting in Jo constantly grappling both with making choices and with the angst this generates. Frequent stimuli presenting different options create a 'fallacy of variety' (Schwartz 2004). But her lack of skill in being able to make sense of those differences establishes a permanent state of choice as burden. Despite far fewer options her anxiety transmits to the political sphere, corroding Jo's electoral experiences. Her subsequent political choice became just another chore to face.

Narratives from those who were prompted to write about the election
Lesley is a late-thirties working mother who mentioned the election frequently in two very distinct ways. In passing comments, where such encounters were seen as trivial, the election interfered with pleasurable activity. The election was also referred to in a very specific and thoughtful manner; on these occasions Lesley dedicated time to pay close attention to it. It was quite clear that these two types of encounters were meaningfully different to her: even her handwriting reflected it (neat when she talked of the 'planned' encounters). For her the purposeful encounters included watching two Party Election Broadcasts (PEBs), reading the leaflets delivered to her house and a discussion with her husband two days before polling day. She allowed a limited amount of election stimuli to matter, ensuring that the vast majority could be discarded without guilt. This sense of duty led her to methodically allow certain moments to be dedicated to the election in order to provide her with sufficient material to fulfil her obligation.

This self-regulating behaviour was not evident in her consumer acts, for example when she discussed the organisation of a family holiday. Here what might be called casual engagement with all sorts of external stimuli was considered useful and she granted mental access to it as it arose. Lesley takes her responsibilities as both consumer and citizen seriously, recognising that this manifests itself in the decisions and choices she faces. However, clear demarcation lines are well established regarding the extent to which this responsibility is actualised in politics; these are far less apparent in consumption. Her desire to meet her civic responsibility without undue complexity coupled with the relative stability of the political offerings meant Lesley required limited stimuli to help with her political choice. However, the importance attached to the act of choosing who to vote for ensured that she took it seriously, and by keeping it distinct from consumer choice its significance was preserved.

Pete is a family man with three teenage children and a wife who doesn't work. He referred to the election on seven occasions throughout the period. Six relate to a specific salient issue: the Longbridge car plant's imminent closure. He too was threatened with redundancy whist the diary was being compiled. The Longbridge coverage and the election coverage merged into one for Pete, especially early on. To him it was 'One and the same thing . . . the real test of any government [is] how they treat their own people when the chips are down'. The coincidence of the redundancy issue being salient to Pete at this time, and of it hitting the headlines at the start of the General Election, left him extremely deflated when it became 'yesterday's news'. The treatment

Longbridge received in the media personified the distance he perceived between 'them' and 'us', and was at the root of what is 'wrong with the lot of them'. Having voted in all previous General Elections, this time he experienced a conspiracy of circumstances that alerted him to his lack of agency. His job insecurity and a family trip to New Zealand planned for 2006 dominated his other diary entries. Both suggested Pete often does not feel in control of situations, resorting to a mildly fatalistic approach on such occasions. He leaves most consumer choices to his wife, dismissing them as 'boring details'. He expresses surprise at other people's apparent ability to differentiate between most brands. Consequently, Pete faces choice quite infrequently and this may exacerbate his feelings of pain when he becomes aware of it. Insecurity regarding his agency generated fatalism in order to cope with subsequent anxiety. Specific electoral circumstances caused a heightened sense of meaning to be attributed to the outcome of the election without any corresponding increased feeling of control. The resulting frustration ultimately led to a rejection of all his political options: Pete became a non-voter but the label apathetic is far from accurate.

Geoff is in his late forties, has a long-term partner and an adopted son. There is a reference to the election on every page of his diary. He confessed to making a deliberate effort 'to ensure the diary was interesting'! Geoff happily admits to being 'the kind of person who knows what I want and I go out to get it . . . I usually do and that feels good . . . if I don't, tough – that's the world for you.' This notion of himself transfers well to his consumer sphere and the way he goes about buying. 'Yep, a bit of a wheeler-dealer Del Boy character, I know.' He wants to make decisions, wants to be proactive whenever he can and confidently pushes boundaries. What is striking is how this is not a skill he believes he can transfer to the political arena. His 'bargain hunting', 'consumer as challenger' stance cannot easily be articulated in the electoral context, where he sees little room for negotiation.

Geoff is adept at 'pigeonholing' situations he faces, depending on the likelihood of being able to use his ability to influence the situation in his favour. Once a circumstance is deemed to offer little capacity in this regard he resorts to plan B: a quick instinctive decision. Angst is confronted and certainty established by Geoff's belief in his own self-determination. Consumption offers an ideal context where he can demonstrate his skills of judgement. A maximiser approach works as motivation to take on the challenges presented. The nature of the political structures that restrict Geoff's sense of control means to engage in this sphere is to accept a role deemed to be too passive. But he cannot quite bring himself to ignore electoral choice completely; instead he commits minimal resource to his decision, so reducing the chance of dissonance in the outcome.

Rosemary is an unattached professional in her early thirties. She is unlike other participants in at least one very significant way: she was someone who 'looked forward to' and 'enjoyed' the election period! She particularly enjoyed the extended coverage and analysis: the idea of extra references to politics whilst there was an election on. Rosemary watched several of the PEBs, and 'loved' the *Channel 4 News* spoof PEBs too. She recorded her favourite programmes and even postponed a few social occasions in order to watch what she considered to be highlights like the Paxman interviews. Rosemary is conscious of her mild outsider status when it comes to politics: 'Some of my friends must think it's a bit sad, but that's me and they know it'. Her attitude to politics reinforces her sense of individuality and is used to demonstrate her opinions. The election was not about helping her make a choice but about her expressing her prior knowledge and well formed political views before a wider audience.

The superficiality of much of the consumption that dominates many of her friends' lives could temporarily be superseded by her without too much bother. Her own consumption patterns fits her world view well: 'I try to make ethical purchases and I definitely refuse to use Asda . . . cheap is for good reason: they pay the lowest wage to their workers and suppliers and so on.' Her linking of consumer choice and broader political issues was also unique among the participants in this study. Making such a link heightened her sense of being in control. Experiencing individuality in a political sphere adds to her own sense of uniqueness. The choosing of a candidate was peripheral to her – indeed, given her strongly held opinions, was not considered a choice at all. The election allowed the judgements she made to be much more visible and, in a way that resonates with Miller's work (1995, 1998), she managed to sustain such judgements, albeit with far less visibility, through making politically motivated consumption choices.

Emergent themes

The participants generally considered politics to be a circumspect external object. Commonly it was referred to as something that was done *to* them that infringed on normal life. Electoral encounters were overwhelmingly framed as an interference, imposing on their lives. Not surprisingly during an election period, where the extent of persuasive stimuli is greatest, the choices these stimuli posed generated feelings of irritation and annoyance, rarely pleasure. The characteristics of participants' engagement ranged from treating it as a challenge to be overcome through to purposeful avoidance. To most the nature of the electoral choice they faced nagged away in the background. The tension this generated was alleviated by avoidance tactics. Valid political options were considered to be very limited, many of the participants' nominal consideration was to vote or not, then whether to vote for one party or another. However, the narrow range of the options did not signify that such choice was considered to be simplistic. The meaning attributed both to how participants decided and to the eventual outcome of this decision were highly personalised. Elements of an expressive approach were witnessed, as were situations where a primary choice was made not to engage in political choice. For some, an intensification of agency, for others, a sense of powerlessness was exacerbated with electoral choice.

Whether participants perceived themselves in terms of being helpless or sovereign was something largely determined before the election campaign began. Occasionally, electoral encounters contributed to a heightened sense of having choice (Mary and Lesley). An experience characterised by 'gain through pain' was evident; electoral encounters were hard work but contributed to improved levels of self-confidence in making a decision. Equally, for some participants (Ray and Sue) election encounters added to their sense of having no real choice. Where little prospect of influence was apparent, the effort required to choose was not considered worth while. Individualised strategies for coping when faced with electoral choice were extensive. These included: ensconcing oneself in a single salient issue; allocating set times to engage in such considerations; being decisive early on in order to avoid further need to think about the choices faced; and using it as a platform to demonstrate the ability to make independent judgements. Participants developed unique coping mechanisms permitting politics into their lives only on their terms.

Exercising choice in consumption performed a compensatory role, allowing the individual to justify whatever specific strategy they employed with regard to electoral choice. Reflecting on consumer decisions, participants were adept at articulating clear, rich purpose. Most participants talked of the diversity of consumer choice creating satisfaction. Within this sphere a blend of enjoyment and utility could be achieved. It was referred to by several participants as the ability to engage in activity that made them feel not only pleased but also good about themselves. By augmenting variety and experimentation, boredom was easily avoided. Consumer activity stimulated conversation and thinking in a way highly congruent with Douglas and Isherwood's work (1986), as the topic of conversation was focused on things the participants cared about, not on the products *per se*. The sheer number of options they faced pained some participants, and this feeling was exacerbated by the number of persuasive external stimuli they encountered. For a few participants their cautious approach to marketing communication activity was transferred into open hostility to much of the election campaign material. An acute awareness of having potential as choice-making beings prevailed in consumption and was manifest in diverse ways. At one extremity, participants placed great emphasis on their being able knowingly to choose, looking for opportunities to test and challenge themselves through such actions. Others purposely limited the scope of their own choice with ease, showing indifference to much beyond these self-imposed boundaries. At the other extremity, participants consciously carried with them what might be called mildly fatalistic tendencies. Those occupying the outermost positions, fatalists and confident self-determinists, tended to take a consumer choice approach to interaction with the political sphere. For the other participants two dominant practices were apparent. Engaging in consumer choice helped them dismiss any angst that they felt over their political choice. They did not carry their well developed consumer-as-choice-maker approach into the political sphere, largely because of the perceived constraints imposed by various political structures.

Conclusion

This chapter introduced a range of consumer-related discourses and potential meanings attributable to choice. However the overall findings acknowledge a point highlighted by Edwards (2000), namely that actual practice is likely to be simpler and more static than the plethora of related theories might indicate. The diversity found was largely between the various participants, not from individual participants. From this glimpse into the lives of a small, diverse group of the electorate we can learn about electoral choice through privileging the electorate as a consumerist choice-maker. First, compartmentalisation of their life is rife, appearing to be second nature: events and experiences are readily allotted specific mental spaces. Consumer choice and political choice rarely occupy the same space. Second, most have a well developed ability to avoid choice situations deemed likely to cause anxiety or 'unnecessary hassle'. At its most severe this is manifest in a form of 'fatalism on tap': available when deemed appropriate. Combined, these first two points indicate a degree of what Coleman (2005) calls reflexive remixing of culture taking place. Because the political sphere is objectified, whilst the consumer sphere merges into their subjectivity, there is far less scope to recast politics. Inability to personalise experience in this life sphere means it is less appealing to our sense of agency and is easily cast as peripheral. Fourth, much talk and thought about intended action leads to no deed actually taking place. This was especially apparent in a political sphere characterised as unfamiliar, distant, without immediate consequence and seen as hard to participate in. As one participant commented, our preference for a certain colour of curtains is easily actualised whereas, for example, our opinions on Iraq are far harder to actualise. Fifth, because the attachment of importance to something is largely an individual process, a sense of agency is readily and widely realised. Lots of small choices, typically located in consumption, add up to meaningful self-determination when it occurs in a life sphere regarded as essential. Finally there was little evidence that participants recognised any direct causal relationship between the outcome of electoral choice and their consumer life sphere. This goes some way to explaining why political choice was framed as an imposing burden. It also illustrates that for many there was little sense of valid attachment to any electoral choice they went on to make.

Consumer culture, and with it a sharp sense of being free agents, shapes the character of our citizens in a fairly subtle way. Value, worth, scope and ethicality are comfortably constructed and experienced in many of our consumer engagements. On balance most of the participants are, in effect, saying that the price of being independent, bouts of anxiety, is worth paying because of what they gain from choice in consumption. For that reason the political sphere can be, and often is, seen as rather insignificant. This is not a demonstration of the electorate's superficiality and shallowness, more an expression of their ability to engage a plethora of life-affirming choice in their consumer sphere. The nature of political choice is frequently regarded as burdensome. That said, the electoral encounters commented on by the participants made an impact of sorts. They were noticed, they did generate deliberation, and sometimes they were considered poignant. Occasionally such encounters jolted participants into facing electoral choice in a new way. They helped increase the self-confidence of a few participants in terms of their ability to choose more wisely. For another participant such encounters offered assistance in fulfilling their sense of duty. Regardless of whether such election encounters resulted in behavioural change, at the very least they temporarily afforded greater significance to the existence of political choice and to some extent framed that choice in a different way from the dominant consumption mode.

References

Brewer, J. (2000), *Ethnography*, Buckingham: Open University Press.

Bromley, C. and Curtice, J. (2002), 'Where have all the voters gone?' in A. Park, S. Jones, L. Jarvis and K. Thomson, (eds), *British Social Attitudes: The Nineteenth Report*, London: Sage.

Brownlie, D. and Saren, M. (2004), 'The Limits of Language: Marketing Praxis and Discourse beyond Words', paper presented to the Academy of Marketing conference, Gloucestershire University, July.

Campbell, C. (1987), *The Romantic Ethic and the Spirit of Modern Consumerism*, Oxford: Blackwell.

Campbell, C. (2004), 'I shop, therefore I know that I am: the metaphysical basis of modern consumption', in K. Ekstrom and H. Brembeck (eds), *Elusive Consumption*, Oxford: Berg.

Coleman, S. (2005), *Remixing Citizenship: Democracy and Young People's Use of the Internet*, Dunfermline: Carnegie UK Trust.

Comaroff, J. and Comaroff, J. L. (2000), 'Millennium capitalism and the culture of neoliberalism', *Public Culture* 12 (2): 291–343.

Corner, J. and Pels, D. (2003), *Media and the Restyling of Politics*, London: Sage.

Csikszentmihalyi, M. (1975), *Beyond Boredom and Anxiety*, San Francisco: Jossey-Bass.

De Certeau, M. (1984), *The Practice of Everyday Life*, Berkeley CA: University of California Press.

Denzin, N. (1997), *Interpretive Ethnography: Ethnographic Practice for the Twenty-first Century*, Thousand Oaks CA: Sage.

Dermody, J. and Scullion, R. (2005) 'Young people's attitudes towards British political advertising: nurturing or impeding voter engagement?' *Journal of Nonprofit and Public Sector Marketing* 14(1–2): 129–50.

Douglas, M. (1996), *Thought Styles*, London: Sage.

Douglas, M. (2003), 'The consumers' revolt', in D. Clarke, A. Marcus and K. Housiaux (eds), *The Consumption Reader*, London: Routledge.

Douglas, M. and Isherwood, B. (1986), *The World of Goods: Towards the Anthropology of Consumption*, London: Routledge.

Edwards, T. (2000), *Contradictions of Consumption: Concepts, Practices and Politics in Consumer Society*, Buckingham: Open University Press.

Firat, A. and Dholakia, N. (1998), *Consuming People: From Political Economy to Theatres of Consumption*, London: Routledge.

Gabriel, Y. and Lang, T. (1995), *The Unmanageable Consumer*, London: Sage.

Gardiner, P. (2002), *Kierkegaard: A Very Short Introduction*, Oxford: Oxford University Press.

Giddens, A. (2002), 'Living in post-traditional society', in U. Beck, A. Giddens and S. Lash, *Reflexive Modernisation*, Cambridge: Polity Press.

Gordon, W. and Valentine, V. (2000), 'The twenty-first-century consumer: a new model of thinking', *International Journal of Market Research*, spring–summer, pp. 185–206.

Hammersley, M. and Atkinson, P. (1995), *Ethnography: Principles in Practice*, London: Routledge.

Harrop, M. (2001), 'An apathetic landslide: the British election of 2001', *Government and Opposition* 26 (1): 206–15.

Hogarth, R. (1987), *Judgement and Choice*, Chichester: Wiley.

Messerley, J. (1995), *An Introduction to Ethical Theories*, Baltimore MD: University of Maryland.

Miller, D. (1995), *Acknowledging Consumption*, London: Routledge.

Miller, D. (1998), *A Theory of Shopping*, Ithaca NY: Cornell University Press.

Neuman, W. (1994), *Social Research Methods: Qualitative and Quantitative Approaches*, Boston MA: Allyn & Bacon.

Putnam, R. (2000), *Bowling Alone*, New York: Simon & Schuster.

Rose, N. (1993), 'Government, authority and expertise in advanced liberalism', *Economy and Society* 22 (3): 265–6.

Roubiezek, P. (1964), *Existentialism: For and Against*, Cambridge: Cambridge University Press.

Scammell, M. (1995), *Designer Politics*, Basingstoke, Macmillan.

Schwartz, B. (2004), *The Paradox of Choice*, London: Harper Collins.

Sen, S., Gurhan-Canli, Z. and Morwitz, V. (2001), 'Withholding consumption: a social dilemma perspective on consumer boycotts', *Journal of Consumer Research* 28: 399–417.

Sullivan, R. (1995), *An Introduction to Kant's Ethics*, Cambridge: Cambridge University Press.

Watts, M. (2003), *Kierkegaard*, Oxford: Oneworld.

Whyte, W. (1981), *Street corner society; the social structure of an Italian slum*, Chicago: University of Chicago Press.

9

Local political marketing: political marketing as public service

Darren G. Lilleker

For many members of the UK's electorate an election campaign is nothing more than a spectator sport which takes place in faraway corners of the UK and that is out of touch with their daily lives. Not so for those voters who reside in the key marginal seats: victory there can often determine which party forms a government. In 2005 the local dimension was seen to be more important than usual. Parties fought a sustained 'ground' war alongside the traditional, mass-media 'air' war, using both nationally devised and disseminated communication as well as localised campaigning by those who sought to be elected as constituency representatives. This increased importance is informed by arguments which suggest that the centralisation of campaigning has led to the disengagement and recent drop in turnout in the UK (Lilleker 2005a), as well as being a response to party strategists' recognition that voters need to be communicated to as individuals. Thus an attempt was made to create an integrated campaign on two levels: the national, or macro, and the local, or micro.

The role of the national campaign is to set out the key promises of each of the parties, it tends to be leader-focused and relies largely on mass media attention. In contrast the local campaign focuses on making the party promises and messages relevant to actual voters, on the doorstep as well as in personalised literature from the candidate; the local media play a secondary role. Due to the propensity for interpersonal communication, local campaigning offers greater opportunities for political marketing in terms of building strong relationships between candidates and their parties and the electorate. However, in this arena marketing has to be more than the slick salesmanship and spin associated with political communication in recent years. If politics is to be made relevant, then voters need to recognise the importance of politics in Westminster and see changes in their own lives and environment that result from government policy. Equally, within an increasingly consumerist society, voters will ask potential representatives and

governments, 'What will you do for me?' or, taking an overtly consumerist perspective, 'Why should I bother making a choice?' (see
Scullion, Chapter 8 above).

News coverage often reduced the contest to a straight fight between
the party leaders, Blair, Howard and Kennedy, a contest into which
the electorate as individuals had very little input. However, in each
of the 646 constituencies in the UK, once the 2005 election was
called, candidates had to fight for the support of local voters and, the-
oretically, it is their success or failure locally that then determines the
national election result. What is unclear is how these two campaigns,
the national or macro-campaign and the local micro-campaign, con-
verge within the minds of voters. Are they seen as integrated, an
extension of one another, and so local candidates are simply perceived
as the local representative of their party, just as the local branch of
Dixon's or W. H. Smith is a representative of a larger company, or is
there some level of separation? In other words, can a candidate earn
a personal vote, based on their campaigning, or work as incumbent,
which will then outweigh negative feelings towards the party they
represent?

Getting inside the voters' minds as they stand in the voting booth
selecting whose name should earn their vote is impossible, to a large
extent; this chapter, however, investigates the influence of local political activities on voting attitudes. The first section outlines local
political marketing strategy and then this model is applied to three
marginal constituency contests. Following this analysis, the chapter
then assesses the effectiveness of the micro-campaign. The overall aim
is to set out and test the effectiveness of a model for political marketing at the constituency level as well as to test the extent to which it is
possible to disentangle the complexities of voting behaviour. At the
core of this aim is an assessment of whether voters do actually vote for
candidates or whether elections are simply referenda on the performance of Prime Ministers and the potential offered by the alternatives,
and whether party loyalty overrides the service element of the role of
an elected representative. This study employs marginal constituencies
as the focus, as it is expected that an MP with a low majority in their
constituency will provide a better, and higher-profile, level of service
(Lilleker and Negrine 2003; Jackson and Lilleker 2004), while in turn
their opponents will have greater resources at their disposal, thus
making for a high-energy campaign that should mobilise supporters
and persuade undecided voters (Denver and Hands *et al.* 2001).

Should micro-campaigning work?

The extent to which the local dimension of an election campaign has any form of effect has been long debated. The classic position, as put forward by Butler's 1951 Nuffield study, was that an incumbent was worth no more than around 500 votes; add that to the loyalists within a constituency and that was all the votes that could be counted on, a position reiterated by Ivor Crewe's analysis of the 1992 General Election and the 1987, 1992 and 1997 Nuffield studies (for a review see Pattie and Johnston 2003: 384). The received wisdom is that it was the national campaign, and perceptions of the performance of government, that were the key influential factors, as television enables voters to have greater access to the party leaders, and it is the reportage and attendant commentary that 'swamp any local endeavours' (Butler and Kavanagh 1997: 210) to persuade voters of the efficacy of any particular candidate or party. Such a notion is encapsulated in the US-election edict 'It's the economy, stupid', that it is the relative strength or weakness of the economy and future perceptions of competent management that are the key factors voters consider; and the observation that it is governments that lose elections, not opponents who win them, or individual candidates who make a difference. In the UK there has been some deviation from that. While the Thatcher victory in 1979 seems to have been the result of the perceived mismanagement of the economy by Callaghan's Labour government, Blair's 1997 landslide was more the result of universal mistrust of Major's Conservatives. While it is proven that Major's popularity dipped and failed to recover after the economic collapse following Black Wednesday (Lilleker 2005a), other factors were argued to be at work. The allegations of sleaze levelled at many senior Conservatives, the youthful vigour of Labour's front bench and the feeling that 1997 was 'time for a change' all have been argued to have played a part. However, none of these elements indicates that the local, micro-level elements of a campaign had any real effect.

What are often ignored in psephological studies are the 'odd' results. It is often the case that some seats fall independent of national swings or manage to buck all trends, making polls and pollsters seem to be no better informed than tealeaf readers. The national swings may follow a long-term trend, and can react to events within a campaign; however, there are also locally specific results that can be explained by nothing more than locally specific events. This indicates that it is not simply the national campaign, perceptions of leaders and their parties, or the predictions for economic stability, that are the sole drivers of voting behaviour; alongside personal partisan attachment, which still exists across the nation, there are other factors worthy of exploration. Thus we find constituency campaigning enjoying increased interest among election analysts and party strategists as elections see a series of fragmented swings, often dependent on local contextual factors, which are often disguised by reports of the national swing. Within the marginal, or party's target, seats campaigning is more intense, voters are encouraged to vote tactically for their second choice, or the 'best of a bad bunch' (see Lloyd, Chapter 2 of this volume), allowing a degree of predictability; however, as MORI research found in marginal seats, the results were far less predictable than could be expected (Baines and Mortimore 2005). This is due to the undecided voters, or swingers, within these constituencies, who are likely to vote but are seeking cues for guidance throughout the campaign – sometimes right up to the point of entering the voting booth.

While studies of local election campaigning enjoyed something of a heyday during the 1950s, such studies were largely qualitative and aimed at understanding the process. These studies observed a highly efficient machine designed to 'get out the vote' (Bealey *et al.* 1965: 29–31; Denver and Hands 2001: 74). However, things have moved on significantly, societal changes have led to an increase in the number of floating voters and greater fluidity in voting behaviour; equally, technology means that parties have far greater means at their disposal for reaching voters and building an integrated campaign with a local and national dimension. It is argued that the targeting of these resources has a significant impact on election results: what was once seen as the exclusive preserve of the Liberal Democrats' by-election machine is now a common feature of the campaigning of most of the parties. The strategy is to identify constituencies which could be persuaded to vote for the party's candidate, and then concentrate all available resources at the swingable voters within that constituency in order to win their sympathy and their vote. This strategy is seen to have been highly effective for the Liberal Democrats, and studies of the 1997 and 2001 General Elections also found a high degree of synergy between levels of campaign spending, the energy put into a campaign and, *ceteris paribus*, gaining a favourable result.

The groundbreaking research of David Denver and Gordon Hands (1997, 2001) found a clear link between the strength of campaigning, or the intensity of the campaign, as indicated from questionnaires to campaign agents, and an increase in the share of votes by parties. There are discrepancies in the results, most likely to be the result of national factors, given that the data were based upon the 1997 General Election and the context of the Labour landslide and collapse of the Conservative vote. However, data from the 2001 General Election, where the result was a foregone conclusion and there was a national sense of *ennui*, appear clearer. The key findings were that the Conservative campaigns were able to mobilise supporters, while intensive campaigns conducted by Labour and the Liberal Democrats had a significant effect on the support for the other party when weighted for the 1997 result, incumbency and regional differences. The data also suggest that one reason for the Conservatives failing to make an impact was the low number of intensive campaigns across the constituencies (Denver *et al.* 2001).

The major criticism of such research, as Pattie and Johnston point out, is that 'they are not able to demonstrate whether the constituency campaign has any influence on individual voters' (2003: 385). Pattie and Johnston's data, derived from calculations of campaign spend and voter responses to the British Election Survey on recall of the campaign, indicated that challengers were most likely to benefit from targeting resources but that all parties could have some effect upon both turnout among their voter segments and persuading voters to support them – particularly among the undecided, floating voters. These findings are corroborated further (Denver *et al.* 2003; Johnston and Pattie 2003), yet the measures rely on there being a link between voter exposure to campaign communications and their choice to vote and over the choice of candidate. The data show that there are also national factors at play, such as Conservative campaigns having a positive effect on Labour support and the issue of tactical voting between Labour and Liberal Democrat supporters; furthermore there are instances of inconsistency between campaigns, meaning that misallocation of resources could see high spend but a negative effect. Within the studies it is almost impossible to weight for all of these factors, as one cannot know the extent to which each factor was influential at the point of marking the cross on the ballot paper.

A further concern is that, within the marginal constituencies, it would be expected that there is little disparity in terms of the intensity. Parties with a narrow majority will endeavour to prioritise their national mailings and phone-bank calling in these constituencies, as will parties that feel they have a good chance of stealing the seat. Equally the candidates and their parties will be encouraged to work harder, resources will be placed at their disposal and personnel are often drafted in from neighbouring safe constituencies as well as from central office. Thus what may be missed from previous research is not the extent to which the local campaign is effective, but that certain elements may be more effective than others. These may be the tactics employed by one party and not by their opponents, or messages that are constructed better or disseminated in ways that appeal to the local electorate. Straight measures will not detect these factors. Equally, the extent to which the incumbent is important is difficult to quantify. Though research suggests that a hard-working constituency MP can earn a personal vote (Cain *et al*. 1987), it does not mean that they necessarily campaign much harder to gain this, but that they adopt a service marketing approach over the full course of their tenure.

Therefore, while it appears that many measures indicate that there is a local campaign effect, it remains difficult to know exactly what component of that campaign was successful, how it reinforced or mediated against national campaign influences and thus what factors coalesce in the minds of the voters when they make their electoral choice. Thus it is perhaps simpler to argue that there remains a great deal of uncertainty as to how voters process the campaigns and which factors are influential when they enter the polling booth.

Micro-level political marketing strategies

Little existing literature on local constituency campaigning focuses on issues such as relationship building and permanent campaigning (for exceptions see Jackson 2003; Jackson and Lilleker 2004); the key variables are usually perceived to be the strength of campaigning, the intensity of leafleting and canvassing, the venerable art of getting the loyal supporters out, what is referred to as 'knocking up', and the use of technology to identify and reach the floating voters. However, such behaviour is little more than viral salesmanship, particularly if it is concentrated solely on the six-week period of the campaign, once every four or five years, and is not built upon a foundation of long-term interaction and service delivery. Given that such activities have limited success in the marketing of fast-moving consumer goods or major service providers, and in fact are often discredited as an interpersonal communication tool for being more of an annoyance than a mode of reaching consumers (Westmyer *et al*.1998), why should these activities be successful for a political campaign? In the sphere of commercial service provision direct mail is useful for building an 'incremental perception', as is other advertising and public relations activity (Fam and Merrilees 2001: 9); thus it can be posited that a range of activities must be conducted in order to gain what political scientists refer to as the 'incumbency factor' (Krasno 1994) or to appear as a representative who could earn a high level of personal support (Cain *et al*. 1987). It is therefore appropriate to look beyond and behind the campaign in order to assess how political marketing can inform the micro-level of political activity.

The role of a constituency MP is similar to that of a service provider who is engaged in simultaneously providing support for existing customers while ensuring that new customers are garnered (Butler and Collins 2001). They can be likened to the old-fashioned insurance agent, the Man from the Pru[dential], who as part of the community will know all of their customers and so can offer a human interface between the individual and the larger organisation. While within the insurance business such activities have largely been replaced by twenty-four-hour call centres, the MP remains a key figure within a constituency, expected to take up casework on behalf of those they represent. Casework can consist of campaigns which benefit an area, attracting industry or leading campaigns for improving the infrastructure, or those that focus on individuals, helping with benefit claims, supporting applications for disabled access to private properties or whatever is brought to the surgery. Such activities are argued to be a priority for MPs that have increased exponentially over recent years (Rush 2001) and they argue that such activities have some impact, though it remains difficult to quantify the effect (Negrine and Lilleker 2003).

The provision of such services often occurs beneath the media or public opinion radar: a strongly service-oriented MP may find the majority of constituents still argue they have little contact with their representative, thus publicity is important in terms of ensuring that the constituency are aware of the dedication to duty. Many MPs now use periodic mailings to advertise their campaigns, often using a moniker such as 'The MP reports back': Liberal Democrats have long produced *Focus*, for Labour *The Rose* is a key aspect of their permanent campaigning, while Conservatives use an annual publication, *Westminster Reports*. These newsletters' function is to communicate to the broader constituency, informing the electorate that the MP is active and working hard as a representative.

Election communication should largely reinforce this image, both for incumbents and for challengers who have been active in local politics. Often the latter serve on the local council to establish a base of support. It provides a combination of national political messages and local examples that are blended to promote both the candidate and the party (Nimmo 1999). However, the important aspect of the communication is to reinforce the role of the MP as a 'customer advocate' (Butler and Collins 2001: 1032), building on permanent campaigning activities and turning these into a set of pledges to their potential electorate; thus there is a natural disadvantage faced by challengers. To a greater extent than the national parties, it is the candidates who 'dispatch promises, favours, policy preferences and personalities to a set of voters in exchange for their votes, voluntary efforts, or contributions' (Kotler and Kotler 1999: 6). It is this service, or indeed the potential for this service, that is argued to be of value to 'a critical mass of constituents' (Butler and Collins 2001: 1035). Clearly this factor could act as a tangible element that can be used to differentiate candidates in an era when parties appear to offer little but an alternative management team. Currently there is little evidence from research among voters, yet it appears that the potential for earning a personal vote has motivated many MPs to engage in service provision (Butler and Collins 2001; Rush 2001; Lilleker and Negrine 2003; Negrine and Lilleker, 2003; Jackson and Lilleker, 2004).

The potential for effective representation, or service, can also be a strength promoted in the election communication of challengers in constituencies. Where an MP is less than active in either service provision or ongoing communication, a locally active challenger, possibly a councillor, can undermine the position of an MP among constituents who are dissatisfied with the perceived 'lack of representation' (Lilleker and Negrine 2003). This was reflected in discussions of future strategies by representatives of all three major parties in the lead-up to the 2005 General Election. Speaking at the Elections and Opinion Polls Specialist Group Conference in September 2004 and the Political Marketing Conference, February 2005, Labour strategist Greg Cook and Dominic Schofield, former Conservative Head of Policy and PPC for Battersea, argued the importance of enhancing the constituency service function. As one candidate reflected after their 2001 defeat, 'I think we've all got to be Liberal Democrats these days' (Lilleker and Negrine 2003: 70), highlighting the requirement to emulate both the target seat strategy but also the way in which candidates market themselves to the local electorate.

The existing evidence of the effectiveness of the micro-campaign and the literature on local political marketing strategies can be combined to produce a model for activity. In the later stages of a government, possibly two years prior to a General Election, candidates will be in place and building up a profile as an effective, or potentially effective, local representative. This will entail taking on a variety of bits of casework and getting behind any number of local campaigns; there may well be a synergy to party policies, such as Liberal Democrat candidates taking part in anti-student-fees demonstrations, but the activities could also be apolitical and primarily emphasise the service aspect of representation. The election campaign will then highlight past achievements, enforce the image of the candidate as an effective local representative and promote them as a product in themselves. The extent to which the product is part of the national campaign can depend upon a range of factors, usually surrounding the image of the party nationally and locally, but also related to specific political issues prevalent in the constituency as well as individually perceived candidate-related factors: style, ability, localness, values and judgement. The effort or energy aspect of the campaign will be important in getting the message across. Volunteers deliver the periodicals and leaflets and can highlight the work of MPs or candidates on the doorstep, so spend and effort remain crucial. As a result, we can argue, there are two important factors that should determine the result in a constituency if service provision is a key element in voter decision making. First, the permanent activities and related communication, second, the ability to get the message across effectively within the campaign period. At this stage, however, this is simply a model and it does not treat national factors as important. To test the hypothesis underpinning this model, this chapter will assess how voters process the information they receive and measure what effect the campaign communication has that simply reinforces party messages or that sells the candidate and their service provision role.

The local marketing strategies: a case study of three marginals

The data here are drawn from observation research into the campaigns of the three major political parties and that of their opponents in three marginal seats in the county of Dorset, on the south coast. The data gained through observation are supported by interviews with each of the candidates and/or party strategists in each constituency. This section will introduce the constituencies briefly, discuss the party strategies, and account for the similarities and differences between the campaigns in each constituency. (For broader contextual analysis see Lilleker 2005b.)

Dorset Mid and Poole North

This Liberal Democrat constituency, held by Annette Brooke after defeating the Conservative Christopher Fraser in 2001, has both an awkward name and a complex geography. The main hub is the northern sections of Poole's urban conurbation and contains a number of residential suburbs ranging from predominantly social housing in Alderney to the comparatively affluent Canford Magna and Broadstone. However, it also has a substantial rural reach which covers Bere Regis, Wareham and St Martin; it is therefore necessary for an MP with a 384 majority to balance a range of concerns that unite the constituency rather than focusing on one or more key areas.

Brooke is perhaps well placed to achieve this. A local activist, former mayor and school governor, she is perhaps as local as one can get, a point stressed in much of her literature. A highly active and visible MP, it is clear that she follows the local political marketing model well, a factor which is prominent in the election literature. While the traditional message that the contest is a 'two-horse race' enforces the fact that Labour cannot win, having historically polled less than 7,000 votes, literature places Brooke centre-ground as the product. The final edition of *Focus* highlights 'Her achievements are many and she has worked tirelessly to put our area and constituents first . . . Annette cares passionately about our community.' The focus is then upon policy issues, messages adapted from the Liberal Democrat manifesto and reprioritised to be relevant to the local community. Top of her personal manifesto is to be 'tough on crime', rather than leading with tax reforms or the scrapping of student fees, which were prioritised in seats where these messages would have higher salience, though local tax was also promoted among the older voters. The bottom line for the campaign is that Brooke is part of 'our' community, enforcing the notion that party and community are synonymous, and thus Brooke ultimately is positioned as 'the best person for the job' of representative. This highlights a trend in Liberal Democrat politics of being locally focused and having MPs who take the constituency service role extremely seriously. It is interesting that while they appeared in 2001 nationally as the least market-oriented (Lees-Marshment and Lilleker 2005: 19), they appear to have a clearer sense of what the local market requires.

The Conservative challenger, Simon Hayes, from the neighbouring county of Hampshire, relied largely on undermining the Liberal Democrats on the basis of their tax policies. After several failed attempts to steal the limelight, and having failed to establish himself as a local person, owing to Brooke's strong local roots, this seemed most likely to appeal to voters with a propensity to support the Conservatives. Given that residents of the more affluent areas might well have found themselves far worse off had Kennedy become Prime Minister on 6 May, this could well have had resonance among the voters, though it was highly unlikely that the Liberal Democrats would be power brokers in Parliament, never mind forming a government. Thus a problem with this strategy is that the Liberal Democrats are protected from such attacks by their distance from power. The message arguably lacked real credibility, as most voters who re-elected Brooke with an increased majority probably were aware that the only real effect was to ensure the Conservatives had one seat less and, perhaps, Blair retained the premiership for a further term. Without beginning to discuss constituents' attitudes, it appears from the result that Hayes's campaign had little effect. Both he and the inactive and largely absent Labour candidate saw their share of the vote reduced as turnout increased and Brooke was returned with a 5,482 majority. It is this evidence of the success of a local political marketing strategy?

Dorset South

If the answer to the above question is in the affirmative, then this should also be the case in Dorset South, where Jim Knight, Labour MP with a majority of 153 votes, was able to win independent of the national swing from Labour to the Conservatives. The constituency centres on the seaside resorts of Weymouth and Swanage but includes much of the rural green belt that is the Purbecks. While Weymouth contains a contrasting range of demographics much of the area is affluent; however, the main populations centres, Weymouth and Swanage, contain a substantial level of Labour voters which allowed Labour to target the seat in 1997 and 2001, finally winning in 2001 after missing out by seventy-seven votes in 1997.

While Labour since 1997 have been described as the most market-oriented (Lees-Marshment 2001), locally they seem to have had less of a sense of what the local electorate want (Lilleker and Negrine 2006). While this may still be true in many constituencies, former Yellow Pages salesman Jim Knight argued his campaign was just what the Dorset South voters would respond to. Knight's campaign was a combination of the highly professional and technocratic and the traditional. DVDs were produced, call centres worked overtime in targeting voters, but poster wars, meetings, leaflet delivery and canvassing remained the mainstay of the strategy. Central to the campaign message was the candidate himself, as Jim Knight admitted: 'We are trying to sell the product, which is essentially myself' (interview, 17 April 2005). The DVD enforced the image of a man with communitarian Labourist values, but highlighted his priorities for the region: more affordable housing, road safety and investment in education. These reinforced national messages but the DVD ends with a more personalised approach that is indicative of a local political marketing strategy. The close of the three-minute film centring on Knight asks constituents to get in touch. This constituency service role is highlighted on the final leaflet delivered, which records that 'Jim has delivered for local people', having dealt with 5,953 individual pieces of casework. While the decision to go negative was agonised over, his record was contrasted with the potential offered by his challenger, *Sunday Times* (17 April 2005) 'Twit of the Week' Conservative Ed Matts.

Matts's campaign attempted to undermine Knight on local issues; however, it was, as Knight mentioned in his victory speech, a campaign that was 'accident-prone'. Matts won prime-time news coverage after doctoring photographs of himself and fellow Conservative Anne Widdecombe campaigning on behalf of the Kachepas, a family of asylum seekers in Weymouth. The new message, 'Controlled immigration' instead of 'Let them stay', led to calls for his resignation a week into the campaign and is an example of a local campaign intended to reinforce national messages that actually damaged his own and possibly the party's image. Furthermore, the use of photos of Matts with a Labour-supporting Olympic medallist and his claim that Knight would support the closure of a middle school he was actually campaigning to keep open led to further criticism locally. While some claim all publicity is good, in Matts's case it seems to be false. Whether the visits of high-profile party luminaries such as John Reid, Patricia Hewitt and Margaret Hodge helped Knight or not is debatable; similarly was Blair launching the election campaign on Weymouth beach a positive? In the end, however, Knight increased his vote despite a slight decrease in percentage share, Matts's vote was cut, with the Liberal Democrats and a range of small party candidates gaining. Interestingly, the Respect candidate made little impact. There are questions raised by this campaign. Was it Knight's hard work and positive messages that enabled him to beat off anti-Labour sentiment post-Iraq and defy the polls, or was it the case that Matts's campaign was actually the factor that swung it? Knight claimed it was a tribute to the South Dorset Labour Party. However, research did suggest there was a reasonably strong 'Matts effect' that may weaken assumptions regarding the power of the local marketing strategy. This is because Matts was able to shore up Labour support, generating a vote against himself as opposed to a positive vote for Knight, yet the choice made suggests that Knight's image was an influential factor.

Dorset West

Despite its fame as the home of the proto-socialists the Tolpuddle Martyrs, Dorset West is historically a Conservative stronghold. The main town of Dorchester is the most demographically varied, the surrounding area is largely rural and affluent, perhaps the only exception being parts of the other large town: Bridport. The Conservatives' majority has narrowed since Oliver Letwin took over the seat in 1997, the Liberal Democrats have increased support in the area and Dorset West was target No. 12 as part of the strategy of decapitation of the Conservative Party by defeating key members of the party's Shadow Cabinet. The strategy failed, in all cases. The Liberal Democrats were, however, perceived by some sections of the Conservatives as a major threat in many constituencies.

It is for this reason that the Conservatives targeted negative messages towards voters who were less than loyal Conservatives and might have considered the Liberal Democrats as a viable alternative. In seats like Dorset West it is possible that the Liberal Democrat tax policies were unattractive to many, a factor that was exploited vociferously by Conservatives. The success of a raft of literature, as indicated on the doorstep, led to a sense of palpable confidence among the Letwin team a good seven days prior to the election. However, the leaflets also promoted a positive message regarding Letwin as a local representative. Under the caption 'Getting things done for West Dorset' were listed five achievements and seven promises for the future. However, this message was not communicated across the constituency effectively, and resonated only among those voters who had met him personally in the areas where the campaign was strongest, the rural areas, but not within the Liberal Democrat stronghold of Dorchester town centre. One reason may have been that Conservative campaign communication also always placed the 'Are you thinking what we're thinking?' messages centre stage, so focusing on cleaner hospitals and lower taxation, perhaps salient but not always following what would be expected of a local political marketing strategy.

Liberal Democrat challenger Justine McGuinness exploited this deficit. As a native of the constituency, as well as a resident, she attempted to offer the potential to be a constituency servant in the best Liberal Democrat style. While the anti-Council Tax 'Axe the Tax' campaign was No. 1 priority, McGuinness promoted herself as the people's advocate, often in tandem with local councillors in Bridport and Dorchester, championing playgroups in rural Beaminster, affordable housing in the key towns, and targeting many messages at the poorer elderly voters needing extra care and financial support. She combated Letwin's media prominence by inviting leading Liberal Democrats to the area. However, she was not able to overturn Letwin's slender majority. While there was a small 0.3% swing towards the Liberal Democrats, Letwin's majority in real votes actually increased, perhaps indicating that his mixture of positive and attack messages were successful in mobilising the Conservative vote, combating the stricter local political marketing strategy pursued by McGuinness with self-promotion allied to a largely nationally focused political platform.

Methodology

The key question therefore is how these contrasting styles and strategies influenced the election result? In order to gain an insight into how voters process campaign communication, assess the level of constituency service offered by the incumbent and the potential of the competitors and then make an informed choice in the voting booth based on the combination of national and local factors a mixed-methods approach was adopted. The first wave was a survey posted to 3,000 voters across the three aforementioned marginal constituencies. The respondents represented a cross-section of the key demographics that influence voting behaviour and were selected on the basis that they voted in 2001 and remained on the electoral register at the same address. The questionnaires were also used to recruit voters to take part in focus groups, two of which were held in each constituency during June 2005. The constituencies, as indicated above, were held by an incumbent representing each of the three major political parties but faced strong challenges, the contests saw a Liberal Democrat facing a Conservative challenge, Labour facing a Conservative challenge and Conservatives facing a Liberal Democrat challenge These were chosen as they would be more likely to have received a large amount of election communication, unlike voters in the non-marginals (Pattie and Johnston 2003), and therefore might well have a greater propensity to participate in the election (Denver *et al.* 2003).

While surveys can suffer from non-response error, the acceptable level of returns (30.7%) and the representativeness of the respondents in terms of voting behaviour, age and gender suggest that the data should be reliable and valid within the usual accepted parameters. The respondents' basic details, broken down by constituency, are shown in Table 9.1. The survey was specifically designed to tease out specific reasons for voting, or indeed not voting, for certain candidates including measures on attitudes to the party, the candidate, the perceived strength of the campaign and the perceived representative function of both the incumbent and the candidates. Using regression analysis it is thus possible to assess the effect of each variable upon voting behaviour, disentangling perceptions relating to national and local politics, the strengths of the two campaigning levels and the importance of the permanent campaign and constituency service element of the MP role. The key findings were then tested further in focus groups where participants discussed the importance of constituency service and the extent to which they were aware of MPs' local representative activities, whether these activities contributed to a personal vote for one candidate or another,

Table 9.1 Demographic profile of respondents (n = 966)

Party	2001 %		2005 %		Age[a] %			Gender[b] %		
	Sample	Actual[c]	Sample	Actual	Year	Sample	Actual	M/F	Sample	Actual
Dorset Mid & Poole North (n = 276)										
Con.	35	41.1	35	36.6	18–30	25	25	Male	50	48
Lab.	12	15.5	10	11.6	31–50	33	32	Female	50	52
LD	39	42.0	49	48.7	50+	42	42			
Other	3	1.4	3	3.1						
None	9		3							
Dorset South (n = 336)										
Con.	32	41.6	37	37.9	18–30	36	25	Male	45	46
Lab.	44	42.0	41	41.6	31–50	32	31	Female	55	54
LD	13	14.4	17	15.7	50+	32	44			
Other	3	2.0	3	4.8						
None	13		2							
Dorset West (n = 339)										
Con.	35	44.6	42	46.5	18–30	34	28	Male	45	44
Lab.	21	13.6	10	7.8	31–50	30	36	Female	55	56
LD	42	41.8	42	41.9	50+	36	40			
Other	3		4	3.8						
None	9		2							

Notes:
[a] Derived from local council data.
[b] Derived from *Census 2001: Report for Parliamentary Constituencies* (Stationery Office, 2002).
[c] 100% of actual voters only, non-voters cannot be factored in.

and how these were balanced against party preferences, perceptions of the national party organisations and leaders and the more accepted reasons for voter choice.

Local political marketing: winning the votes or a wasting the resources?

The standard response among political campaigners when asked about the impact of the local dimension is to shrug and suggest that there is greater fear of the effect of not campaigning locally than any real body of evidence for its influence. However, there are certain elements that are seen as of high importance. The first is the incumbency factor. It is seen as having some ability to ensure the success of a candidate, and given the marginality of the three contests could have been pivotal in securing those few extra votes. A key question is, however, do the voters actually notice? There were a number of questions that related to the attitudes towards the incumbent, the most important of which asked respondents to rate their MP, out of ten, for their service to constituents. When looking at the mean scores across different voter groups (Table 9.2) some interesting indications emerge.

Firstly, all the incumbents received a high score (almost 9 out of 10) from those who voted for them. This offers a strong correlation between perceptions of the incumbent and voting. However, that is too simple. The pattern includes a range of voter types, some of whom are party loyalists who will automatically give their man or woman a 10. What is notable is that while the mean scores are lower from opponents' voters the standard deviation (SD) indicates that their service is recognised among these voters also. A couple of comments indicate that this is where national politics come into play: one Labour voter in Dorset Mid argued Brooke was 'an excellent MP, but I can't vote against Labour'; similarly, in Dorset South, Knight was given a 10 by a respondent who 'couldn't vote for him, as I wanted a Tory government'. Therefore incumbency is important, but it does not appear to override national politics. However, it does appear to aid some undecided voters in making their voter choice, particularly when they desire their vote to have some form of influence locally and nationally.

Using a range of statistical analysis tools it is clear that the national and local factors have a strong and significant influence upon voting behaviour. Looking across each constituency, we see how respondents replied to a range of questions about candidates' activities and the national party's image and the strength of association with actual voting behaviour (Table 9.3). The contests where Liberal Democrats

Table 9.2 Recognition of incumbency by constituency and voting behaviour

Incumbent	Con. voter	Lib Dem voter	Lab. voter	Voted for other
Jim Knight	5.5	6.6	8.8	4.0
(Labour)	SD 3.4	SD 1.1	SD 1.2	SD 0.0
Annette Brooke	7.6	8.9	4.7	0.0
(Lib Dem)	SD 2.3	SD 0.4	SD 4.9	SD 0.0
Oliver Letwin	8.7	4.8	2.6	5.8
(Conservative)	SD 0.9	SD 3.8	SD 1.2	SD 3.2

Table 9.3 Association tests for perceptions of candidates and opinion towards parties by constituency

Constituency	Candidate factors	Party factors
Dorset Mid	0.529**	0.618***
Dorset South	0.801***	0.693***
Dorset West	0.455***	0.591***

Note:
** Significance <0.005. *** Significance at 0.000

fought Conservatives witnessed national factors showing far stronger associations than the Labour versus Conservative fight in Dorset South. It appears that in the former situations Conservative candidates earned some votes from fears of giving the Liberal Democrats too much power. Given the relative affluence of many of the voters in these constituencies, it is understandable that those who may not have had a strong allegiance to one party might well adopt an economic perspective when voting. This was explained by one Conservative voter in Dorset West: 'I don't like the Conservatives usually, and would not support Howard as a Prime Minister, but if I was to choose between the policies of them or the Liberal Democrats then it has to be the Conservatives. For me, economically, that choice makes sense.' The reverse was the case in Dorset South. While the contest was close, Knight was able to appear as both trustworthy as a person and the hardest working potential representative. Despite a degree of dissatisfaction with the Labour government, he was able to gain a personal vote that his Conservative opponent could not impact upon. Some respondents who had voted Conservative in 2001 switched to Knight

Table 9.4 Voter choice and influential factors

Factor	Voted Cons.	Voted Lib Dem	Voted Lab.
Best party for country	0.275***	−0.396***	0.144**
Best representative for area	−0.158**	0.326***	0.235**
Candidate who best addressed my concerns	0.092	0.293**	0.108**
Tactical vote	−0.189**	0.219***	−0.037
Best for economy	0.256***	−0.437***	0.222***
Best for public services	0.210***	−0.290***	0.132**
Best on immigration	0.462***	−0.409***	−0.067
Most trustworthy leader	0.073	−0.009	−0.070

Note
** Significance < 0.005. *** Significance *at* 0.000.

in 2005; their responses indicate that they did not see either Blair or Howard as their first choice of Prime Minister (though Kennedy was not rated, either), that they had little favourable to say about either of the parties in contention, but they saw Knight as a better potential representative than Ed Matts. For example, 'Matts proved himself to be a liar, there's enough of them elected already. Jim is an honest bloke, better him and Labour than Matts and his lies.' This highlights the complexity of voter decisions in marginal seats. In terms of voting, therefore, it is possible to identify a range of factors that lead voters to select one party over another; these are shown in Table 9.4.

The data indicate that Conservative and Labour voters largely choose their candidate based on national factors; constituency service is a consideration only where voters feel that they are unable to vote for their first choice owing to that party being unable to win or if they are genuinely motivated to consider constituency service above national political factors. Within the Dorset Mid and West contexts a combination of the two appeared important. Many of the voters who took part in the focus groups were not loyal Liberal Democrats, nor were they staunchly Labour, but they were anti-Conservative. This led them to make a simple choice: it had to be the Liberal Democrat. This expression of tactical selection suggests that constituency service did not play any role, however, and, as is discussed further below, the fact that the Liberal Democrat had 'worked hard for the last ten years locally' in Dorset Mid, and that McGuinness in Dorset West 'showed what a good, hard-working MP she'd make' motivated some members of the electorate; as one voter stated, 'I didn't care who the MP would be, but chatting to Justine made me think that she deserved my vote, that's the only reason I bothered!' In Dorset South the contest came down to personalities and who would be the best representative. Owing to the mistakes made by Conservative candidate Ed Matts, those issues impacted upon voter choice and led Conservative supporters to vote on incumbency and 'the type of representative that this area needs'. This was helped perhaps by a perception that it was unlikely that the Conservatives would form a government, regardless of their vote. Liberal Democrat voters do vote on local factors; there are strong negative associations between percep-tions of the party and voting for them. It is the candidate that is the product in their case, perhaps owing to their distance from power in Westminster; for Labour and the Conservatives, as potential govern-ments, it is a complex combination that can be swayed by local factors where they are relevant. Overall, however, it is the national context that determines the vote. In the words of one focus group participant, 'the campaign is rubbish. I judge who to vote for by who can run a country not an office in Dorchester.' She thus voted for Letwin as prospective Chancellor, not for him as an MP, nor was she sidetracked by the locally focused McGuinness campaign.

Tactical voting: voting for and against governments or supporting individuals

The undecided voters within the marginals may well, as discussed above, simply choose between the two national front runners. However, the party campaigns are also interested in squeezing the votes from those who, for example, live in Dorset Mid, feel Labour are the best party for government, yet are aware that a vote for Labour is a wasted vote and may actually benefit another party, in this case the Conservatives. How do these people view the issue of incumbency and the local factors? We know that those who chose to vote Labour in Dorset Mid and Dorset West rated the incumbents very low on average. Liberal Democrats were far more charitable to Jim Knight in Dorset South, but what of those whose votes were squeezed? Are these the tactical voters who vote purely on the national picture and offer the Liberal Democrats their support on the basis they are not the Conservatives, or are other factors at work?

Table 9.5 Perceptions of parties and voting behaviour

Perception	Voted Cons.	Voted Lib Dem	Voted Lab.
Con. best government	0.621***	−0.333***	−0.283***
Lib Dem best government	−0.217***	0.424***	−214***
Lab best government	−313***	0.002	0.439***
Con. identifier	0.692***	−0.393***	−0.278***
Lib Dem identifier	−316***	0.517***	−0.191**
Lab. identifier	−0.391***	0.233**	0.467***

Note:
** Significance < 0.005. *** Significance at 0.000.

Table 9.5 shows that those voters who view one party as the best government, and who identify with its policies, are most likely to vote for that party. Not an earth-shattering discovery, but indicative that not all votes can be squeezed. However, the interesting voters are those who identify with Labour policies, have some questions surrounding whether Labour are the best government, and who then vote Liberal Democrat. Isolating just those who voted in Dorset Mid and West, where Labour could not win, these voters all recalled receiving leaflets from the Liberal Democrats (only 74% recalled Conservative literature), 65% were visited by or met Annette Brooke and all were visited by a party representative during the campaign. In turn they suggest that the most influential communication was contact with the MP (42%) or party leaflets (32%), above the national media (16%) the local newspaper (5%) and then party Web sites (4%). Unlike the voters who had a simple choice, 'Do I actually turn out and vote for the party I most identify with?', these voters carefully selected their tactics based not solely on the local candidate but definitely on the local campaign, including, naturally, how relevant national messages were made to them personally. What is important here, in the context of a system that sees the floating voters as having the greatest power in determining the outcomes in constituencies such as these, is that the local campaign appears to have greater influence upon them than that which took place through the national mass media.

Some voters in Dorset West and South may have also been influenced by the 'vote swap' campaign, where Liberal Democrats in Dorset South should vote Labour and vice versa in Dorset West; the campaign was led

Table 9.6 Labour identifiers and influences on tactical voting behaviour

Influence	High score awarded for quality or activity	Association with voting Lib Dem
National factors	Best party	−0.469***
	Best government	−0.292**
	Best for nation	−0.492***
Political identity	Strength of Lab. identity	0.389**
	Strength of Con. identity	−0.139**
	Strength of Lib Dem identity	0.128***
Local factors	Relevant	0.894**
	Understands area	0.261***
	Best representative	0.254**
Marketing communication	Recall of leaflets	0.239**
	Liking messages	0.488***
	Presence in constituency	0.292**
	Recall from local media	0.266**
	Visited by the candidate	0.452***
	Visited by party worker	0.206**
	Perception of representative	0.695***

Note:
** Significance < 0.005. ***Significance at 0.000.

by former pop star and Labour and Liberal Democrat activist Billy Bragg via his Web site. But did the candidate also have any impact? It appears that they did. Few of these Liberal Democrat voters believed that they were voting for the representative of the best party for the country, few said that the party was best on any issue apart from public services; they claimed to trust Kennedy but did not see him as a Prime Minister. However, they did claim that the candidate was the best for the area, talked about the local issues of most concern and understood the area (see Table 9.6).

The respondents show that under these circumstances they will vote for an alternative to the party they identify with, and can be swung on local issues and campaign strength. Looking at the identity scores, where they were asked to match themselves to each party, we see this group as having strong Labour identification, followed by Liberal Democrat, but a reasonably low Conservative identification. They have a generally low opinion of the Liberal Democrats nationally, and would not want to see the party govern, but they identified with the candidates. They see them as relevant, understanding the area and its constituents; they like their messages and find the high-profile style of

Table 9.7 Vote switching correlated with local and national factors ($n = 92$)

Factors important for voting		Candidate voted for	
Local	National	had best local profile	represented best party of government
0.845*	0.035	0.745*	0.234**

Note:
* Significant at > 0.01. ** Significant at > 0.05.

campaigning attractive. Clearly it is unlikely that they would support the party in a contest between it and a Labour candidate; switches did occur in some circumstances due to other factors relating to the Iraq war, but in these specific constituencies it seems that a local focus and a high-profile campaign paid off as well. Table 9.7 shows correlations between local factors and national factors among the switchers, a group that constitute 8.9% (ninety-two respondents) of the sample. These data demonstrate that to some voters, a minority perhaps, the local factors are paramount and that such voters may exist nationally in significant enough numbers to swing a close fight such as those focused on here (see also Lilleker, 2005b).

Rethinking local political marketing

Given the marginality of the seats, one could assume that all the candidates with realistic changes were trying to develop a relationship with constituents and attempting to shore up support in time for the General Election. The constituents' perception of the MPs suggests that was definitely the case, as even among non-supporters recognition of their service was high. The problem is identifying how this converts to votes. The voters that were won over to the incumbents came from parties that were unlikely to do well, except for the case in Dorset South, where the fight focused much more upon the efficacy of the candidates. Labour voters were drawn to Liberal Democrats to avoid a Conservative victory, basing their decisions on dislike of the Conservatives and affection for the Liberal Democrat style. Thus it remains the case that national factors have priority. Looking at the hard facts on voting, it is perceptions of competence and trust in the government, or potential government, that dominate voter thinking, not who would be the best MP for a single constituency. Arguably, apart from a minority of voters who will vote purely on local factors, it is only when that choice is forced by local factors, such as who can actually win, or when the national contest is a foregone conclusion, that local factors, and a localised marketing strategy, come into play.

What then is the verdict on a locally focused marketing strategy? It has a role, that is clear. Trust seems to be as important at the local level as at the top of government. Knight was a trusted and highly active local MP; Matts attempted to use aggressive tactics which backfired, earning him infamy in the local and national media. Under these conditions Knight's record as a hard-working incumbent benefited him and won him votes from the Conservatives. Letwin was recognised as hard-working but mainly among his loyal voters: few awarded him the higher scores that Brooke and Knight earned from across the spectrum. The Letwin vote was for a Conservative government; his local activities were an added bonus only and were seen as much less of a factor among Dorset West voters. Letwin's Liberal Democrat opponent clearly has a strong following, one bolstered by Labour converts who were anti-Conservative and were won over to the McGuinness camp by her style and potential for service delivery. While they may be short-term converts they were mobilised, rather than considering their vote a wasted one and staying at home. The Brooke victory in Dorset Mid relies much on a bedrock of Liberal Democrat support and her own personal vote as a former councillor, mayor and now incumbent. She earned much of her support for her local work and thus attracted Labour identifiers.

The important aspect here, as highlighted in the studies correlating spend and effort with the vote, is the campaign itself. The fact that leaflets are seen as influential among voters who are undecided is a key finding, not one that many would expect in the modern cluttered market place. While the majority of leaflets do go into the bin, name recognition and interest in the contest mean that some voters take heed of the messages. This is particularly the case in the marginal constituencies, where voters endeavour to make their vote count but need to be mobilised. As one focus group member put it, 'The media told us how important our votes could be, so I needed to know who deserved my vote.' Leaflets, however, are useful only as follow-up cues. Above all, it is contact with the candidate, the face-to-face relationships, that have the most profound effect. In Dorchester voters felt ignored by Letwin, unlike in the rural parts of the Dorset West constituency; the fact that McGuinness had supported their causes and was prominent in that town earned her support. As one focus group participant argued, 'If she hadn't come round I might have voted Labour, or I might not have voted at all.' Thus the high-profile campaigning allows voters to get a sense of who the candidate is, what they stand for, and how active they may be in serving the community. In the case of the voters who have loyalties to neither of the major contenders, or are uninterested in the contest generally yet feel it their duty to vote, this appears crucial.

Perhaps then candidates are correct in being afraid not to partake in campaigning, and of the effect of not being diligent case workers, rather than being sure of their effectiveness. Under the 'first past the post' voting system, where votes for third-place candidates are wasted, there are some voters who can be won over. It is the local efforts that can achieve that. However, the majority of voters decide on the national issues. Largely it is 'Who do I think should govern?' or perhaps 'Who do I think should not govern?' that dominates decision making in the voting booth – a truth that seems sensible and inescapable in electoral politics despite a push towards local political marketing among Liberal Democrat and Labour strategists and candidates.

References

Baines, P. and Mortimore, R. (2005), 'Marginal Seat Picture offers little Solace to Conservatives', www.mori.co.uk/pubinfo/plb/marginal-seat-picture.shtml, accessed 30 April 2005.

Bealey, F., Blondel, J. and McCann, W. (1965), *Constituency Politics: A Study of Newcastle under Lyme*, London: Faber.

Butler, D. E. (1952), *The British General Election of 1951*, London: Macmillan.

Butler, P. and Collins, N. (2001), 'Payment on delivery: recognising constituency service as political marketing', *European Journal of Marketing* 35 (9–10): 1026–37.

Butler, D., and Kavanagh, D. (1997) *The British General Election of 1997*, London: Macmillan.

Cain, B., Ferejohn, A. and Fiorina, M. (1987), *The Personal Vote: Constituency Service and Electoral Independence*, Cambridge MA: Harvard University Press.

Denver, D. and Hands, G. (1997), *Modern Constituency Electioneering: Local Campaigning in the 1992 General Election*, London: Frank Cass.

Denver, D. and Hands, G. (2001), 'The fall and rise of constituency campaigning', in J. Bartle and D. Griffiths (eds), *Political Communications Transformed: From Morrison to Mandelson*, Basingstoke: Palgrave Macmillan.

Denver, D., Hands, G. and MacAllister, I. (2003), 'Constituency marginality and turnout in Britain revisited', in C. Rallings, R. Scully, J. Tonge and P. Webb (eds), *British Elections and Parties Review* XIII, London: Frank Cass.

Fam, K. S. and Merrilees, B. (2001), 'What do excellent service promoters do differently?' *Services Industries Journal* 21 (4): 1–16.

Jackson, N. (2003) 'The Internet and MPs: Political Gadget, Passing Fad or Vote Winner?' Paper presented to EPOP conference, Cardiff, September.

Jackson, N. and Lilleker, D. G. (2004), 'Just public relations or an attempt at interaction? British MPs in the press, on the Web and 'in your face'', *European Journal of Communication* 19 (4): 507–33.

Johnston, R. and Pattie, C. (2003), 'Do canvassing and campaigning work? Evidence from the 2001 General Election in England', in C. Rallings, R. Scully, J. Tonge and P. Webb (eds), *British Elections and Parties Review* XIII, London: Frank Cass.

Kotler, P. and Kotler, N. (1999), 'Political marketing: generating effective candidates, campaigns and causes', in B. Newman (ed.) *Handbook of Political Marketing*, London: Sage.

Krasno, J. S. (1994), *Challengers, Competition and Re-election*, New Haven CT: Yale University Press.

Lees-Marshment, J. and Lilleker, D. G. (2005), 'Political marketing in the UK', in D.G. Lilleker and J. Lees-Marshment, *Political Marketing in Comparative Perspective*, Manchester: Manchester University Press.

Lilleker, D. G. (2005a), 'Political marketing: the cause of a democratic deficit?' *Journal of Nonprofit and Public Sector Marketing*, 14(1–2): 5–26.

Lilleker, D. G. (2005b), 'The local campaign: management from the centre or chaos on the periphery?' *Journal of Marketing Management*, special edition on the 2005 UK General Election, 21(9–10): 979–1004.

Lilleker, D. G. and Negrine, R. (2003), 'Not big brand names but corner shops: marketing politics to a disengaged electorate', *Journal of Political Marketing* 2 (1): 55–75.

Lilleker, D. G. and Negrine, R. (2006), 'Mapping a market orientation: can we only detect political marketing through the lens of hindsight?' in P. J. Davies and B. I. Newman, *Winning Elections with Political Marketing*, New York: Haworth.

Negrine, R. and Lilleker, D. (2003), 'The professionalisation of media-based campaigning in Britain, 1966–2001: the rise of a proactive media strategy', *Journalism Studies* 4 (2): 199–211.

Nimmo, D. (1999), 'The permanent campaign: marketing as a governing tool', in B. Newman (ed.), *Handbook of Political Marketing*, London, Sage.

Pattie, C. J. and Johnston, R. J. (2003), 'Local battles in a national landslide: constituency campaigning at the 2001 British General Election', *Political Geography* 22: 381–414.

Rush, M. (2001), *The Role of the Member of Parliament since 1868: From Gentlemen to Players*, Oxford: Oxford University Press.

Westmyer, S., DiCioccio, R. and Rubin, R. (1998), 'Appropriateness and effectiveness of communication channels in competent interpersonal communication', *Journal of Communication* 48 (3): 27–48.

10

View from the armchair: why young people took no interest and no notice of the campaigns

Dianne Dean

There has been much recent discussion surrounding the loss of trust in politicians, in particular that many young people are switching off from the democratic process altogether. Marketing has increasingly been used in political campaigning and has largely taken the blame, owing to the association made with techniques such as packaging and spin allegedly serving to disengage the electorate from the political process. However, out of the three groups identified as disengaged from the electoral process – Know Nothings, Guilty Know Nothings and Political Cynics – only the Political Cynics are aware of marketing techniques and their application to political campaigning. Both the Know Nothings and the Guilty Know Nothings are disengaged from the political campaign even before it starts; it is this phenomenon that this chapter addresses and seeks to understand.

Young people's electoral behaviour

The prevailing view is that young people 'don't know, don't care and don't vote' (Heath and Park 1997: 6). That is to say, they have lower levels of knowledge and commitment to the political process and are less likely than older generations to cast their vote. Voting is tradition- ally a low-priority pastime among young people (Furnham and Gunter 1989; Park 1995, 1999). This is supported by the finding of Hiscock (2001) that 44% of eighteen to twenty-four-year-olds did not vote in the 1997 General Election, falling by 2001 to 20% who stated they were 'absolutely certain' to use their vote (Electoral Commission 2001: 11). Although this continued decline is alarming, it is not the full picture. In the 2001 election 40% of young people stated they were participating in some political activities, so the picture is more complex than it first appears (Diplock 2001). Fahmy (1996) identified different levels of

participation: 5% of fifteen to twenty-one-year-olds take part in some
sort of political activity other than voting, and 4% of the sample take an
'active part in a political campaign'. So it is difficult to argue that young
people *per se* are not involved in the electoral process; this reflects the
heterogeneity identified by Gomez and Wilson (2001). What this
chapter hopes to achieve is to build a deeper understanding of how
young people viewed the General Election. What knowledge did they
have of politics, political parties and the issues? Did they feel that any
of the parties specifically targeted them in terms of their needs? Did the
presentational aspects of the campaign have any impact upon their
views?

Explanations have been provided to elucidate low political participation. These range from the lack of relevance to young people to the complexity of politics (White *et al.* 1999; Electoral Commission 2003).
Brynner and Ashford (1994) argue that the person's experience at
school and employment prospects can determine the level of alienation.
Butler and Stokes (1974) suggested that age was a determinant in electoral behaviour and young people become more interested in politics
and political issues as they become older. However, Kimberlee (1998)
argued that owing to social changes, for instance staying on in education and continuing to live with parents, young people do not have the
responsibilities that encourage an interest in politics. Bhavnani (1994)
argues that young people find politics boring and complex and believe
there is little point in voting; in contrast others claim that disengagement results from lack of trust in the political system, politicians and the
media (Dermody and Hanmer-Lloyd 2003; Russell *et al.* 2002). White *et
al.*'s (1999) research supported the established view that many young
people merely follow their parents' electoral behaviour. Denver and
Hands (1990) and Crewe *et al.* (1992) contend young people do not
really enter the electoral process until there is something that mobilises
them, such as paying tax, owning a home or having children, etc.
Mulgan and Wilkinson (1997) suggest that issues such as environmen-
talism and animal rights mobilise political action among many young
people.

Interestingly, research undertaken by Wring *et al.* (1999) suggested
that for some young voters alienation and cynicism did not provide an
accurate picture of their voting intentions. They identified a marked
level of involvement among some respondents who did take part in
political activity at a number of levels, again reinforcing the notion of
electoral heterogeneity among young people. They noted that different
groups demonstrated different characteristics and levels of interest and
participation. These findings are supported by the qualitative analysis of

White *et al.* (1999). White organised groups of young people according to their level of interest and connection with the political system. She identified some groups of young people who did vote and recognised that there were a significant group of people who were not interested and alienated from the political process. Later research on first-time voters in the 2001 General Election supported this (Henn and Weinstein 2002; Henn *et al.* 2002). Nevertheless, the key point is that the decline in the number of young people actually voting is disproportionately steeper than that of other members of the electorate. Therefore, previous research has uncovered different groups of voters, some who are politically active, and an increasing number of young people who are alienated from the political and electoral process. Ansolabehere and Iyengar (1995: 10) claimed that increased marketing activity and negative advertising were polarising the electorate. Was this reflected in the 2005 General Election? Each of the major political parties adopted a different marketing approach. What effect did these have on young peoples' voting intentions?

Methodology

The methodological approach was to use both qualitative research in the form of six group discussions (three male, three female), then twelve individual in-depth interviews (six male, six female), with eighteen to twenty-five-year-olds. Qualitative research was used in order to establish what latent or repressed views, memories or experiences shape these voter's views on politics, political parties and political campaigns. For both individual in-depth interviews and group discussions a quota was set for educational attainment and employment: no educational qualifications and unemployed, educated to GCSE level in a clerical position, and degree-educated in a junior management position. Bernstein's (1971) work showed that education and social grouping had a direct impact upon communication codes, so it would be useful to see how campaign messages resonated with young people from different social and educational backgrounds.

Findings and discussion

There were three key issues that arose from this research. First, how apathy kept many young voters away from the electoral process, with many respondents taking little notice of politicians, party or the election campaign messages. Second, how trust has been significantly eroded: for both Labour and the Conservatives there was little trust. The Labour

Party campaign was seen as slick, superficial and not covering-over the cracks perceived following the debate about war in Iraq and the arguments over weapons of mass destruction. Whilst the Conservative Party, which strongly focused on negative campaigning and fear appeals, failed to engage any young people apart from Conservative loyalists. It is interesting to note that the Liberal Democrats, who adopted a more traditional campaign strategy, focusing on issues rather than negative campaigning, were perceived by young people to be more trustworthy in contrast to the two main parties. Finally, the bad news for the Liberal Democrats: although they were seen as a credible party in terms of relevance of policies and believability their lack of governmental experience ensured that many young voters would not vote for them. It was apparent that they were perceived as a 'third' party and voting for them was a 'wasted vote'. It was immaterial how they presented themselves, as it was clear to many respondents that they did not have the requisite experience to take control of government.

Apathy in its many guises

There is much in the literature that suggests that voters are apathetic, but apathy has also been used to explain non-voters who have a lack of awareness or limited understanding of political issues. Again it is more complex; young voters are disengaged from the electoral process owing to a number of reasons.

Crewe *et al.* (1996: 26) also identified an 'apathetic abstainer'. However, this classification is inappropriate, as the definition of 'abstain', according to the new *Oxford English Dictionary*, is either to 'restrain oneself from doing something' or to 'formally decline to vote either for or against'. This would indicate a level of cognitive processing which the abstainer follows with a conscious decision not to vote. The apathetic abstainers, according to Crewe *et al.* (1996), are more closely aligned with the group identified by Hyman and Sheatsley (1947) as 'Know Nothings'. They are alienated from the political process for a number of reasons. However, this research indicates that 'Know Nothings' are alienated but they don't abstain. Abstention suggests a conscious decision; rather, they avoid the political process altogether, so no deliberate decision is made.

Research from the election identified a number of different groups who did not vote, 'Know Nothings', 'Guilty Know Nothings' and 'Political Cynics'. These groups each had a different view of politics, political issues and the election campaigns. For some there was no interest in how the campaigns were executed or whether they were market-oriented. Indeed, even the 'sound bites' and poster campaigns did not engage this group. For others, the market-led approach merely reinforced their view that politics was about 'selling something' and 'spin', and this further alienated them from the electoral process. The following section segments the respondents into groups based upon their attitudes to the election campaign and politics in general. These groups illustrate how a market approach can alienate rather than engage young people in the electoral process.

Know Nothings

The Know Nothings are not new to the literature, first identified by Hyman and Sheatsley (1947). They are 'unwilling to receive or incapable of encoding information' (Bennett 1988). This chapter suggests that, even with a marketing-oriented approach to campaigning, this group consistently fail to engage in political communications. 'Know Nothings' have no voting intentions and they look on politicians as trying to sell something. Indeed, they treat political communication in the same way as tele-sales representatives, 'slamming the phone down'. When the subject of the election was introduced there was complete silence, and when they were asked what politics meant to them there were many anxious glances and the body language was defensive, with arms and legs crossed and respondents making themselves small to avoid directed questioning. They don't vote, and feel left out, or excluded from the political system. Maybe this would suggest that if the needs of this group were addressed by a more market-sensitive party there might well be an increased level of engagement. However, it is quite clear that the Know Nothings believe they are outside the loop and their needs are not considered. This culminates in a negative attitude to politicians and government:

> Greedy flash cats . . . with big cars . . . they make a lot of money by just talking to people. (Male, unemployed)

Know Nothings are generally members of society who feel excluded both economically and socially.

After the initial warm-up questions about lifestyle and family background, questions began to become more focused towards politics and how it affects them. The questions were framed in a very unthreatening manner but still encouraged a tense silence and shuffling. Two of the group looked at each other almost in panic and drew their legs up beneath them, folding their arms, avoiding eye contact with the rest of the group and the moderator. They were probably the most extreme example of a 'Don't Know', contributing little to the discussion, looking out of the window or at each other and giggling self-consciously. They don't read newspapers apart from the *Sun*, they avoid the news on television, never watch party political broadcasts and avoid politics as much as possible. If political parties genuinely want to engage this group, they seriously need to consider researching their needs and potential modes of engagement. Merely adopting a different approach to campaigning is not enough.

Lack of interest was evident across the lower education groups independent of gender. These voters perceive politics as having little relevance to their own lives. They are quite alienated from the issues as well as the political process, leading to a high level of apathy:

> I just get on with my life. Wouldn't vote. (Male, unemployed)
> If parliament comes on the telly I just switch it over. I've just got no interest at all. (Male, clerical)

They have no understanding of the political codes of communication: the words used are complicated, politicians are perceived as long-winded and Know Nothings believe politicians to be 'posh'. They also find it hard to understand them. The remoteness the Know Nothings feel is related to the different frames of reference and the elaborate communication code used by politicians. They believe that the language employed by politicians is beyond them and would like them to talk in much simpler terms, using the restricted code that Know Nothings themselves use in every day life. The political campaigns have been largely ignored and when they catch them on the news there is exasperation:

> Can't they talk proper English? (Female, unemployed)
> Make things simpler. (Female, unemployed)

This group also believe that politicians are unable to appeal to young people, as they are so much older. They believed politicians did not address the issues that were relevant to young voters, their language style, manner and even dress code was so out of touch with young people.

> They're all so old. No wonder they don't appeal to kids. They're all so boring. (Female, unemployed)

However, there is a dilemma. If political parties attempt to appeal to this group, using a simpler message or techniques of commercial brands that are positioned to attract young people, will they, first, be believable – for instance, William Hague wearing a baseball cap – and second, will they alienate other sections of the electorate?

Among these voters there is a perception that the issues that political parties discuss or debate are of no direct relevance to them. Their perception of politics is that there is no real debate, just oppositionalism for its own sake. When they catch Prime Minister's Questions, they do not engage with the discussion, all they discern is the noise and the arguments. They offered a simplistic approach to the solution:

> Why don't they all club together and maybe they might come up with a bright idea? They don't talk, they just argue – we had that idea months ago and you pinched it off us. (Male, unemployed)
> When they televise the House of Commons you can see them falling asleep and carrying on. No wonder there are so many wars – all stood there arguing with each other – but if they just talked to each other I'm sure they could sort it out sensibly. (Female, clerical)

When they inadvertently catch television coverage of the House of Commons there is little respect for the politicians, These voters do not understand the process of debate and there is little understanding of the issues under discussion. The only issues that they noticed from the campaigns were related to immigration, highlighted by the Conservative Party campaign, but this group noticed it from the newspapers rather than any campaign material. There was a naivety in the discussion which emphasised their exasperation with the system. There was no understanding of the complexities of decision making; they appeared to be oblivious to the relative positions of political parties and the limits to which they can 'compromise'. They also believed that the debates were of no relevance to them and that politicians have no understanding of how 'life really is'. This is where the females in the group were most animated:

> Politicians [are] not brought up on council estate[s], they don't understand. (Female, unemployed)

When asked what democracy meant to them there was silence in both unemployed groups. Ironically, at this point one member of the female unemployed group, who had previously made no comments at all, spoke quite animatedly and confidently about how the vice-presidents are elected in US schools. She was familiar with voting from *Saved by the Bell*, a US teenage situation comedy. So, potentially, such programmes can help educate people who are disengaged from the political process. From a market perspective, it indicates that if the message is presented as entertainment, then maybe there could be engagement. However, it remains to be seen whether this engagement would extend to evaluating campaign messages.

The Know Nothings held simplistic stereotypical views which framed their cognition of political concepts; this was exacerbated by the limited understanding they had of the process of politics and the institutions.

For instance, when the concept of the welfare state was introduced again there was silence until they were prompted gently. The extent of the ensuing discussion was limited, however, with one unemployed male respondent claiming, 'Well, I wouldn't be able to explain it,' There was lack of confidence in the discussions, with many respondents reluctant or unable to respond. The most extensive response was that the welfare state was for 'looking after people' but this female clerical respondent was unable to identify how the welfare state worked or how it was funded. Again language was limited, using a very restricted communication code. In the unemployed group, discussions gradually moved on to taxation but the comments were very superficial, with no understanding of the role of taxation and how it contributes to the welfare state, apart from funding the benefit system. An extract follows that illustrates this:

> 'What does tax do?' (female, unemployed).
> 'Pays people like me to sit at home' (female, unemployed).
> 'Where does tax go?' (female, unemployed).
> 'To taxpayers. I don't know – pays police wages' (female, unemployed).

These young people had little conception of citizenship and would not go to work owing to the low wages and the possibility of taxation. They discuss the methods they employ to avoid paying tax altogether; sometimes they work and claim social security. They see this as getting one over on the system, so they see it as an 'us versus them' situation, as they believe tax is collected for no reason. There is no understanding of what happens to the taxes when they are collected, they made no association with the public services and when prompted believed they went on politicians' high salaries and 'their big fast cars' (male unemployed). There was no ability to broaden the thinking to wider issues related to taxation. When discussing local taxation, there was little awareness of what Council Tax was, with some respondents demonstrating no understanding at all. Understanding of the National Health Service was equally weak, with some totally irrelevant and unrelated comments: 'Vets' bills are ridiculous – it's absurd' (female, unemployed). There were discussions of hospital waiting lists but only if their own family had any experience of waiting what they believed to have been an undue length of time to see a specialist or have an operation.

Even after prompting there was no elaboration upon this. There was no ability to conceptualise political issues; importantly, there was no motivation, either. Although immigration was recalled from the campaign it did nothing to motivate them to engage in the electoral process. This group is most closely associated with the Generation X characteristics of 'disinterested, alienated, and cynical'. However, their cynicism is not articulated in the same way as the next group, Guilty No Nothings, mainly because they have little ability to criticise coherently and consistently. The schema through which they make sense of the world is limited to their own life world, and other concepts are alien and remote. The responses to discussion were very limited short-sentence responses rather than elaborated discussion. Their body language indicated feelings of alienation and boredom with the whole political process. Their perception was that it was corrupt and did nothing to help them, ideas consistent with their general lack of trust in politicians. They spoke in stereotypical language, using many sweeping generalisations that demonstrated their lack of understanding of the political system. When a concept such as democracy was introduced, some of the female respondents reacted with sideways glances and giggled to each other. Gentle probing caused participants to avoid eye contact with the moderator; their posture was defensive, arms folded, avoiding the question.

The Know Nothings demonstrated the least ability to conceptualise political issues, as well as demonstrating the lowest level of motivation among all the groups. This group were represented mostly, as would be expected, both among males and females, in the unemployed group. However, there were also some respondents sharing the same characteristics in the female clerical group. Among them all information sources are avoided rather than sought out. The motivation variable, which determines their identification and personal relevance to the political system, shows that there is no interest in this at all, with total disengagement from the system and political parties in general. They had very little knowledge of the election, and little interest; even when prompted about issues related to terrorism and the war in Iraq, there was limited discussion. If political marketers want to engage this group, they need to identify what is salient to them, as well as making politics in general more relevant to their life experiences. They also need to present messages in easily understandable language, using the same restricted code of communication used by the Know Nothings. Using different media such as television programmes or celebrity endorsement may also be helpful but this approach could be at the expense of alienating the other voter groups in the electorate.

Guilty Know Nothings

These are a curious group, mostly educated to degree level and articulate, but they are still alienated from the electoral process. This group's awareness of the political system and avoidance of any political information was similar to Know Nothings. However, there were two characteristics that set this group apart from the Know Nothings. One is their ability to conceptualise abstract political issues and second that politics was perceived as so vitally important that they felt overawed by the issues. For this group, although their motivational levels were quite low and there was little interest, this was driven by a lack of understanding of the codes of political communication. Despite their strong conceptualisation of everyday issues and their articulation employing an elaborate communication code using a more extensive vocabulary, indicating a capacity for political cognition, there was a lack of familiarity with political concepts and they were unfamiliar with the political process. This leads to an alienation which drives their lack of participation in the political process. They were also conscious of the need to be involved in the political process, having a strong understanding of the notion of civic responsibility. This group thought politics was an important and responsible activity. They believed it should be taken seriously, and as they became older they felt guilty as they should know more about politics and the alternatives on offer. The respondents in this group who had children had the greatest feelings of guilt. Although they said they were not interested in politics 'for themselves' they recognised that they should do something to make the world or the country better for their children. In this instance the galvanising issue was the environment, and this generated considerable discussion. Thus the style of campaigning is crucial; for the Guilty Know Nothings the promotional campaign should be responsible. In their opinion, this responsible campaign should be serious, the issues should be outlined clearly and cogently. They believe that politics should not be undermined by negative campaigning, which frustrates them because they believe politics to be so important.

The Guilty Know Nothings were predominantly 'female with a degree' or 'female clerical'. They were disengaged from the political process in that they had never felt any engagement, they had never voted, and they found politics boring:

> I'm just not interested in it, although I would like to know more about it.
> (Female, degree)

Politics for this group was difficult to understand, and remote from their everyday life. They were concerned about issues but believed they did not know enough about them to make an informed decision:

> It just all seem so complicated. Where do you start? Its all above my head.
> (Female, degree)

At the present moment in time there is little to motivate them into elaborating political information, and the campaign did little to change that view. Although they felt ignorant of the political process, they perceive politics as important but the complexity of the issues made it difficult to follow:

> I mean, it does affect you and sometimes it is a bit indirect in a way, but I think you should be interested in it, although it's a bit boring, but I think you should listen to things. (Female, degree)

The importance they attach to the understanding of politics meant that they were reluctant to get involved in the process until they were sufficiently informed to make an educated decision. Equally, the fact that they knew that they should be involved in the political process but were not added to their feelings of guilt: almost a Catch 22 situation.

> I'd rather do it properly and I just thought I'd rather not vote. I mean, next time I definitely will find time to look into it more and find out more about it. I was pretty mad that I didn't, like I didn't have a say. I mean, all those women [Suffragettes] tying themselves to railings so I could have the vote. So next time I will, but I didn't really feel I – I don't know it, was kind of fake. I wasn't simply 100% behind it. (Female, degree)

There is a possibility that this respondent was reacting to the spin surrounding political campaigning. Guilty Know Nothings need a responsible election rather than spin and 'yah, boo' political campaigning. The Liberal Democrats' leader, Charles Kennedy, recognised this problem, declaring that their political campaign would be honest and positive, focusing upon issues rather than deploying negative campaigning.

This group did not vote during the 2005 election as they felt that politics was too important. They felt that the feeling of obligation was too much for them to get involved, given their lack of understanding. Instead, they believed that they really should pay attention to the issues, as voting was a responsible activity relating both to civic duty and also to the implications of their voting action.

> I didn't think about it myself, so I didn't think it was fair to vote if I wasn't 100% sure of what I was voting for. (Female, degree)

Voting without understanding the issues was deemed 'irresponsible' (female, degree) and the implications of a casually cast vote would be too much to bear, so abstention was more appropriate at the time until they could build up enough knowledge of the issues to vote responsibly. This group demonstrated the capacity for cognition but there was a serious reluctance to overcome the barriers to political involvement.

There was a palpable feeling of guilt among this group, a feeling that they should get involved and know more about it:

> I was going to say I ignore it. I feel that I should know about it and would
> love – love? – like to be interested in it. I know who does what, and know
> why they believe in all that. I think it's because you feel obligated to do so,
> because they are running the country and you should take more interest
> in who runs the country and what they think about it but I do ignore it but
> I always say I'm going to start reading the papers, watching the news more.
> (Female, degree)

However, this was tinged by frustration that politicians do not really
help this process, as they never answer a question directly. They use an
elaborate code of communication that is unfamiliar to many respondents. This was resented as they believe that politicians obfuscate the
issues when they fail to answer questions directly. This was a major
criticism of politicians. Many in this group believed that they should
simply 'just speak the truth' (female, clerical); there was no understanding demonstrated that there was more than one view and that
political ideologies and party perspectives colour the position the
parties adopt.

> You get frustrated with it. I watch the BBC's breakfast news programme in
> the morning. You get frustrated. Whenever a direct question is asked you
> never get a direct answer back. (Female, degree)

There was no apathy or boredom in this group; it was more a feeling
of estrangement from the process due to the complexities of the political process and the time it would take to learn about the issues. There
was also little political discussion in their households. Interestingly, this
group did indicate a range of triggers that would make them participate.
One respondent reflected the findings of Butler and Stokes (1974),
among others, that age was an important criterion, as her knowledge of
politics had increased as she became older.

> It's getting easier for me. I used to . . . when it was on the news I didn't
> know who was who, and so I wasn't interested, and I watch the news more.
> I'm getting more interested because I'm understanding it more as I'm
> getting older. It's getting more interesting for me. (Female, degree)

This research also identifies life-stage changes such as marriage and
having children also affecting political involvement, supporting the findings of White *et al.* (2000). The ability to conceptualise political issues
generally was quite limited, primarily owing to lack of awareness rather
than ability, a factor recognised by the respondents themselves. When
prompted they were primarily concerned about health and education
and became aware of these as political issues through personal experience. For instance, the National Health Service was related to when

their children were born; the education system to when their children started school. Clearly, salience is a key motivational factor with this group of women.

Another interesting finding arises from discussions about politics and parental influences. Clearly this is a group of women who are non-confrontational and this relates to how they engage in political discussion. They avoid talking politics at home with their families, recognising the adversarial nature of political discussion. Politics were rarely discussed in the family home, and, although most knew how their parents voted, they did not really oppose or challenge them.

> I have never been particularly involved. My dad is quite strongly Conservative, and my mum was, but she has gone towards the Liberal Party, and my grandparents are very strongly Conservative as well. (Female, degree)

These familial political preferences are claimed to be highly influential (Butler and Stokes 1974). Such claims are evidenced by discussions surrounding when respondents married and the spouse had a different political allegiance. The motivation to maintain harmony in the family was more important than partisanship.

> My other half is a member of the Labour Party. He is really strongly involved. I felt it would be irresponsible to vote, because I don't pay enough attention and was probably influenced by my parents' politics, and I thought maybe for the wrong reasons, so I didn't. (Female, degree)

The desire to avoid confrontation was possibly a reason for avoiding political debate and campaign stimuli, as this is competitive and adversarial. When discussing their understanding of politics and campaign issues they acknowledged their limited understanding. There was a perception that they probably should start to think about political issues. The level of ability to process information, and analyse new information alongside their existing knowledge, was evident in the transcripts, where discussions were quite articulate, discussion was demonstrably longer and the vocabulary employed was much more varied than other groups. However, when political concepts were discussed, the guilt resurfaced, as they had little knowledge but felt they should have. They were able to articulate abstract issues but political issues were largely too remote for them to evaluate. For Guilty Know Nothings, promotional activity could engage them, first, by reducing the adversarial nature of campaigning; second, by bringing to an end negative campaigning and, finally, by engaging in responsible election campaigning.

Political Cynics

The Political Cynics displayed a similar characteristic of disengagement but, in their case, disengagement came from alienation with the system. There was little respect for politicians and the political system was claimed to be quite undemocratic. Among this group there was a lack of trust in politicians and the political system, with much cynicism of politicians in general.

> All smiles. They all smile. (Male, unemployed)

Political cynics believe that, rather than using an elaborate language code to illuminate particular issues, this group believe that they use this to conceal their true motives. This group are the most cynical of the use of marketing and promotion in political campaigning: they see it as superficial and 'spun'. The most damning comments came from the male degree-educated group, who evidenced the greatest cynicism:

> Liars, on the whole . . . They all seem full of promises and then you don't see a lot following that. The Labour government, for example . . . (Male, degree)

Another claimed:

> I don't like politicians, to be honest. I don't really take much notice . . . [They are] not very trustworthy. That's the general impression I get. (Male, degree)

There was some knowledge of proportional representation (PR) in this group and a discussion arose about which political system was most democratic. These respondents were the only group to recognise that one vote will not make a great difference to the overall outcome of an election and saw the reluctance of the Labour government to introduce PR as being in defence of their own self-interest. This degree of cynicism was also evident when talking about the two-party system. There was broader discussion of political concepts and the alternatives in this group but also recognition that the current system hindered smaller parties.

> With the two-party system I know that they [the Liberal Democrats] could get in. (Male, degree)

However, when looking at their motivation to get involved in the electoral process, this is very low, as they do not believe the newspapers, as they are perceived to be politically biased and untruthful. There was a view that the political parties manoeuvre the press within this group and they spoke most vociferously against 'spin'. Indeed, this was the only group of non-voters who understood the term 'spin'. Therefore even the information they gained from the media was processed with a degree of cynicism. Some members of this group also demonstrated a level of apathy; although a significant number of respondents in this group had voted in the 1997 election, there was a perception that they had been duped. All parties were the same in that they need to keep most of the people happy most of the time and retain the *status quo*. The following quote sums up this group's feelings well:

> They [the government] run the country for the people. In general, they are often worried about who they'll offend instead of doing what they feel is right for the country. They'll see how little they can offend with what they do. (Male, degree)

This group believed that there had been little change between one government and the next. There was no optimism among this group when the Labour government was first elected, even though some had voted Labour and had a Labour background. Many have a very negative view of politics in that they view politicians as corrupt, self-interested, or both:

> they seem to do it for their self-interest. There seems to be quite a lot of corruption, and they should be serving the public interest. (Male, degree)
>
> Yeah, I think the local ones are probably more untrustworthy than the national ones, 'cos there's a lot more media attention. When you think how many people actually do get caught nationally it makes headlines, 'cos it's a real scandal, but at the local level in the councils there's probably loads of fiddles going on, probably a lot greater. (Male, degree)

For the Political Cynics politicians and political parties are 'all the same' but they observe events from a distance, making judgements but claiming uninterest, owing to the perceived corrupt nature of the political system. This group used elaborate communication codes and were able to understand political rhetoric. This is evidenced by strong cynicism about Tony Blair among this group; he was seen to be shallow and superficial, with a 'shiny' smile. Political Cynics were conscious of the marketised nature of the political product which is presented like a brand with core values (such as the five-item pledge card) and spun accordingly. They were most concerned about the debate on weapons of mass destruction and the justification for the war in Iraq. For this group, this was damning evidence that Tony Blair was a 'liar'.

This group was predominantly male and degree-educated. They occasionally watch the news, but claim not to take a great deal of notice; they rarely watch current affairs programmes. Political Cynics watched political affairs quite assiduously in order to observe when promises are broken; they actively seek evidence of marketing activities, but they do this to reaffirm their view that politics is manipulative, unethical and politicians are untrustworthy. This group had a demonstrably high ability to conceptualise political issues and a strong awareness of a number of political issues; they recognised the difficulty of government, the balancing of promises and the accommodation of different interest groups but seemed to have a very pessimistic view of the outcome.

> [It] doesn't matter who's in government, either Conservatives or Labour. Nothing seems to change. (Male, degree)

Political Cynics claim to have little interest in the democratic process; they do not believe in it, and they possess little interest in elections or politics in general, but they claim that this results from a low level of trust in the political system.

> I think they are all the same, to be honest . They all seem to care about the media, what's in the papers. Nothing seems to change from one to another. (Male, degree)

Political Cynics also indicated that their attitudes persisted after an election, as they find promises broken. One respondent believed that the continued success of the Labour Party was purely down to the dissatisfaction with Conservative policies; they see little positivity related to any aspect of the political process. This results in little interest in, or recall of, political communication, party political broadcasts especially, except the communication could be used to reinforce their negative views.

> I can remember watching one. It was like it wasn't that subtle. They didn't tell us what they were going to do, they just picked on what the Conservatives hadn't done. I just couldn't believe that this had been allowed. (Female, degree)

Among these respondents their cynicism about PEBs was related to the notion that they were like advertising. They recognised the hooks and symbols used in classical conditioning and likened PEBs to propaganda. Propaganda had negative connotations within this group and was strongly associated with manipulation.

> Yeah, now you mention, I do remember watching that one. It's just glossy, like advertising. There's nothing really there. It's just, I suppose, they're trying to aim at people like us who aren't obviously that involved and don't take that much of an interest and try to hook in that couple of minutes. For me it just doesn't help. (Female, degree).

For this group there was no distinction between persuasion and manipulation; they had a negative perception of all promotional activity, as it was all seen as superficial, glossy advertising lacking any substance. Out of all the media channels used by political marketers, posters had the greatest level of recall but little notice was taken of message content. However, this lack of awareness could be due to the fact that they wanted to emphasise their cynicism; they wear it as a badge of honour, by not showing that they could possibly be influenced by political messages. They remembered the 'demon eyes' and derided that as another attempt to use marketing tools to manipulate potential voters; the 'pigs might fly' poster was further used to justify their cynicism. Overall their view is blamed on the use of negative campaigning; this group found it more distasteful than any of the other groups, as it further enforced their view of politics as a dirty business. For this group there is little opportunity to influence their voting decision; their attitude to abstention appears to be quite resolute. Their cynicism of the media and any political communication is built on a belief that they are able to decode and deconstruct the messages so they could avoid being fooled by what they perceive to be a type of propaganda.

Interestingly, the political party that did command some respect was the Liberal Democrats. Political cynics perceived Charles Kennedy as a credible leader, an honest, genuine sort of man. His approach to political campaigning, relying on a more in-depth communication of policies and a refusal to engage in negative campaigning, was respected by the Political Cynics. However, this is where the frustration with the political system arose, as they believed that, although his party was credible, the system would not enable it to get into power; they blamed the other parties. This group have well developed selective perception, they regularly reinforce their cynical view of promotional campaigns by searching out the right stimuli. It is difficult to see how this group will ever engage in political discourse, as the levels of trust have been so severely eroded.

Conclusion

In summary, young non-voter groups are much more diverse than the literature suggests and the reasons for alienation or abstention are complicated, dependent upon a host of variables including, but not limited to, background, education and also, for some, previous experience. However, as these variables are also interrelated, and vary over time, these factors add to the complexity. To a great extent education determined the cognitive capacity of the uninvolved groups and this in turn determined how they engaged with political communication messages and the campaign itself. For instance, the Guilty Know Nothings and the Political Cynics were most likely to come from degree-educated groups, whilst the Know Nothings were identified most strongly in the clerical and unemployed groups. When exploring the attitudinal components of their beliefs, from an affective perspective, both the Know Nothings and the Political Cynics distrust politics but they differ in their cognitive structures. For the Know Nothings politics is meaningless and irrelevant, whilst Political Cynics believe politicians are all the same and the political system is sleazy and unethical. On the other hand, Guilty Know Nothings have a similar cognitive capacity to the Political Cynics and are capable of understanding complex elaboration codes but are unfamiliar with the language and communication codes of politics. This leads to their diffidence towards politics: although they believe it is important and serious, they also think it is too difficult to identify with. They either do not vote but feel guilty that they should vote given its importance or feel they should not vote, as this legitimises a corrupt and elitist system.

The promotional campaigns used by the political parties failed to engage these groups of voters at the 2005 election for three main reasons. First, the Conservative Party promotional strategy of fear and negative campaigning merely reinforced the Political Cynics' view of how marketing and propaganda are intertwined, nor did they engage the other two non-voter groups. Second, the Labour Party, with the focus on presenting the party as a brand, had little effect in engaging any of the non-voter groups. Finally, the Liberal Democrats' attempt to engage the electorate in a more considered, cognitive campaign was more believable, Charles Kennedy's presentation was perceived to be honest but the lack of experience and the inability to win were key concerns. Marketing is not spin, branding is not just superficial packaging. If political parties are to use marketing techniques they need to use them to inform and engage the electorate rather than alienate them by using communication codes that are perceived as being meaningless or duplicitous.

References

Ansolabehere, S. Iyengar, S. (1995), *Going Negative: How Political Advertisements Shrink and Polarise the Electorate*, New York: Free Press.

Bennett, S. E. (1988), 'Know Nothings' revisited: the meaning of political ignorance today', *Social Science Quarterly* 69: 476–90.

Bernstein, B. (1971), *Class, Codes and Control* I, *Theoretical Studies towards a Sociology of Language*, London: Routledge.

Bhavnani, K. (1994), *Talking Politics: A Psychological Framing of Views from Youth in Britain*, Cambridge: Cambridge University Press

Brynner, J. and Ashford, S. (1994), 'Politics and participation: some antecedents of young people's attitudes to the political system and political activity', *European Journal of Social Psychology* 24 (2): 223–6.

Butler, D. and Stokes, D. E. (1969), *Political Change in Britain: The Evolution of Electoral Change*, London: Macmillan.

Butler, D. and Stokes, D. E. (1974), *Political Change in Britain: The Evolution of Electoral Change*, London: Macmillan.

Crewe, I. (1996), 'Partisan loyalties: dealignment or realignment?' in G. Evans and P. Norris (eds), *Critical Elections: British Parties and Voters in Long Term Perspective*, London: Sage.

Crewe, I., Fox, T. and Alt, J. (1992), 'Non-voting in British General Elections, 1966–October 1974', in D. Denver and G. Hands (eds), *Issues and Controversies in British Electoral Behaviour*, Hemel Hempstead: Harvester Wheatsheaf.

Denver, D. and Hands, G. (1990), 'Issues, principles or ideology? How young people decide', *Electoral Studies* 9 (1): 19–36.

Dermody, J. and Hanmer-Lloyd, S. (2003), *Negative Media: Another Nail in the Democratic Coffin*, London: Goldsmiths.

Diplock, S. (2001), *None of the Above: Non-voters and the 2001 Election*, London: Hansard Society.

Electoral Commission (2001), *Election 2001: The Official Results*, London: Politico.

Fahmy, E. (1996) 'Young people's political participation: results from a 1996 MORI Omnibus survey. Online at www.radstats.org.uk/no070/article3.htm.

Furnham, A. and Gunter, B. (1989), *The Anatomy of Adolescence: Young People's Social Attitudes in Britain*, London: Routledge.

Gomez, B. T. and Wilson, J. T. (2001), 'Political sophistication and economic voting in the American electorate: a theory of heterogeneous attribution', *American Journal of Political Science* 45 (4): 899–914.

Heath, A. and Park, A. (1997), 'Thatcher's children?' in R. Jowell *et al.* (eds), *British Social Attitudes: The Fourteenth Report, The End of Conservative Values?*' Aldershot: Gower.

Henn, M. and Weinstein, M. (2002), 'Do you Remember the First Time? First-time Voters in the 2001 General Election', paper presented to the Political Studies Association conference, Aberdeen, April.

Henn, M., Weinstein, M. and Wring, D. (2002), 'A generation apart? Youth and political participation in Britain', *British Journal of Politics and International Relations* 4 (2): 167–92.

Hiscock, D. (2001), 'The apathy generation', *The Guardian*, 9 May.

Hyman, H. and Sheatsley, P. (1947), 'Some reasons why information campaigns fail', *Public Opinion Quarterly* 37 (1): 279–90.

Kimberlee, R. (1998), 'Young people and the General Election of 1997', *Renewal* 6 (2): 87–90.

Morgan, B. (2001), 'General Election Results, 7 June 2001', House of Commons Library. Online at www.parliament.uk/commonslib/research/rp2001/rp01–054.pdf.

Mulgan, G. and Wilkinson, H. (1997), 'Freedom's children and the rise of generational politics', in G. Mulgan (ed.), *Life after Politics: New Thinking for the Twenty-first Century*, London: Fontana.

Park, A. (1995), 'Teenagers and their politics', in R. Jowell, J. Curtice and A. Park, *British Social Attitudes, Twelfth Report*, Aldershot: Dartmouth.

Park, A. (1999), 'Young people and political apathy', in R. Jowell, J. Curtice, A. Park, K. Thompson and L. Jarvis (eds), *British Social Attitudes: The Sixteenth Report*, Aldershot: Ashgate.

Russell, A., Fieldhouse, E., Purdam, K. and Kalra, V. (2002), *Voter Engagement and Young People*, London: Electoral Commission.

White, C., Devine, F. and Ritchie, J. (1999), 'Voter volatility: a qualitative study of voting behaviour at the 1997 General Election', *Social and Community Planning Research*, January.

Wring, D. (1999), 'The marketing colonisation of political campaigning', in B. Newman (ed.), *A Handbook of Political Marketing*, London: Sage.

Wring, D., Henn, M. and Weinstein, M. (1999), 'Young people and contemporary politics: committed scepticism or engaged cynicism?' in J. Fisher, P. Cowley, D. Denver and A. Russell (eds), *British Elections and Parties Review*, London: Cass.

11

Conclusion: was 2005 the year political marketing came of age?

Darren G. Lilleker, Nigel A. Jackson and Richard Scullion

Traditionally, politicians have rejected the idea of marketing playing a role in politics, implying that it necessitates creating the policies that voters want. Rather, politicians have suggested that they create a vision of what society *should* look like, and then seek to persuade voters that it is the best way forward. To some the adoption of political marketing signals the first stirrings of critical change in this outlook. That it is the voter, even if it is at this stage a small segment within the electorate, whose vision of society is imprinted upon party policy. If so it may be indicative of the future direction in party behaviour, particularly at election time. This final chapter returns to the three key broad areas of the book – the political offering, the communication strategies and the electorate's views – in order to assess the electoral practices from a marketing perspective. Here we also return to the central enquiry of this research collection, the extent to which the electorate actually do play a role in shaping these three elements of the parties' character and behaviour, in order to gain an understanding of how political marketing is practised in the context of a UK election.

The contributions of the campaign context to political marketing

First, however, it is important to understand how the electoral and political context of the 2005 General Election shaped the framework within which our contributors operated. Changes in the constituency boundaries, the reduction in Scottish seats and the low turnout in 2001 all helped to set the scene. However, the dominant electoral context, which shaped the campaign, was the 'first past the post' electoral system, which had particular resonance for political marketing. First, it reduced the choice of the electorate. It is possible to buy the same brand of soap powder in supermarkets all over the UK, yet there is a vast array of choices for the consumer. In most cases, however, electors had only three 'real' choices, and this is not uniform across the nation. In many cases the 'real' choice was between two, and in the safe seats there was no real potential to have any influence over the result at all. Second, only a fairly limited number of seats affect the final outcome of the election; as a result parties focus most of their campaigning effort in the closely fought marginal seats. In marketing terms this means that identifying and tailoring messages to very small segments of the electorate has a disproportionate effect on the final result. The majority of the electorate are increasingly aware of their being largely taken for granted and left to experience a distant tele-visual campaign. Third, the importance of these target seats opens up a potential schism in the campaign strategy. It appears that there are now three distinct campaigns: one aimed at the masses, transmitted via the media; a traditional constituency ground war; and a nationally orchestrated and targeted campaign aimed towards key voters. Thus in target marginal constituencies there are two styles of campaign in competition: a highly marketised and propagandist one from the national party offices and a lower-key relational approach building on service provision. There are a number of questions this raises for political marketing. First, does it mean that party marketing is aimed purely at a small segment of voters, so excluding the majority from product development and communication design? Second, are parties attempting to develop aggregate policies or aggregate messages that will catch the majority of voters across the nation? Finally, what are the effects upon the voters?

It appears from our analysis that there is little real attempt to engage with voters directly in designing the product, not even the key floating voters in the target seats. There are attempts to both lead and follow the public agenda, with Labour acting as the follower to the greater extent. However, the predominant strategy is to design communication that will appeal to the voters at different levels. The targeted direct mail will highlight specific issues of relevance, and will offer a message that is designed to appeal; national campaigns sell the parties on broad platforms and offer the impression of 'listening'. Voters, it appears, see through this. Many of them, it seems, are largely not engaged. While in the target marginal seats they are mobilised for a variety of reasons, they largely recognise many campaign communication techniques as marketing. Is this a problem with politics, political marketing as it is deployed or the consumers?

Marketing – or just packaging?

One way to read this book is to argue that we are witnessing rhetorical marketing in the contemporary political campaign. If enough professional campaigners and political commentators say marketing is happening (and enough of us spend time debating the issue) then it is! There is, however, a significant proviso in taking such a stance: people can see through the rhetoric! A marketing orientation imbues organisations and individuals with a certain way of viewing the world. It means more than placing priority on looking for neat and mutually rewarding ways of matching one's 'offerings' with the needs and wants of potential customers. It also means accepting changes in a political offering, and that politics in all its guises – from policy and delivery processes through to the structures of the system itself – should be most sensitive to those outside the political organisation. Our contention is that this responsiveness should be born out of a belief that it is the right way to conduct our affairs rather than begrudging expediency.

Most of the chapters in this book bear witness to increased professionalism in terms of how the campaign itself was organised and implemented. Several chapters demonstrate that the 2005 election saw improved, more systematic, adoption of marketing techniques – from central call centres canvassing those most likely to influence the electoral outcome to the controlled communication channels (advertising, direct mail, etc.) sticking tightly to a predetermined set of messages. All imply that political actors use the language and logic of marketing more frequently and perhaps a little more comfortably than once was the case. Parties segment and target voters, recognise they are probably brand managers in various manifestations and are concerned about developing positive 'relationships' with core groups. If marketing equates with promotion then it would appear quite unproblematic to conclude by congratulating the political parties for their enhanced use of commercial marketing practices.

However, read together, the chapters present a far less positive picture for political marketing in terms of its practice during the 2005 General Election. The story that emerges as we take stock of all nine chapters is one that might have been typical of many commercial organisations some twenty years ago when they 'discovered' the wonders of marketing! That is to say, when they thought that marketing was simply a different way of selling what they were good at producing. Following the structure of the book, we see first that there is little sense of a market orientation at the root of policy formation or, in marketing terminology, product development. Linked with that finding, second, we observe modest attempts to apply a marketing outlook within party organisation to ensure it is focused, integrated and offers some semblance of being responsive to external stakeholders. However, finally, we also find an audience who, whilst they may have noticed the extra gloss, did not believe anything of significance had changed, from their perspective. Just as research can be used to support a position already adopted rather than help determine that position, so marketing seems to have been widely used when and where it fitted the prior agendas of the main players, and this market orientation seemed to fit most easily into the communication stage of the campaign process.

Plotting the orientation through the political process

There is little evidence to suggest that the core political offerings were determined by insightful appreciation of the specific wishes of the electorate. Ormond and Henneberg's analysis of the party manifestoes offers conclusions that are remarkably analogous to the overall sense we gain from this collection of work: evidence of a cautious and at times selective market orientation. Savigny's chapter (4) does point out the acceptance by the political parties of managerialism that, in part, has replaced ideology as a driving force. She argues that both main parties now have an underlying ontological commitment to market-led solutions to political issues, a situation which has clear implications for democratic dialogue. Ormond and Henneberg's notion of gravitational centrist forces (chapter 2) may well be a result of this acceptance that the market simply has to play a leading part in the development of a political programme. Lloyd's chapter (3) reveals how the parties have a quite sophisticated understanding of the differentiating role of branding and that they try to utilise both functional and emotional benefits where possible. However, she argues that the positioning territory considered acceptable leaves little room for distinction other than in terms of transient personalities. In addition she says that, despite the highly professional approach to branding, much of the electorate ends up buying into the least bad option. Thus we appear to be observing the emergence of a market place full of negative brands. Apparently paradoxical conclusions can be drawn by overlapping the findings from these first three chapters: to the degree that a market orientation has impacted the political products it has served as a force for convergence, not difference.

A market orientation is most evident in the strategic approach to 'getting the message out'. Dermody and Hanmer-Lloyd's chapter (5) illustrates well how all three main parties act as a commercial brand with regard to the promotion of their image and the construction of integrated messages, but they note that this of itself does not add up to a market orientation. A development mirrored in Gaber's chapter (6), where he discusses the battle for the media agenda indicative of a selective market orientation: utilised when it is seen as beneficial.

Rhetorically Labour were most market-oriented, because their messages most closely matched public priorities as shown in polls; however this does not suggest that the policy direction was determined by interaction with the public, only that they were influential over the party communication. Jackson's chapter (7) also demonstrates a move in the direction of the political parties' use of new media as a more substantive marketing tool. He argues this is currently most potent as an internal marketing device; this is symptomatic of an approach that uses marketing pragmatically, here and there, to key segments when necessary, but marketing as a philosophy is not allowed to inform all behavioural aspects at all times.

The response to this rather patchy approach to political marketing by the parties, from the electorate's perspective, seems to have been 'Can't spot the difference.' Supporting this argument, Scullion's chapter (8) suggests the election could not have been anything other than marketing-oriented, given that the electorate are comfortable consumers while at best being reluctant citizens. In other words they bring a consumerist perspective to bear regardless of the political parties' actions. However, while consumers view politics through a marketing lens, politicians appear to be content with a sales approach. Dean's investigation (chapter 10) of young potential voters supports this view, as she found that the campaign simply did not connect, regardless of approach; indeed, Labour's more 'slick' style fed the existing cynicism of some. Somewhat ironically Lilleker's chapter (9) shows that a more traditional approach to campaigning, on the doorstep, face to face, listening to the concerns voters raise, appears to be viewed positively and can contribute to a propensity to vote. This perhaps represents a truer form of market orientation, yet a fear is that it may be employed only for cynical purposes: to nurse a small majority and attempt to retain power in a marginal constituency where every vote matters and any advantage can be crucial. If we were to plot the degree of market orientation apparent, following the structure of the book, we might see something like that outlined in Figure 11.1.

Explanations for the shape of this orientation

Conversations with the electorate at a macro-level, however 'big' they are, do not directly shape the manifesto pledges or the codified political language utilised. The holy grail of the so-called 'middle ground' leads to an election being fought over a narrow set of issues discussed within a limited remit. The essences of the political offerings remain shades of a left–right spectrum governed by the structural impediments to

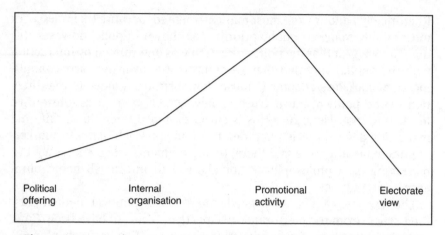

| Political offering | Internal organisation | Promotional activity | Electorate view |

Figure 11.1 Market orientation manifest in the General Election of 2005

engagement – most people being in 'safe seats', where an overriding sense of it not mattering prevails. Greater central control and consistency-enabling technology do mean the main parties were more able to present a united front. So an internal market orientation of sorts is detectable alongside a more sporadic external market orientation. Whether this is adhered to by party members in order to improve electoral chances rather than because it is considered to be a better form of politics is debatable. With huge spin machines, the use of commercial communication agencies and greater understanding of message control and manipulation, the promotional campaigns were, in many ways, comparable to those designed for commercial brands. However, the messenger remains the political class who at best are misunderstood but can also be treated with suspicion; at worst they are detested by much of their audience. The market they operate in, 'mainstream politics', remains a marginal and tainted one to many, and the political players in the heat of electoral battle largely ignore this defining problem. The electoral system rewarding the winner regardless of overall turnout, and indifferent to the number of votes cast not in support but in dismay at the alternatives, means any shift in market orientation can easily be dismissed as mere window dressing.

Future research agenda

This book has made concluding remarks that suggest political marketing is currently practised in a rather disjointed manner that places great emphasis on the middle stage: communicating the product offering and paying only 'lip service' during product development to the role of the political consumer. At a broad level further research needs to better understand *why* this is the case by, for example, focusing on the attitudes of the political classes towards the idea of a market orientation. Is there serious miscomprehension about what this notion actually is or are there other reasons for resisting its full import into the political arena? More specifically each chapter raises specific questions and issues that can usefully be taken forward by future research projects.

When focusing upon their discrete elements of the product Ormrod and Henneberg argue in Chapter 2 that the party manifesto should take into account elements of what they call the Strategic Political Postures, in order to create a political offering that distinguishes itself from the competition. Are such postures noticed and if so how are they interpreted by the various stakeholders the manifesto is aimed at? Lloyd says in Chapter 3 many voters are unable to differentiate between the main political brands using anything other than personally relevant heuristics and consequently governments are more likely to be elected on the basis of appearance over substance. Whilst in Chapter 4 Savigny sees convergence around policy issues, and nonpolicy issues resulting in decisions for voters being reduced to 'which campaign team had implemented the best marketing strategy', this means that research is required that investigates the consequence of such changes on the legitimacy of governments chosen with, perhaps, less consideration than which take-away to buy on the way home this evening.

Similar questions are also raised through the study of the development of communication and the reactions of the receiver. Dermody and Hanmer-Lloyd demonstrate in Chapter 5 how promotional marketing tools are currently being used in election campaigns with an emphasis on creating distrust and suspicion of the competing political parties, whilst Dean (Chapter 10) suggests the promotional campaigns used fail to engage the groups of voters most disengaged because the campaigning merely reinforced the political cynics' view of how marketing, as propaganda, is used by politicians. How, in this lose–lose situation, where the source of the message destroys the credibility of whatever message it is, can forms of mass communication play a positive role in tackling aspects of the democratic deficit? Gaber notes in Chapter 6 that there is not a media agenda but in fact six separate dominant agendas, all competing for attention and all, to some extent, influencing each other. This may sound like a positive endorsement of a plural democracy operating well. However, if we dig beneath the surface might it actually be revealing some type of 'matching game' is taking place where each is trying to second-guess in order to 'fit' the agenda they feel is likely to be the winning formula?

In Chapter 7 Jackson claims evidence that the parties have most of the basis of a relationship marketing strategy in place through an evaluation of their Web sites. He argues that most parties particularly recognise the importance of membership recruitment opportunities that the Web provides. Given that an election can be only a snapshot, how can parties use the Internet, especially e-mail, to build strong, mutually beneficial and fruitful relationships between election campaigns? The answer to this may be not with e-communication but with local interaction. Lilleker argues in Chapter 9 that the verdict on a locally focused marketing strategy is that it has a role; it can develop and maintain trust between local politicians and active members of the electorate (see also Coleman 2005). Lilleker states, 'Above all, it is the contact with the candidate, the face-to-face relationships that have the most profound effect,' though this is limited to a few rather than the majority of voters. Future research needs to test whether what were once viewed as the peripheral aspects are growing in importance among voters who need to feel that the state and its political organisations are interested in them, as citizens and consumers of policy, rather than seeking power and using marketing communication as a tool to exploit a weak market place.

Linking with this, Scullion demonstrates in Chapter 8 that, currently, electoral choice is often seen as rather insignificant and that this is in part because consumers have a well developed ability to engage a plethora of life-affirming choices in their consumer sphere. A fuller understanding of an electorate acting primarily as consumers might frame what politics comes to mean is required. A better understanding of the consumer, the way that they process politics and political messages, and the effects upon behaviour, is argued to be crucial for a connection to be constructed between the public and political spheres (Coleman 2005). This is analogous to the development of a true market orientation, where political representatives actually do represent, thanks to being 'in touch' with the electorate, and actively maintain a channel of communication that nurtures mutual trust and understanding. The challenge for those who see this as a goal is: how can it be put into operation?

Clearly this list of potential research agendas is not meant to be either exhaustive, nor does it reflect the priorities of any of the individual authors. These questions are here to act as stimuli to the reader, to encourage further thoughts and work in this area. Political marketing offers a range of explanatory tools, as well as some that would prescribe behaviour; as yet, though, there is much understanding that is under-developed. These questions offer some routes that might rewardingly continue the exploration into understanding what political marketing *actually* is, what it does and the nature of its potential.

The future of political marketing?

This final section then purports to answer a rather broad and somewhat nebulous question, particularly given the context for this study being limited to a single election in one country. Perhaps this distance between what the political class do and what is comprehended by much of the electorate is the fundamental question that students and scholars need to consider at this juncture. The analysis of the three components of an election campaign – the party offering, the attendant communication and the way that the communication was received and processed – indicates that political marketing is not necessarily a feature of elections in the UK. What evidence is there for this statement? If we posit that political marketing indicates not merely the adaptation of various concepts drawn from the world of consumer product development and associated communication, but that it is the adoption of a marketing philosophy, whereby market forces influence all aspects of an organisation's behaviour, then clearly this is simply not happening. Marketing as a discipline is about much more than communication, and indeed communication should by definition be secondary to the development of the product. In contrast it seems that, in the political sphere, communication is prioritised above all other aspects of behaviour. It is suggested that politics is packaged (Franklin, 2004), that political behaviour is designed to be communication-friendly; however, this does not indicate a marketing philosophy. What it suggests is that marketing informs one aspect of behaviour only. It may determine the nature of communication, and even the subject. However, the parties standing for election did not present clear evidence that the political solutions they offered were those desired by the market. Perhaps actually the nature of the communication reinforces this conclusion, given the extent to which the major parties led with a negative message about their opponents, instead of offering a consistently positive message about the future of the nation should they be elected.

The evidence presented suggests that the political campaigner at the turn of the twenty-first century employs a magpie approach to the design of an election campaign. Magpies are birds that steal things that are shiny; politicians in turn are stealing techniques that offer rewards. The problem is that, just as magpies line their nests with milk-bottle tops as well as the occasional jewelled pendant, politicians may also steal something that looks glossy but has no value to the consumer. For magpies the appearance is sufficient; consumers seem to feel that politicians think along similar lines.

In terms of the party offerings, these were packaged within a discourse of dialogue. Rhetorically parties were either following the public consensus or they were leading but within a discourse of shared understanding. Thus they attempted to reflect authenticity in their offering, they offered themselves as the repositories of the public will, an almost Rousseauesque conception, yet this is hardly evidence of a marketing philosophy. What is lacking is a grounded understanding of exactly what the public desire from the political product, a conception that appears to be far beyond what is currently on offer: a neo-liberal management team who appear self-obsessed, rather than focused on serving their consumers.

Thus it appears that political marketing may be nothing more than a veneer which tries to obscure the actuality of *Realpolitik*. Parties sell themselves as being consumer-focused yet actually the process of government is perhaps far too complex to be led by market forces. Thus a party is able to adopt a market orientation while in opposition, as was the case with New Labour 1994–97 (Lees-Marshment 2001), but this must be abandoned as it gets closer to taking power. Perhaps this is the conundrum at the heart of the modern political landscape. Consumers have an expectation that governments should do the bidding of those who give them their vote; in many ways they may have some instinctive feeling that the vote is payment and they should receive a certain level of service, perhaps even access, in return. However, a government acting in the post-9/11 global economy is unable to act in this way. The economy is driven by the international community with which a nation trades, foreign policy is governed by alliances as well as broader concerns for global security. What room is there for governments to follow public opinion, and in the long term would they be thanked for doing so?

If the process of exchange is a flawed premise through which to understand voting behaviour, then marketing, in its various guises, is not going to be a panacea for the problematic political landscape inhabited by our political parties. Could it be the case that as voter partisanship shrank, and the advertising gurus and marketing consultants moved in, the process of disengagement was exacerbated? That the consumer, who faces millions of different marketing stimuli in any average week, will happily accept organisations as diverse as shampoo manufacturers and banks to sell their wares using similar techniques, but perhaps expect something different, maybe something quantifiably better, from aspirant political leaders? Is it the use of negativity, because it appears to work for the eventual victor, for example for the Republicans in the US in 2004, glossy sloganeering, because it works for HSBC, or tele-marketing, because it works in conservatory sales, that helps turn voters away from electoral politics?

The answer appears to be mixed. Largely voters are disengaged from the process, and the market called 'traditional politics' is not attractive to them. Politics is externalised to their ordinary lives and debates during the elections are irrelevant and detached from their lives. Only at the local level, when there is a real interface between the politician and the voter, is there any indication that an electoral candidate is awarded value. Elsewhere, and even among those who vote, but vote on national politics, the situation seems to echo Lloyd's conclusion that the person selected is the best of a bad bunch, not the person who is desired to be the Prime Minister. Even among those who value their MP there is a cynicism about politics beyond the confines of their constituency. Interesting, then, that the glossiness is largely eschewed by those candidates who feel they have been awarded what Jim Knight, Labour MP for Dorset South, described as 'permission to contact' their electorate (Lilleker, 2005).

So where does this leave political marketing? Should we recommend a return to a more locally focused, non-marketised form of campaigning and relegate the whole concept to the dustbin of failed electoral techniques and realms of academic study? This is the fundamental question which we feel this analysis raises. Perhaps what is required is for political actors to gain a complete understanding of what the public desire from their elected representatives. Maybe if politicians attempt to discover why voter-consumers externalise electoral politics, and the young feel that electioneering is irrelevant to their everyday lives, and act in a way to reverse these trends of disengagement, then a renewed interest in election campaigns can emerge. Does this suggest the employment of a marketing philosophy or a shift away from an ontological perspective that promotes the power of market forces and for parties to lead public opinion while being honest about the realities of the modern political environment? However, this raises some further questions. First, do they try this but their arguments are lost amid the rest of their salesmanship? Second, even if they do present a non-marketised communicative message, do voters now see nothing but the sheen?

Our evidence suggests that we are able to analyse some facets of party behaviour by employing marketing concepts, yet it is more difficult to apply marketing in order to explain all party inputs and outputs.

Concepts such as brands and branding, and that of a marketing philosophy, seem to lack sufficient fit. Equally, marketing does not fully explain why one party appears victorious; it may be the market leader, but why? Labour were a tarnished brand, yet won; however, across the nation a series of mini-battles saw a much more diverse picture, suggesting more is at work than simply a single marketing campaign. Thus we could resort more successfully to more traditional terrain, campaign intensity at the local level, issue salience or emotional partisan attachment as explanatory – all of which can be part of a marketing strategy but would not constitute political marketing. Maybe it is safe only to argue that the party with the best marketing and news management strategy and which sells itself best *can* win over some of the electorate – but perhaps only those voters who are willing to base their voter-decision upon merely this type of criteria.

Marketing can explain this from the consumer perspective, however. The key factor that emerged from the analysis of voter reception was that the differences between the Labour and Conservative Parties had blurred to the point of intangibility, while the Liberal Democrat brand lacked sufficient credibility. The offering was unclear, as in 2001 Labour and the Conservatives largely focused on the same issues, in fact the wedge issue of Europe was abandoned, leaving fewer points of differentiation. Clearly the major parties all led on issues of salience; however, the promises remained vague. Therefore the consumer is left unsure which brand to trust. Equally, apart from the voters mobilised in the marginal constituencies, most voters found the election irrelevant to them. There were some aspects that were salient, particularly in terms of the agendas, but largely this was swamped with parties' negative messages and the media focus upon process rather than policy; thus we find the media also complicit in the process of disengagement.

Unlike consumer marketing, political marketing in its current form does not engage fully with the life of the voter-consumer. Why is this? One main reason is that at the most fundamental level none of the parties is really conducting marketing as any other organisation would understand it. The approach is largely sales-oriented, meaning they are simply concerned about selling their product to the masses. The voter-consumer desires a more personalised and relevant approach which may well be beyond their reach. As has been the case previously, there is little hard evidence that parties allow the voters to inform policy in any real sense (Lilleker and Negrine 2006). This returns us to our critique of the parties as magpies. Rather than adopting marketing to inform their behaviour they pick a few techniques, some to engage with core voters, some to attract the floating voters, but this pick-and-mix approach does not appeal to the voters. Some will vote out of duty, some will be drawn in by the glossy coating of the campaign, others will use rational or emotional approaches to their decision; yet we return to the choice being limited and uninformed and for many a trivial one. Should marketing be deployed properly, can it form those connections that appear to be demanded? Or is this actually a fallacious argument; is it the fact that marketing is inappropriate in a political context? Equally, and returning to actual party behaviour, is campaigning now simply about gaining sufficient votes to win an election and actually the democratic deficit does not matter?

This raises the thorny question of whether parties have any motivation to consider their behaviour to any profound extent. Due to the 'first past the post' election system, would parties wish to engage the voter, especially given that currently enough vote for them to give them victory? Parties actually pursue the votes of the few in order to win those micro-contests that are most likely to enable them to win the overall battle. Parties will attempt to mobilise 'their' vote, as well as demobilising the voters who will not support them. If gaining power is a zero-sum game, in which ethics are optional, and when a contest can be won by adopting an electoral professional campaigning model, what role is there for real marketing? Currently the role ascribed for marketing is to attempt to cut through the clutter within the modern promotional society and sell politics to the voters. However, direct communication appears to be failing. Evidence suggests that high-profile, proactive and service-oriented candidates can get a message across, but the majority of voters' information is gleaned from the mass media. Given the media treatment of politics, this can do nothing to reverse the trend of disengagement. As Gaber notes, Labour may be able to tie their messages to the media and public agenda but if the message is irrelevant or mistrusted this is insufficient for engaging a public cynical and distrustful of political candidates.

Marketing's function is to satisfy consumers; politics as it currently operates consistently fails to do so. Maybe politics cannot be market-oriented, if it is all about leading and not following. The problem is that consumer expectations are far higher than can be delivered by those who perform within the constraints imposed by 'the art of the possible'. Yet perhaps this is missing the trick. Politicians need to understand their consumers, present their cases in a way that combines the best practices of politics and of marketing. We could contend that the failure of the political sphere to engage the public is because marketing is deployed purely for the promotional aspects of party behaviour, thus the marketing is peripheral: perhaps it is correct to claim the parties are using 'bad' marketing. Parties claim they are 'guided', 'informed' by and 'synergistic' with public opinion. Parties listen and act, we are told; but in the UK in 2005 few voters believed it to be the case. Perhaps then political marketing, as it is practised, is at a crossroads. Parties should implement the full marketing philosophy, starting with policy development and the structure of the political organisations, or should abandon marketing altogether. What appears to be happening is the gap between political and public is growing, and it does not seem to be too wild an assumption to suggest that political marketing, as it is currently practised in the UK, is one key cause.

References

Coleman, S. (2005), *Direct Representation: Towards a Conversational Democracy*, London: IPPR.

Franklin, B. (2004), *Packaging Politics*, 2nd edn, London: Edward Arnold.

Lees-Marshment, J. (2001), *Political Marketing and British Political Parties*, Manchester: Manchester University Press.

Lilleker, D. G. (2005), 'The local campaign: management from the centre or chaos on the periphery?' *Journal of Marketing Management*, special edition on the 2005 UK General Election, 21(9–10): 979–1004.

Lilleker, D. G. and Lees-Marshment, J. (2005), 'Conclusion: towards a comparative model of party marketing', in D. G. Lilleker and J. Lees-Marshment, *Political Marketing in Comparative Perspective*, Manchester: Manchester University Press.

Lilleker, D. G., and Negrine, R. (2006), 'Mapping a market orientation: can we only detect political marketing through the lens of hindsight?' in P. J. Davies and B. I. Newman, *Winning Elections with Political Marketing*, New York: Haworth.

Index